The Negro in the Civil War

The Negro in the Civil War

by
BENJAMIN QUARLES

New introduction by

WILLIAM S. MCFEELY

A DA CAPO PAPERBACK

Library of Congress Cataloging in Publication Data

Quarles, Benjamin.
   The Negro in the Civil War / by Benjamin Quarles: new introduction by
William S. McFeely.
      p.   cm. — (A Da Capo paperback)
   Reprint. Originally published: Boston: Little, Brown, 1953.
   Bibliography: p.
   Includes index.
   ISBN 0-306-80350-X
   1. United States — History — Civil War, 1861-1865 — Afro-Americans. I.
Title.
E540.N3Q3   1988
973.7'15 — dc19   88-34295
                                                                                          CIP

This Da Capo Press paperback edition of *The Negro in the Civil War*
is an unabridged republication of the edition published in Boston in
1953, here supplemented with a new introduction by William S. McFeely.
It is reprinted by arrangement with Little, Brown and Company.

Copyright © 1953, by Benjamin Quarles
New introduction copyright © 1989 by William S. McFeely

Published by Da Capo Press, Inc.
A Subsidiary of Plenum Publishing Corporation
233 Spring Street, New York, N.Y. 10013

All Rights Reserved

Manufactured in the United States of America

To Roberta

Introduction to the
Da Capo Edition

"WHAT IS AMERICA?" is a curious question with which to begin a book that allows for no doubt. Benjamin Quarles's *The Negro in the Civil War* celebrates, without equivocation, the active participation of black Americans in their own emancipation. In Quarles's view, an America going about the business of freedom, as he is certain it was in the Civil War, is America at its best. And yet the author lets his question stand. By doing so, he forces us to confront the paradox of people achieving freedom in one century and still seeking it in the next.

In 1904, when Benjamin Quarles was born, the bloody revolution that freed his people—in which they freed themselves—was only forty years in the past. The ardor of the struggle still glowed, but many people's understanding of why the battles had been fought had dimmed. White Americans, North and South, were engaged in a protracted hesitation waltz of reconciliation. For black Americans there were no such niceties. The war's promise had been blighted by relentless poverty and a debt system that locked a whole people in gaunt place. Their efforts to assert themselves as citizens during Reconstruction had been thwarted in the 1870s and their attempts to organize to meet economic and political needs during the Populist revolt in the 1890s had been met with the grim methods of social control: disenfranchisement, gruesome lynchings, and insulting enforced segregation.

A half century later, when Quarles, born in Boston and educated at Shaw University and the University of Wisconsin, was at the height of his power as a historian (his masterful biography, *Frederick Douglass*, appeared in 1948) there were signs that the fight for freedom might be resumed. *The Negro in the Civil War*, published first in 1953, before the *Brown* decision, before Rosa parks and Martin Luther King, Jr., was a hint to his people that if the struggle was to be won, they, collectively, would have to do the struggling. And, of course, they did in a second—and this time non-violent—revolution of emancipation.

Now, yet another generation later, for men and women of Professor Quarles's splendid talent and tenacity and, as always seems to be the case in these matters, luck, the promise—in almost full measure—has been fulfilled. But most of the celebrating seems to be coming not from these discerning people, but from those who are happy to put the whole subject of black Americans aside. Others determined that there be no such neglect are aware that many, far too many, descendants of the slaves that Professor Quarles wrote about are still bound by a poverty which, if now urban rather than rural, is as pernicious as ever. Benjamin Quarles's people are still asking, "What is America?"

The Negro in the Civil War is written with grace and force. There is wonderful life in Quarles's story of black activists converting a war to save the Union into a crusade to end slavery, in his accounts of black soldiers in battle. If the book has a deficiency, it is the absence of any questioning of war as a device for achieving even the most desirable social change. It is wrong to say the book has been superseded; it is entirely right to say that every inch of the book as been worked over by scholars since it was written. The sea islanders struggling to be independent farmers, which Willie Lee Rose wrote about in such loving detail, are here. So too are the black men gone to war who have had Glatthaar, and many more historians. The torments and hopes of war refugees, which have commanded the attention of a phalanx of scholars whose consciences and curiosities were aroused by the Civil Rights Movement, are also here.

Eric Foner, by moving the era's start from the conventional 1865 back into the war years in his comprehensive work, *Reconstruction*, responded to the central message of Quarles's work. The slaves were ready for freedom and ready to fight and suffer to achieve it. And Professor Quarles can take perhaps his greatest satisfaction, as the dean of the scholars of emancipation, in the work of some of his fellow Marylanders. At the University of Maryland, Ira Berlin and his associates edited, as the first volume of their massive project documenting the process of the move out of slavery of 4,000,000 people, *Freedom: The Black Military Experience*. That book, in powerful first-person accounts, tells the story again that Quarles told. Black Americans were participants in, not recipients of, emancipation.

Quarles is a deceptively simple writer. His crisp attention to detail and to narrative can permit the unwary reader to miss his subtlety. As in his *Black Abolitionists* and *Frederick Douglass*, there are often psychological insights that are strikingly current. As an example, one chapter title in *Civil War*, "Portraits in Sepia," suggests the need for scholarly inquiry into a realm of the history of Afro-Americans usually left to gossip: the question of color. The subject of how differences in pigmentation have been perceived and how those differences affect the elusive concept of race is now receiving the concentrated attention of historians. Once again Professor Quarles has put us to work.

There is a reason, other than the utilitarian one that it will be exceedingly helpful to have it again readily accessible, to be glad that *The Negro in the Civil War* is back in print. There are few scholars, anywhere in the academic world, of greater generosity or dignity than Morgan State University's distinguished professor emeritus. On his eighty-fifth birthday, he deserves Da Capo's small tribute. And, on otherwise discouraging days, we readers of his book, rather than ducking away from his daunting question, "What is America?", can brighten the vision a bit with the thought that perhaps Benjamin Quarles himself is as good an answer as we are likely to come up with.

WILLIAM S. McFEELY
Athens, Georgia
January 23, 1989

Foreword

WHAT IS AMERICA? A clue to a nation's character is revealed when a crisis comes; in a time of troubles a nation's culture crops out. Certainly during that fateful span of the Civil War — the only great war in the hundred-year period in world history from Waterloo to Sarajevo — this query received an illuminating answer.

Up to the time of that wager by battle between the North and the South, the significance of America lay in the circumstances of her origin — she had been conceived in a revolutionary war fought in the name of certain inalienable rights, and she had become a world symbol of those human freedoms. Many observers in the Old World, however, wondered skeptically whether the American experiment in equality and democracy, so bright with early promise, could survive the shock of a long-drawn-out war. Would not an America in travail lose sight of her avowed mission?

The Civil War not only swept aside these misgivings but succeeded significantly in enlarging the compass of American democracy. For when the smoke lifted from the battlefield, gone was a disfigurement that had embarrassed the country since the days of the Founding Fathers.

These men, who had met in Philadelphia in the summer of 1787, sought to frame a document which would secure the blessings of liberty to themselves and to coming generations of Americans. They had brought great gifts to the task of forming a union, for they were men of public affairs, men of learning, and they had a paternal love for the young nation which a short decade ago they had begotten.

They had wrought well in general, but they had stopped short of the goal of human liberty. Themselves men of property, they had scrupulously avoided any interference with chattel slavery. Moreover, many of them expected slavery to die soon of its own weight, its failure to pay cash dividends. "Slavery," said one delegate, "will be but a speck on the horizon." However, that system, strengthened greatly by remarkable improvements in cotton culture, grew as the country grew, centering almost exclusively in the South.

But by mid-century the slave system had come under bitter attack. In turn the plantation owners had become increasingly sensitive to criticism, finally succeeding in stifling freedom of thought and freedom of discussion below the Potomac. They did not stop there. In attempting to protect slavery, Southern Congressmen advocated laws that seriously endangered the principles, so revered in America, of freedom of petition, freedom of transit and trial by jury. By 1861 thoughtful Americans had reached an inevitable conclusion: chattel slavery imperiled civil liberties. It must go.

The Civil War was thus waged in the name of preserving the Union — the American experiment in democracy; and in containing an institution — chattel slavery in the South — which threatened American liberties from within. But the war did more than checkmate slavery; it delivered a deathblow. The abolition of slavery had become a national goal only in the later stages of the war, and was accomplished in piecemeal fashion. Nonetheless, however halting her antislavery action during the course of the war, America, as the land of the free, inevitably moved in the direction of her high calling.

The Civil War was a revolution in many ways; hence it is open to a hundred and one interpretations (the above interpretation included). But on one point there is common agreement: without slavery there would have been no resort to arms. Hence the slave was the key factor in the war. But the Negro's tale was not merely a passive one; he did not tarry in the wings, hands folded. He was an active member of the cast, prominent in the dramatis personae. To him freedom was a two-way street; indeed he gave prior to receiving.

North and South the Negro bestrode the stage. The quarter of a million Negroes north of the Mason-Dixon line, schooled over the years in public affairs by the colored convention movement and the abolitionist crusade, acted as a whip and spur to the Lincoln administration. Acting in concert with whites of like outlook, they prodded mayors, governors, and public opinion at home and abroad. Thousands of them went to training camps and then embarked for Southern ports, ready for the smoke and din of skirmish and battle. Negro women, like Harriet Tubman, served as nurses. Others formed ladies' aid societies to help the boys in blue, and some went down as teachers to work with the newly freed slaves.

The role of the three and a half million Negroes in the South reached epic proportions. From the moment of the first drumbeat, three groups of slaves were in rehearsal for freedom. Those who remained under the Stars and Bars for the entire war took on graver responsibilities. The South quickly became a vast military camp, and slaves were immediately impressed for noncombatant service in the army. As waiters, orderlies and teamsters, they were under enemy fire. Not far behind the lines, and frequently within them, were the military laborers who threw up the foundations for the artillery, built the forts and dug the entrenchments. Those who remained on the home front supplied the skills for the factories that sprang up, and the brawn for working the mines. On many plantations field hands assumed the task of overseers; house slaves too grew in authority.

A second group which prepared itself for freedom were the contrabands, those slaves who came into the Union lines whenever

the Federal troops drew near. Many of them settled on the plantations which their fleeing masters had abandoned. Here they made
a crop as paid laborers, or lessees, or actual owners. Other thousands, fameless and unrecorded, followed in the wake of the
armies, doing the heavy work. Many who came into the lines
brought with them, in General Abner Doubleday's opinion,
"much valuable information which cannot be obtained from any
other source." Many contrabands became guides and spies.

The third Southern Negro group that fitted itself for freedom
comprised those in the armed services. From the ranks of former
slaves came the bulk of the 180,000 Negroes who enlisted in the
army, and the more than 29,000 who manned Union ships. By the
middle of 1863, as the Secretary of the Navy confided to his
diary under date of June 6, "all of our increased military strength
now comes from Negroes." To their soldierly qualities a host of
competent witnesses bore testimony.

As if one final requirement for freedom were necessary, these
soldiers and contrabands showed a remarkable zeal for self-
improvement. To learn to spell, to write one's name instead of
making one's mark — this was their first and most cherished goal.
In the army, their officers became their teachers. The contrabands
learned their letters from teachers recruited in the North by
church groups. Instructor and pupils assembled in a cotton barn,
an old kitchen, or a "praise-house," with the New Testament as
the textbook.

Thus when slavery was abolished by constitutional amendment
in December 1865, the Negro took the intelligence calmly. It was
not news. For when the first gun roared he had scented freedom
in the air, and by the time Lee's men had stacked their muskets
at Appomattox, Negroes everywhere had become free *de facto*,
their own exertions having measurably been a factor.

The Negro's constructive role did not end with striking a blow
for freedom. He brought to his freedom a spirit of forgiving and
forgetting. He showed no vindictiveness toward his former mas-

ter; there was no hatred in his heart. Of course there were instances like that of the colored maid in Mississippi who announced
to her mistress that "answering bells is played out." But in general
the Negro stood to let bygones be bygones and to start afresh
in a spirit of amity. "Prayin' and lovin'," said Joseph Clovese, last
of the Negro Civil War veterans, "are the greatest needs" of the
sons of men. Ex-infantryman Clovese's observation was made in
1948, on the occasion of his hundred and fifth birthday, but his
words echo the sentiment of the mass of Negroes, particularly
those in the South, at the close of the Civil War.

But — and here is the real tragedy of the postwar period — such
a spirit was unequal to the aroused passions and hatreds engendered in the South by four long years of sacrificial struggle
in a cause that lost. Doubtless it was expecting too much of
Southerners. Still vivid at the end of the war were the searing
memories of Yankee atrocities which had been so imaginatively
described by Southern poets, politicians and newspaper editors
patriotically bent on steeling morale. It would be difficult for a
white Southerner to reach an understanding with a group which
to him had become the symbol of his defeat. For him it was the
wormwood and the gall. Imagine the somber memories of those
who loved the South and who had "dared for her to fight from
Lookout to the sea." Even white Southerners without bitterness
toward the Negro could not escape the chagrin of remembering
that at Milliken's Bend a Negro soldier had taken his former
master into camp, a prisoner, and that among the first Union
troops to enter the surrendered cities of Charleston and Richmond were marching blacks. And could reasonableness go far
with such a Southerner as the one who during General Butler's
occupation of New Orleans in the summer of 1862 kept a "Son-
of-a-bitch book," in which was entered the name of everyone
who collaborated with the Yankees by taking the Union oath of
allegiance, and the street corner where he should be hung?

But the attitude of a fixed place for the Negro would yield, in time. "I know of no country where the conditions for effecting great changes in the settled order of things, for the development of right ideas of liberty and humanity, are more favorable than here in these United States." The man who spoke these words was an ex-slave. The occasion was a meeting called in 1857 to ponder a Supreme Court decision, just handed down, which held that a Negro could claim none of the rights and privileges of citizens of the United States. Yet this speaker, Frederick Douglass, did not doubt that America would rise to her goal of freedom for all.

His faith was not misplaced. The day was soon to come when America was to do a far better thing than she had ever done. A shot which rang out in the harbor at Charleston before dawn's early light on April 12, 1861, heralded the breaking of that day. The Negro was ready. This is a record of that readiness.

In these chapters I have attempted scrupulously to confine myself to statements from sources that pass muster as to scientific scholarship. The generous use of direct quotations reflects an effort for accuracy as well as for liveliness. Since in three instances I have used reconstructed dialogue, it might not be amiss to say that not a single line in quotation marks is of my own composition. I have tried to guard carefully against giving any misleading impressions by using out-of-context citations. To one change I confess: in conformity with modern usage, I have capitalized the word "Negro" whether the quoted passages did so or not.

So rich and varied was the role of the black man in the war that much that he did must be treated in brief compass, and many Negroes who are worthy of mention must go unchronicled in these pages. It is hoped that their history-conscious descendants will understand. Another difficult "leaving-out" decision concerned battles: of the fifty-two military encounters in which colored soldiers took part, which ones could be bypassed with least regretting? The five battles herein highlighted are representative from the standpoints of geographic distribution and participating personnel. Two of the actions, Battery Wagner in South Carolina and Port Hudson in Louisiana, involved regiments composed largely of free-born Negroes — the volunteers at Wagner were recruited in the North, and those at Port Hudson were made up primarily of New Orleans "free men of color." In the other three military actions described in these pages — Milliken's Bend, Nashville and Petersburg — the black regiments were composed of ex-slaves respectively from Mississippi, Tennessee, and Maryland and Virginia jointly.

It is a pleasure to express my appreciation to those who provided grants to assist in making this study. For such stipends I am grateful to President A. W. Dent and the Board of Trustees of Dillard University, and to the Carnegie Foundation for the Advancement of Teaching.

My thanks are extended to the staffs of the Boston Athenæum, the Boston Public Library, Rare Book Room, the New York Public Library, Room 300, the Library of Congress, Manuscripts Division, and the National Archives of the United States, War Records Office. Jean Blackwell, curator of the Schomburg Collection of the New York Public Library, was quite helpful in giving me carte blanche to that excellent repository of Negroana. Mrs. Dorothy Porter, librarian of the Moorland Foundation at Howard University, Washington, D. C., continuously and graciously made available both the rich collection she superintends and her own extensive knowledge of matters bibliographical concerning the Negro. I also wish to thank the University of Chicago Press for permission to quote from B. A. Botkin's *Lay My Burden Down* (1945), and John Hope Franklin for permission to include a passage from his edited study, *The Diary of James T. Ayres* (Springfield, 1947).

To those who critically read selected chapters in manuscript, notably Howard H. Bell, of the Library of Congress, and Harold Smith of Kentucky State College, I am most appreciative. For suggestions as to style, I owe much to Mrs. Adelaide James

Ward, formerly editorial assistant of the *Journal of Negro History*, who gave the middle chapters a careful going over. This acknowledgment, which I am happy to record, is made in gratitude rather than in implication, for there were times when no amount of cautioning could restrain my invincible preference for ending a sentence with something that dangles. For assistance in reading proofs, I am indebted to my wife, Ruth Brett Quarles, and to Marcus B. Christian.

BENJAMIN QUARLES

Contents

The Negro in the Civil War

CHAPTER I

So Nigh Is Grandeur

TONIGHT we'll sleep in Fort Wagner," said a black soldier, fixing his bayonet and peering into the gathering darkness on Morris Island, South Carolina, in the early evening of July 18, 1863. As he spoke he craned his neck in the direction of famed Battery Wagner, less than half a mile away along the sand bar. But from that formidable earthwork held by the Confederates, all was dark and still — there issued no glimmer of light, no noise of preparation to join battle. The other Negro soldiers of the Massachusetts Fifty-fourth said nothing; each man was preoccupied with his own thoughts in these final moments before the assault.

A few minutes earlier, at 6 o'clock, no less a personage than Brigadier General George C. Strong had appeared before the regiment, accompanied by his two aides and two orderlies. Strong was mounted on a superb gray charger and was in full military dress down to white gloves. A yellow bandana was loosely knotted around his neck. The black soldiers remembered the details of his appearance — he was destined that fateful night to be mortally wounded. Strong asked the Fifty-fourth if they would care to lead the attack on Wagner. A cheer went up from six hundred throats. Then, taking the flags from the color sergeants, the general waved them aloft in anticipation of victory.

The men had a soldier's respect for Strong, who eight days

earlier had been the first man to step ashore on Morris Island, leading his entire command in person. They were pleased that he had been considerate enough to ask them to spearhead the assault instead of simply issuing a command. Strong's thoughtfulness showed he knew that the regiment had spent the last two nights on the march through sand and peltering rain, and that no regular issue of rations had been made to them since the evening of July 16, nearly fifty hours previously; hardtack and coffee had been their fare for two days.

After Strong's appearance the weary regiment had nearly an hour to relax before wheeling into line. Commanding General Quincy A. Gillmore had decided to begin the assault on Wagner at twilight, so that the storming party would not form too distinct a target for the Confederate batteries on the nearby islands — James, on the extreme left and Sullivan's and Fort Sumter in the front. As the Fifty-fourth awaited the formation of the column of regiments in its rear in the deepening darkness, and in the strange quiet with the great guns hushed, the thoughts of the men ran forward to the task immediately ahead, and backward to the organizing of their regiment some months ago.

The task immediately ahead was sobering — the storming of a fortified position held by both infantry and artillery. It was not easy for a commanding officer to compel the most seasoned troops to advance under a rain of fire from artillery emplacements supported by the incessant barking of small arms: few lessons of the war were learned at greater cost than this. And Wagner was one of the strongest single earthworks ever constructed.

Located on the northern end of Morris Island where the width narrowed to less than a hundred feet, Wagner was practically unapproachable from its water faces. Along its northern sea face lay a deep moat with a sluice gate and three guns. On the east Wagner was bounded by the ocean and on the west by Vincent's Creek and the impassable marshes. At the southern face — the only approach to the battery — the Confederates had mounted two guns and one mortar which swept the shallow and shifting sand beach and gave a flanking as well as a direct fire on an advancing column. The battery's guns stretched across the length of the island, from water to water. The fort itself was constructed of compact sand. Its parapets and traverses were thick and high, and a ditch in front added to its impregnability. For the protection of its garrison when enemy fire became hot, the battery boasted a capacious bombproof capable of sheltering nearly eight hundred men.

The Union forces wanted Wagner for an important reason: Morris Island, on which the battery was located, was one of the approaches to the city of Charleston. The main ship channel flowed along the shores of Morris Island so that a fleet of enemy ships attempting to reach Charleston would find it necessary to run the gantlet of Wagner, less than six miles from the city. Morris Island was also an outpost of Fort Sumter, the key to the harbor defenses of Charleston. Hence, another reason for capturing Wagner was to get within a more effective breaching distance of Sumter, only 2600 yards away. And with Sumter reduced, the Union fleet, so reasoned the Northern joint command, would be able to push on into Charleston without resistance.

For Charleston was the goal. The name of that proud city was anathema above the Potomac. Charleston, to those in the North, was considered the cradle of secession, the nursery of disunion. In that capital of South Carolina lived a class-conscious gentry which styled itself "the chivalry of the South," and was disdainful of all things Yankee. "See Charleston and forever envy her citizens," stated the inhabitants with the air of announcing a simple truth. In Charleston, writes Avery Craven, even death lost its sting if one were buried in St. Philip's or St. Michael's. Charleston's capture was desirable not only because that city was the seat of rebellion and the symbol of haughty pride; the capital of the Palmetto State also had a great economic importance. It was one of the two chief points through which supplies and munitions from abroad found entrance into the beleaguered Confederacy.

With a view to seizing Wagner, a Union flotilla loaded with troops from nearby Folly Island had crossed Lighthouse Inlet on July 10th, and effected a landing on the southern end of Morris Island. The Confederate forces, lacking sufficient heavy gun power and infantry strength, fell back to Battery Wagner.

Impressed by the great strength of Wagner, the Union command decided to erect counterbatteries on the island. Then, with the co-operation of the guns of the Federal fleet, it might be possible to tranquilize Wagner's armament, demoralize her defenders, and thus mount a successful attack. Bringing up a siege train from Folly Island, the Union forces proceeded to place on Morris Island forty-one pieces of artillery at distances ranging from 1300 to 1900 yards of the fort. By July 18 all was ready for operation "softening-up." From General Gillmore's headquarters had come the command: in order to dismount the enemy's guns, shells should be exploded in or directly over Fort Wagner.

The morning of July 18 broke bright and beautiful: "The God of day," wrote Confederate officer Robert C. Gilchrist, "rising to the splendor of his midsummer glory flung his red flame into the swelling sea, and again performed the miracle of turning water into wine." The Federal forces made the most of the perfect weather. Their land batteries opened up the cannonading from the south side, and were soon joined by six ironclads — the *New Ironsides, Weehawken, Montauk, Patapsco, Nantucket, Catskill* — and a complement of other warships, including three gunboats (*Wissahickon, Seneca,* and *Ottawa*), and the double-ender, *Paul Jones,* a converted merchantman mounting a heavy gun at each end. From a distance of a few hundred feet these Union vessels poured a remorseless stream of shells into Wagner's east side. The pounding was particularly strong from the guns of the flat-bottomed U.S.S. *New Ironsides,* a three-decked armor-clad whose turret mounted the heaviest cannon on any ship that had ever floated. The log of the *New Ironsides* for July 18 reveals in staccato entries something of her role:

At 12:15 opened on Fort Wagner with 150-pounder rifle.
At 1:12 opened on Fort Wagner with port broadside.
At 5 opened with No. 4 gun with 5-second shrapnel.

The tempest of iron hail rained against Wagner was perhaps unparalleled in naval history: "Nothing like the rapid discharge from heavy artillery has ever been seen or heard before on this continent," wrote the Richmond *Examiner* for July 24, 1863. The air was filled with a bursting volley of iron as the shells struck Wagner's slope and bounded over her parapet. Other shells ricocheted across the ground and on into the water, throwing up huge masses of sand and volumes of sea. The whole Confederate-held end of the island emitted smoke like a furnace, and the horizon was fitfully illumined by the flashes of flame belching from the monster guns on land and sea. "My estimation," reported Southern General W. B. Taliaferro, in command at Wagner, "is that not less than 9000 solid shot and shell were thrown in against the battery during the eleven hours the bombardment lasted."

At four in the afternoon, Taliaferro gave the order to silence the fort's guns which up to then had been making a few feeble, token responses. The Confederates had decided to reserve all their remaining firepower for the sterner test of the forthcoming assault. When Wagner's batteries went silent, the Union command was elated, believing the enemy's armament had been irreparably damaged and that the defenders of the garrison were disabled or demoralized. This was to prove a miscalculation.

To the men inside the fort every minute was leaden-footed: "the sun seemed to stand still and the midsummer day to know no night." But they had foresightedly managed to protect their light guns with sand bags and to bury their fieldpieces in the sand. Moreover, despite the terrific bombardment, there were only eighteen casualties among them — four killed and fourteen wounded. And of the four dead, two were without a mark — the concussion had forced the breath from their lungs and collapsed them into corpses. When the Union bombardment subsided, the unobserved Confederates came up from their bomb-proofs and sand pits, exhumed their buried cannon, remounted their guns, and manned the ramparts. They were ready for the assault they knew was imminent.

❧

As the Negro soldiers awaited the bugle call in the ominous silence, the reveries of many of them went back over their brief regimental history. The Fifty-fourth had come into existence largely because of the zeal of John A. Andrew, war governor of Massachusetts, who led the movement for Negro troops. In January 1863, at his request, Andrew had received authorization from Secretary of War Edwin M. Stanton to organize a colored regiment of volunteers to serve for three years.

But Massachusetts had a very small colored population from which to recruit; within the first six weeks a scant hundred volunteers had signed up. Andrew anxiously summoned George L. Stearns and persuaded him to head a committee of prominent citizens to superintend the raising of black recruits. In a short time Stearns's committee collected $5000; abolitionists and public-spirited Bostonians gladly made subscriptions to the fund. Thereupon Stearns advertised widely; a call for enlistments in the Firty-fourth was published in dozens of newspapers from east to west.

To speed up the work, Stearns employed recruiting agents, obtaining the services of such Negro leaders as Frederick Douglass, William Wells Brown, Charles Lenox Remond, Martin R. Delany, Henry Highland Garnet, J. Mercer Langston, J. W.

Loguen, George T. Downing and Stephen Myers. These agents were required to write to Stearns every evening, giving a summary of the day's work; they were required to send in a statement of expenses every week. In two months Stearns had organized a line of recruiting posts from Boston to St. Louis. Soon the quota was raised, and 1000 Negroes representing every state in the country, plus a quota from Canada, were learning the manual of arms at the camp at Readville, Massachusetts.

The commissioned officers were white. On this point many Negroes, particularly those in Boston, voiced a strong criticism, perhaps keeping a number of young colored men from volunteering. But some of the criticism against white officers was quieted when it became evident that Governor Andrew was interested only in the highest type of men. Andrew felt that good officers would help to overcome the prejudice against Negro troops. Moreover, superior officers were necessary since the Fifty-fourth was the first colored regiment to be raised in the free states and its success or failure would be closely watched. "Young men of military experience, of firm Anti-slavery principles, ambitious, superior to the vulgar contempt of colour, and having faith in the capacity of coloured men for military service"; such were the qualifications, wrote Andrew, that he had in mind.

To take command of the regiment, Andrew approached Robert Gould Shaw, then captain of the Massachusetts Second Infantry. A handsome young man of great personal charm, Shaw came from a wealthy and socially prominent family, and had attended school in Switzerland and college at Harvard. Captain Shaw hesitated for a day over Andrew's offer; he knew many of his friends would disapprove and that he faced ridicule and ostracism. But "he inclined naturally toward difficult resolves," as William James expressed it, and he accepted. As indicated by the Muster-in Roll, Shaw was made a major on April 11, and a colonel on May 13. His example in becoming an officer of the Fifty-fourth was followed by the scions of other well-to-do families. Most of these officers were very young; the average age of the officers of the regiment was twenty-three.

On May 18 Secretary of War Stanton telegraphed Governor Andrew to notify the Fifty-fourth to report to General David Hunter, Commander of the Department of the South, with headquarters at Hilton Head, South Carolina. On that morning at 11:30, Andrew went to the Readville camp to present to the regiment four flags which friends had procured. Along with Andrew nearly 3000 visitors made the trip, including such notable abolitionists as William Lloyd Garrison, Wendell Phillips and Frederick Douglass. As the sun beamed in the cloudless sky, Negro pastor Leonard A. Grimes opened with the invocation. Thereupon the governor presented the flags to Colonel Shaw. "I know not, Mr. Commander," remarked Andrew, "in all human history, to any given thousand men in arms, has there been committed a work at once so proud, so precious, so full of hope and glory as the work committed to you." In his brief and gracious response, Colonel Shaw expressed the hope that the Fifty-fourth would have the opportunity to show that Massachusetts had not made a mistake in entrusting the honor of the state to a colored regiment.

Ten days after Stanton's letter to Andrew, the Fifty-fourth left its Readville camp and came to Boston to debark. The regiment had been scheduled to march directly to the wharf, but so great was the public desire to see the Negro soldiers that a review had been arranged. On the morning of May 28, the city had an expectant air. The national colors flew everywhere, as if in celebration of a holiday. One hundred policemen were on duty to clear the streets and keep order. Although not known to the public, additional reserves of police were held in readiness, for it was not certain how Boston, liberty-loving though it was, would respond to the novel sight of Negroes in military dress.

The excitement mounted as the Negroes marched through the downtown streets on their way to the Common. Observers noted the flags presented to the regiment ten days earlier at Readville: among them was a national flag presented by the young colored women of Boston; another, showing the state colors, was a gift of the Colored Ladies' Relief Society, and a third, donated by "a large and patriotic committee," was an emblematic banner of white silk with the figure of the Goddess of Liberty, and the inscription, "Liberty, Loyalty, and Unity." Sure to catch the eye were the regimental banners of superb white silk, adorned on one side by the coat of arms of Massachusetts, and on the other side by a golden cross and a golden star, with *In hoc signo vinces* beneath. This exalted exhortation to conquer by the sign of the cross was expressive of the belief that the mission of the Fifty-fourth was a holy crusade.

Thousands cheered the impressive spectacle — no such reception had been given to the preceding fifty-three Massachusetts regiments. The poet John Greenleaf Whittier forsook his pacifism for an hour to get a glimpse of the marching blacks. It was the only regiment he viewed during the war, and he never forgot the scene. The face of spectator Frederick Douglass was flushed with pride as his two sons, Lewis and Charles, stepped along the line of march, their Enfield rifles swinging to the beat of Patrick Gilmore's martial music.

On jammed Boston Common the troops passed in review before Governor Andrew, the mayor of the city, and Senator Henry Wilson. The eyes of twenty thousand onlookers followed the motions of the marching men, who made an excellent appearance. A reporter from the Boston *Transcript* commented upon "the general precision attending their evolutions," and "their ease and uniformity in going through the manual."

In front rode Colonel Shaw, his head erect under his high felt army hat with cord. Young Shaw sat well on a horse, and as his mother, Sarah Sturgis Shaw, watched her beloved and only son, she murmured, "What have I done that God has been so good to me?" Another spectator, the talented seventeen-year-old Negro,

Edmonia Lewis, never forgot how handsome he looked; a year later when she sculptured a bust of him, she drew heavily from that vivid memory.

From the scene of the dress parade the regiment marched to Battery Wharf. En route the band played the John Brown song "while passing over ground moistened by the blood of Crispus Attucks," a Negro who was the first patriot to shed his blood in the Revolutionary War. One of the soldiers of the Fifty-fourth had just written a poem whose lines remembered Attucks:

> O give us a flag, all free without a slave,
> We'll fight to defend it as our fathers did so brave.

Shortly after one o'clock the regiment boarded the *De Molay*, made ready for her maiden voyage. Three hours later the lines were cut and the steamer eased from her moorings, bound for Port Royal, South Carolina. "Glory enough for one day; aye, indeed, for a lifetime," said Negro leader William C. Nell, an eyewitness.

The six weeks following their arrival at Beaufort, on Port Royal Island, were days of hardening up. There was more, however, than camp life and discipline. The Fifty-fourth was ordered to sack and burn the little town of Darien on the Georgia coast, an operation which their colonel found distasteful and barbarous. Shortly afterward, on James Island, in the early morning of July 16, the Fifty-fourth, fighting alongside white troops, acquitted itself well during a sharp skirmish.

On that same night, July 16, the black soldiers left James Island and marched to Coles Island. From there they embarked to Folly Island on the morning of the fateful July 18. That day they marched to the upper end of Folly Island and late that afternoon, they were ferried to Morris Island. Here General Gillmore, the greatest artillerist produced by the war, and now in command of the Department of the South, had constructed the siege lines preparatory to another attack on Wagner.

The testing time had come. Despite their exhaustion, hunger and wet clothes, the black soldiers were anxious to acquit themselves like men. They had something to refute. Still rankling in their minds were the familiar charges that the Negro was too grossly ignorant to perform the duties of a soldier intelligently, and that blacks were not fit to wear a military uniform because they belonged to a degraded, inferior race, lacking in manly qualities. This assault on Wagner would furnish an answer to these belittlers.

❖

It was half-past seven, and the Union forces had formed in three brigades, the first brigade of six regiments being led by the Massachusetts Fifty-fourth. To the east a heavy fog had gathered over the sea, enveloping the warships of Rear Admiral John A. Dahlgren's South Atlantic Squadron. In front loomed Wagner, silent and defiant.

Robert Gould Shaw stopped pacing up and down and stepped forward for a final word. In the dusk the silver eagle on each shoulder of his officer's jacket was hardly visible, and his light blue trousers had meshed their color with the shadows. The young colonel reminded the men that much depended on their conduct that night. He spoke calmly; if he had any feeling that he himself stood on the brink of eternity, he did not betray it. He urged the soldiers to make sure their bayonets were secure.

The signal was given. At the command, "Attention," the men straightened up, and the metallic tones of the bugle sounded the advance. Over the half mile of Morris Island sand the storming blacks led the way, with their colonel in the vanguard. On they came with a cadenced tramp. No sentinel hoarsely cried out in challenge; from Wagner came not a shot.

The defenders of the battery were waiting for the Union soldiers to get within two hundred feet of the fort. Not only would the enemy troops then be within short musket range, but they would encounter two obstacles unknown to them. One was a defile made by an easterly bend of Vincent's Creek and its marshes. At that point the land mass between the sand hillocks and the sea had narrowed almost in half, and the men on the right would have to walk in water, thus making the regiment break line. The other obstacle was a ditch with four feet of water.

As the Fifty-fourth broke ranks while passing the defile, Battery Wagner, miraculously it seemed, lit up with a withering sheet of flame and fire from bastion to bastion. Wagner had become a volcanic hell, vomiting shot and shell with deafening explosions. "As the enemy advanced," reported Confederate General Taliaferro, "they were met with by a shower of grape and canister from our guns and a terrible fire of musketry from the Charleston Battalion and the Fifty-first North Carolina." Simultaneously with Wagner's first volley, the rebel guns on the nearby islands, James, Sumter, and Sullivan's, opened up a rapid fire.

As the Fifty-fourth staggered under this shock, the wounded screaming and falling, the command came to charge at double-quick time, so as to close sooner with the enemy. Stopping up their ragged gaps, stepping over the bodies of their fallen comrades and stumbling across the pits dug by Wagner's shells, the soldiers quickly reached their second unexpected obstacle — the ditch.

Without hesitation they plunged forward and downward. The ditch was not wholly enshrouded in darkness; cannon flashes illumined it. The soldiers might have preferred total darkness. For as they swept across the ditch, the howitzers in the bastions poured down a raking fire, up and down the line. A shell would explode, clearing a space of twenty feet. The black soldiers would close up again, on the run.

Those who survived the musketry's fire had a final hurdle — the parapet. They had to climb up the sloping sides of the fortification and effect a lodgment. The lionhearted Shaw led the troops, shouting, "Forward, Fifty-fourth." As they groped up the seamed and jagged face of the fort, the air was suddenly filled with exploding hand grenades. The Negro troops pressed upward, ignoring the harvest of death. "I had my sword-sheath blown away while on the parapet of the Fort," wrote Lewis Douglass to his father. "Swept down like chaff, still our men went on and on."

The darkness proved a distinct disadvantage to the storming Union forces, who were in unfamiliar surroundings with no visibility. One of the officers of the Fifty-fourth, Luis F. Emilio, later related that he felt like crying with Ajax, "Give us but light, O Jove! and in the light, if thou seest fit, destroy us!"

Despite all obstacles, Shaw and some of his men reached the top of the parapet, and for a few moments there was a bitter hand-to-hand struggle — the blacks with their bayonets and the Confederates with handspikes and gun rammers. Standing on the parapet, Shaw waved his sword and shouted to his troops, "Rally! Rally!" A moment later a bullet pierced his heart and he fell forward into the fort. "I saw his face," said a survivor. "It was white as snow, but in every line was that courage which led his men to the very crest of that wall of death."

A dozen blacks fell simultaneously with their leader, among them the color sergeant carrying the national flag. Before the flag slipped from the relaxing fingers of the stricken bearer, William H. Carney of Company C sprang forward and seized it. Born in Norfolk in 1840, Carney at fourteen had "attended a private and secret school kept by a minister," and "in my fifteenth year I embraced the gospel." In New Bedford young Carney had done odd jobs for a living, while still retaining his inclination toward the Christian ministry. Despite wounds in his legs, in his breast, and in his right arm, Carney planted the flag upon the parapet and flattened himself on the outer slope for protection, remaining in that position for half an hour.

The desperate struggle could not be long protracted. The outnumbered Union troops were etched against the horizon, furnishing an easy target. The supporting regiments had not moved up rapidly enough to take advantage of the first fierce onslaught. Human courage had reached its limit, as the frightful blasts of the Confederate artillery took their sanguinary toll. Nurse Clara Barton never forgot the carnage: "I can see again the scarlet flow of blood as it rolled over the black limbs beneath my hands, and the great heave of the human heart before it grew still."

Checkmated, the colored regiment fell back, firing at the shadowy figures above as a parting gesture. The surviving black soldiers made their limping way back to the friendly darkness of the sand hills. Among them was the almost lifeless Carney, exhausted by the loss of blood and creeping on one knee, but still bearing aloft the colors.

With the repulse of the Fifty-fourth the other regiments of the first brigade recoiled. The second brigade, numerically weaker than its predecessor, then took up the gage of battle. They were joined by several of the black soldiers, eager for a second try.

The re-enforced second brigade gallantly stormed the fort, actually succeeding in gaining a foothold on the battery's southern salient. For two desperate hours they held on. But they were met by men as brave and determined as they. Moreover, these Confederate forces had been strengthened between assaults by the opportune arrival of Colonel G. P. Harrison's Thirty-second Georgia, ordered to Wagner by General P. G. T. Beauregard, commanding the Department of South Carolina, Georgia and Florida. The augmented Confederate troops poured shot into the salient, the Union forces sustaining severe losses. The Union commanding officer, Colonel Haldimand S. Putnam, was shot dead. The brigade fell back, the sound of the Rebel yell mingling with the thunder of their volleys.

With the repulse of the second brigade the Union forces called a halt. The high command had learned a lesson, at heavy cost:

Battery Wagner was impregnable to assault. "Praise be to God. Anniversary of Bull Run gloriously celebrated," wired Beauregard to Joseph E. Johnston and three other Confederate generals. In tones more restrained and somber did the reporter of the New York *Tribune* describe the aftermath:

> The battle is over; it is midnight; the ocean beach is crowded with the dead, the dying and the wounded. It is with difficulty that you can urge your horse through to Lighthouse Inlet. Faint lights glimmer in the sand-holes and rifle pits where many a poor and bleeding soldier has lain down to his last sleep.

The balance sheet of casualties reflected the outcome of the assault. The Rebel casualties totaled 174 killed and wounded, including officers. The Federal total reached 1515. Of these Union losses the Massachusetts Fifty-fourth sustained more than that of any other of the ten regiments participating in the attack — its 247 Negro casualties being higher than the Confederate total. "De Forest of your city is wounded," wrote Lewis Douglass to his fiancée, Amelia Loguen of Syracuse, "George Washington is missing, Jacob Carter is missing, Charles Reason wounded, Charles Whiting, Charles Creamer all wounded."

Following the long night of July 18 the Sunday morning sun unveiled a grisly scene at Wagner. Men were lying in grotesque positions, their fingers and legs stretched rigidly out. Still to be heard were the cries and moans — some for help, others for water. The Confederates removed the wounded. The more than three hundred mangled bodies they buried in common graves in front of the fort, near the beach; Wagner was one military operation from which the embalmers would make no capital.

Under a flag of truce the Union command made unfruitful inquiries about Colonel Shaw. According to John T. Luck, a captured Northerner, the Confederate commander, Johnson Hagood, said to him:

I knew Colonel Shaw before the war, and then esteemed him. Had he been in command of white troops, I should have given him an honorable burial; as it is, I shall bury him in the common trench with the Negroes that fell with him.

Nearly twenty years later Hagood denied any recollection of making such a remark, but he did not deny that Shaw's body had been pointed out to him.

Such an unusual disposal of the body of an officer of Shaw's rank certainly seemed to be a premeditated indignity for his having been so foolhardy as to have taken a Negro command. At any rate, throughout the North the story of Shaw's burial excited great indignation. Soon the phrase attributed to Hagood became a war cry: "We have buried him with his niggers."

At Beaufort, with its over 95 per cent Negro population, the day after Wagner was a day of distress. In the morning the *Cosmopolitan* arrived with the nearly 150 wounded soldiers, and with the sad news of the repulse. The first to come off the boat were the injured who had to be borne on stretchers, the silent crowd eager to lend a helping hand. Then filing down the gangplank came those wounded combatants who did not need to be carried, many of them limping. Through the lane of damp-eyed spectators they made their way to the edge of the crowd where they climbed aboard the waiting wagons.

At the hospital they were objects of tender care. Sea Island Negroes furnished an oversupply of beef and chicken broth and stimulants. Among the volunteer nurses was the beautiful young Negro schoolmiss, Charlotte S. Forten, who had hurried over by rowboat from St. Helena, six miles away, where she was engaged in teaching the former slaves. With the other volunteer nurses, Miss Forten wrote letters for the men, and sewed up bullet holes and bayonet cuts. "Sometimes," wrote she, "I found a jacket that told a sad tale — so torn to pieces that it was past mending."

Like the other Negroes who had known him, Charlotte was deeply pained by the news of Shaw's death. Three weeks earlier

she had had tea with the officers of the Massachusetts Fifty-
fourth, and had been charmed by their young colonel: "What
nobleness of soul, what exquisite gentleness in that beautiful face."
In her diary of July 6, Miss Forten had jotted down a remembered incident:

> Tonight he helped me on my horse, and after carefully ar-
> ranging the folds of my riding skirt, said, so kindly, "Good-
> bye, if I don't see you again down here, I hope to see you
> at our house."

The Negroes showed their great regard for Shaw by collecting
money to erect a monument to his memory. The Fifty-fourth
raised $2832 for the monument, a truly remarkable exercise in
giving, and the freed slaves in the Sea Islands contributed to the
fund. Something of the high esteem that Negroes held for Colonel
Shaw was expressed by a colored versifier of a later generation,
Benjamin Brawley, in his poem, "My Hero":

> And Lancelot and Sir Bedivere
>   May pass beyond the pale,
> And wander over moor and mere
>   To find the Holy Grail;
> But ever yet the prize forsooth
>   My hero holds in fee;
> And he is Blameless Knight in truth,
>   And Galahad to me.

Along with other admirers of Shaw, the colored people could
share the glowing mood of exalted enterprise so beautifully expressed by Ralph Waldo Emerson in those memorable lines whose
inspiration, as the poet informed Shaw's father in a letter of
September 10, 1863, was the brave young colonel:

> So nigh is grandeur to our dust,
> So near is God to man,
> When duty whispers low, *Thou must*,
> The youth replies, I can.

Wagner had a sequel. From a purely military point of view the assault was a costly failure, but Wagner was an event which could not be measured in terms of immediate success. Wagner was not simply another of the Civil War's 2400 recorded military engagements. The storming of that slaughterhouse furnished the severest test of valor and soldiership: the assaulters were cast in the role of *enfants perdus* — expendables who would pay the forfeit of their lives. In the dread twilight on that barren Carolina shore the Fifty-fourth fixed beyond recall the Negro's right to the title of citizen-soldier.

At Wagner the Negro sealed his devotion to the cause of freedom. "Remember, if I die," wrote a noncom to the girl he left behind, "I die in a good cause." This sergeant of the Fifty-fourth and many of his black comrades in arms were fighting for freedom in the round — not a low relief freedom for themselves alone, or for their group alone, or for the Union alone, but for freedom wherever there was oppression.

In their goal to win this freedom they had fought valiantly at Wagner even though the attack had been badly mismanaged. None of the usual preparations for mounting an assault had been made: no line of skirmishers had been sent out; no guides had been provided to lead the column over the unfamiliar terrain. None of the men of the Fifty-fourth had had a musket in his hand more than eighteen weeks prior to the assault, and the regiment had had no experience or practice in the storming of a fortified work. And yet under enemy fire they had shown dauntless courage and determination. Such an achievement could not fail to win widespread respect. For, as Robert Dale Owen observed, in commenting on the valor of Negro troops, "Though there are higher qualities than strength and physical courage, yet, in our present stage of civilization, there are no qualities which command, from the masses, more respect."

Wagner was a turning point in the war. The valor of the 600 enlisted men of the Fifty-fourth opened the floodgates for the fresh army of more than 180,000 Negro soldiers who would infuse new spirit into a war-weary North. This brave black regiment thus blazed a path which would wind its way to Appomattox.

But even during the first two years of the war, before the Fifty-fourth kept its rendezvous with death on the parapets of Wagner, the Negro had been playing a role that was both heroic and significant. That role, and the obstacles he overcame in achieving its realization, furnish the first portion of this book's story.

Strike any other mortal blow
And use extremest rigor
But lest you "irritate the foe,"
Oh, do not touch "the Nigger!"

CHAPTER 11

They Also Serve

ON APRIL 12, 1861, a member of the Ohio state legislature
rushed into the chamber at Columbus in great excitement
and, scarcely waiting to catch the eye of the presiding officer,
made a dramatic announcement, "The Secessionists are bombarding Fort Sumter." Instantly the proceedings came to a halt and
a hush fell upon the assembly. Then the silence was broken by
a clear voice exclaiming, "Glory to God." The speaker was a
slim, plainly dressed, elderly woman with bright eyes. Abby
Kelley Foster had given "the best years of her useful life to the
redemption of the Negro from slavery," wrote one of her colleagues, William Wells Brown, who considered her the Joan of
Arc of the abolitionist crusade. A follower of Garrison and Phillips, she did not bite her tongue, and was in the habit of causing
"the truth to make a sensation by making it sensational."

The news which had evoked her outburst came as a shock to
the North, but there was little of real surprise. For nearly four
months the Union garrison at Fort Sumter had stood in need of
re-enforcement. One of three forts in the Charleston harbor,
Sumter was a dark, damp, gloomy-looking stronghold, its construction incomplete. Nevertheless on December 26, 1860, its
commanding officer, Major Robert J. Anderson, had transferred
his men to Sumter from Fort Moultrie since the latter was easily

assailable from the neighboring sand hills. All during the winter months Anderson's small band of sixty-one enlisted men, seven officers and thirteen musicians anxiously awaited re-enforcement.

In early April Anderson's food supply had become so depleted that he faced surrender to the Southern Confederacy, now established after an organizational meeting at Montgomery, Alabama, on February 4. Anderson's plight called for action and President Lincoln decided to send a relief expedition. The Confederacy, however, had something to say. Learning that Sumter was to be re-enforced and reprovisioned, the Confederate Secretary of War, Leroy P. Walker, wired the commander at Charleston to "reduce the fort." General P. G. T. Beauregard received the telegram on April 11. The next morning at daybreak the bombardment began. After forty hours under fire, "Anderson has hauled down the United States flag on Sumter and run up the white flag," in the exulting words of onlooker Robert Barnwell Rhett, Jr., editor of the Charleston *Mercury*.

"The last ray of hope for preserving the Union peaceably expired at the assault on Fort Sumter," wrote Lincoln in his first annual message to Congress. On the day of the fort's surrender, he drew up a proclamation for volunteers — the regular army numbered only 16,367 officers and men. Placarded on bulletin boards the next day, Monday, April 15, the proclamation requested from the militia of the several states 75,000 men to put down "combinations too powerful to be suppressed by the ordinary course of judicial proceedings."

The response was everything the President could have hoped. For the attack on Sumter angered and solidified the North. All past differences of opinion were forgotten as patriotic feeling welled from Maine to the Pacific. Everyone rallied to the flag. "A flame of fire seemed to run through the whole North," wrote a Boston abolitionist. "A month before the gun was fired at Sumter, it would have been dangerous for any antisecession man to express his sentiments; the next day after, it would have been dangerous for anybody to have said a word in favor of secession, even in the worst parts of the city." In brief compass, a Negro editor described the response: "The whole North, East and West are in arms. Drums are beating, men are enlisting, companies forming, regiments marching, banners are flying."

No laggard as a patriot, the Negro was not inattentive to the eagle's scream. Here was an opportunity to fight in what he took to be a crusade for liberty. Frederick Douglass confessed to a feeling allied to satisfaction at the prospect of a conflict: "Standing outside the pale of American humanity, denied citizenship, unable to call the land of my birth my country . . . and longing for the end of the bondage of my people, I was ready for any political upheaval which should bring about a change in the existing condition of things." William Waring, pastor of Toledo's colored Baptist Church noted that "from the hour of the uprising, the Negro was a new man." Joseph T. Wilson, who himself sought to join up, observed that "at the sound of the tocsin at the North, Negro waiter, cook, barber, bootblack, groom, porter and laborer stood ready at the enlisting office."

One eager Negro, aged sixty-five, insisted on going to war in an unenlisted capacity. Nicholas Biddle, a runaway slave, had come to Pottsville, Pennsylvania, where over the years he had made a living selling ice cream in summer and oysters in winter. Two days after Lincoln's call for volunteers, Biddle attached himself to the Washington Artillerists. The captain of the artillerists, James Wren, had wired Governor Andrew Curtin, offering the services of his unit for the defense of the nation's capital. The land and water approaches to Washington were easily accessible (as the British had demonstrated during the War of 1812), and Southerners were clamoring for its capture. Hence, the speeding of volunteers to that city to prevent its seizure.

When the Washington Artillerists, in company with the National Light Infantry, left Pottsville, Biddle, aged but "full of alacrity," made the trip with them. At Harrisburg, where they stopped overnight, he was an object of curiosity and delight to the colored population. Here the Pottsville troops were joined by three additional companies from Reading, Lewistown and Allentown.

When the five companies entrained for Baltimore, Biddle was with them. En route one of the soldiers joshingly remarked that Biddle might be caught by plug-uglies in Baltimore and sold down to Georgia. Asked whether he was afraid, the former slave replied, "See here, Misser Roberts, I's goin' to Washington a trustin' in de Lawd, and de debbil himself and the other Plug-Uglies can't skeer me. *You* better look out."

Arriving in Baltimore shortly after noon on April 18, the troops prepared to go from one railroad station to another since the city afforded no through rail connection to Washington. Trouble was in the air, for Baltimore sentiment was strongly Southern, and it was touch and go as to whether Maryland would stay in the Union or attempt to throw her weight with the Confederacy. Moreover, news had just reached the city that neighboring Virginia had passed an Ordinance of Secession.

With the Pennsylvania troops, 530 strong, as they strode the streets of Baltimore en route to the southern depot, marched Biddle, "in military dress," and in step "at the rear of the artillerists and immediately in front of the infantry." A mob followed them, throwing stones, hissing, jeering, and shouting, "Welcome to Southern graves." Particularly was Biddle an object of ire. The cry was raised, "Nigger in uniform," and one bystander yelled, "Kill that ––––– ed brother of Abe Lincoln."

A moment later Biddle was struck in the face "with a missile hurled by a rioter and cut so severely as to expose the bone." He would have fallen but for the support of First Lieutenant James Russell. The troops arrived at Washington in the early evening. Although small in number and but partly armed, they were received with great joy. When Congress met in July, in response to

Lincoln's call for a special session, the House passed a resolution tendering its thanks to them.

The Biddle episode was no *opéra bouffe*, either. The Baltimore populace had caught the sight of blood, and the next day when the Sixth Regiment of Massachusetts Volunteers set foot in the city a full-scale riot broke out. Ten thousand Baltimoreans crowded around the troops, and the subsequent jostling cost the lives of four soldiers and twelve civilians.

After the Baltimore experience Biddle dropped out of sight, although one day his friends at Pottsville would engrave on his tombstone:

> His was the proud distinction of shedding the first blood in the late war for the Union, being wounded while marching through Baltimore with the first volunteers from Schuylkill County, 18 April, 1861.

But Biddle's attitude was typical of the Negro's response. Frederick Douglass urged the colored men to form militia companies. His exhortation was unnecessary.

As was the customary practice among whites, the initiative in recruiting soldiers was taken by local leaders. When this leader (often self-designated) had rounded up a sufficient number of volunteers, he would offer them to the governor for enrollment into the state militia. In the early stages of the war much, therefore, depended upon community initiative, the technique of enlistment emphasizing states' rights.

Possibly the first group of Negroes to take organized action were those in Boston. Within thirty-six hours after Lincoln's call, a monster meeting was called at the Twelfth Baptist Church. The pastor of this church, Leonard A. Grimes, had been a prosperous hackman in Richmond who had used his earnings to assist runaway slaves. For this he had spent two years in a Richmond jail, and while there had come to the conclusion that he should preach. In Boston he made the Twelfth Baptist Church a center for public meetings.

The well-traveled William Wells Brown found the meeting "crowded as he had never seen a meeting before." The Stars and Stripes were cheered "most vociferously." The resolutions committee left no doubt that the Negro was anxious to leap for the knapsack and musket. "Our feelings urge us to say to our countrymen that we are ready to stand by and defend the Government with 'our lives, our fortunes, and our sacred honor.'" The colored people "have their souls in arms," and were eager for the fray. Another of the resolutions affirmed that "the colored women could go as nurses, seamstresses, and warriors if need be." The concluding resolution committed the group to "organize ourselves into drilling companies so that when we are called on we shall be prepared to make a fitting response."

Elsewhere the story was the same. In Providence a company of 106 Negroes organized by Samuel Dorrer offered to accompany the First Rhode Island Regiment as it left for the front. In New York City, wrote Horace Greeley, "a number of Blacks quietly hired a public hall and commenced drilling therein, in view of the possibility of a call to active service." A group of the city's leading colored citizens sought an audience with the governor in order to speak for Negro enlistments. A white New Yorker informed Secretary of War Simon Cameron that "a black regiment from this city could be put into the field in thirty days." And he added significantly, "Efficient and accomplished white soldiers are waiting to lead it." At Philadelphia Thomas Bowser "issued a soul-stirring and patriotic address to the colored people," with the result that "two regiments of colored men are now being formed." A correspondent of the New York *Tribune* sent word from the Quaker City: "The blacks here are drilling on their own hook. They could muster 5000 here easily." Gerrit Smith, perennial friend of the Negro, offered to equip a colored regiment with uniforms and arms, it being not uncommon for a rich man to outfit a unit.

From a Washington Negro came a letter to the War Office

offering the services of "300 reliable colored free citizens" for the defense of the city. The writer, Jacob Dodson, would have it known that "I have been three times across the Rocky Mountains in the service of the country with Frémont and others." If anyone wished to confer with him, concluded Dodson's letter, "I can be found about the Senate Chamber, as I have been employed about the premises for some years." In the seething city of Baltimore, "300 to 400 of our most respectable colored residents made a tender of their services to the city authorities," reported the *Sun* on April 23. Mayor George W. Brown assured them of his thanks, informing them "that their services would be called for if they can be made in any way available."

Cleveland's colored citizens responded in like vein. At a meeting on April 19, they expressed their desire to prove their loyalty and to put themselves in a position to defend the government. "Resolved," ran one of their statements, "that today, as in the times of '76, and in the days of 1812, we are ready to go forth and do battle in the common cause of our country." They pledged themselves to organize a military corps without delay. In another Ohio community, Albany, the Negroes formed a military company, the "Attucks Guards." The colored women of the town presented a handmade flag to the volunteer company.

The Michigan Negro was not to be outdone in patriotism. At Detroit a "superior" military band, organized in May 1860 by Captain O. C. Wood, sought to enlist. A Battle Creek physician, G. P. Miller, assured the War Department that the colored man was anxious to fight for the maintenance of the Union. To this end Miller solicited the privilege of "raising from 5000 to 10,000 freemen to report in sixty days to take any position that may be assigned to us (sharpshooters preferred)." Should this proposal be unacceptable, added Miller, these men would fight as guerrillas "if armed and equipped by the national government."

Throughout the North, in town after town, the Negro's response was a patriot's response. From Negroes in Canada, too, came offers to bear arms. A Negro citizen, in a letter to a Boston daily, expressed the general sentiment: the Negro "will go where duty shall call . . . not as a black man, but as an American. He will stand by the side of his white brave fellow-countrymen." Taking note of these widespread and spontaneous offers, a Negro editor observed, "It now remains for the government to accept their services." There was the rub.

For as promptly as the Negroes volunteered their services, just as promptly were those services declined. There seemed to be a common sentiment that the only military command that Negroes should hear was, "As you were." In Providence the police officials sent word that the drilling exercises of the Negroes were "disorderly gatherings" and would therefore be broken up. New York's chief of police notified Negro companies to discontinue their drilling else he would be unable to protect them from the public wrath. Negroes in Cleveland were informed by H. B. Carrington, the State Adjutant General, that the Ohio constitution did not permit him to issue an order for their enlistment. Ditto, said Governor William Dennison. "In Boston, Providence, New York, Philadelphia, Cleveland and Columbus, black men have offered their services and have been rejected," reported the *Standard* in early May.

The national government echoed local sentiment. To Dodson's letter the Secretary of War immediately returned a curt note, a single sentence in length: "In reply to your letter of 23 instant, I have to say that this Department has no intention to call into the service of the Government any colored soldiers." Miller's letter from Michigan brought a more courteous reply from the Acting Secretary of War. Wrote Thomas A. Scott, "The Department fully appreciates the patriotic spirit and intelligence which your letter displays, and has no doubt that upon reflection you will perceive that there are sufficient reasons for continuing the course thus far pursued in regard to the important question upon which your letter is based."

The unwillingness to consider Negro enlistments resulted in part from a widely held belief that the war would be over in ninety days. Mr. Greeley's daily assured the nations of Europe that "Jeff Davis & Co. will be swinging from the battlements at Washington at least by the 4th of July. We spit upon a later and longer deferred justice." A Philadelphia sheet predicted an even shorter existence for the Confederacy: "This much-ado-about-nothing will end in a month." The Chicago *Tribune* wanted the commotion localized: "Illinois can whip the South. We insist on the matter being turned over to us."

There was a more deep-seated reason for refusing colored volunteers – the North sought to avoid anything relating to the Negro. Congress had not been in session three weeks, before both houses passed a formal declaration of intention which affirmed that the war was being waged to maintain the supremacy of the Constitution and to preserve the Union, and not to overthrow or interfere with slavery.

The North was yet a long way from inscribing upon its banners, "Freedom for the Slave," and it did not propose to be stampeded in that direction by the abolitionists. Rights for Negroes must still be measured out in homeopathic doses and administered with a long spoon. The South was gone, true enough, but the Border States remained. In the Midwest, moreover, there were thousands who were bound to the South by ties of origin and sentiment. Border and Midwest states were ready to pounce on the government for anything that could be construed as pro-Negro. "At Washington I found that the mere mention of a Negro made the President nervous, and frightened some others of his cabinet much more," wrote a staunch friend of the Negro, the Unitarian clergyman, Moncure D. Conway of Cincinnati (who in the spring of 1862 showed his own lack of nervousness by personally shepherding a squad of thirty-one of his father's slaves in a two weeks' trek from Falmouth, Virginia, to Yellow Springs, Ohio).

State governors, their ears to the ground, did not dare act contrary to the assertions that this was a white man's war, and that white volunteers would not shoulder arms with the Negro. "We don't want to fight side and side with the nigger," wrote nineteen-year-old Corporal Felix Brannigan of the seventy-fourth New York Volunteers to his sister. "We think we are a too superior race for that." That the Negro was inferior, that "Negro blood" was different from other blood, was America's most deeply rooted misconception; and in a people's war, such as the Civil War, the prejudices of the man in the street frequently dominated the actions of elected officials and the attitude of the military.

Many Negroes would not permit these refusals to wet-blanket their ardor. Some went into the navy, "for Jack has never been squeamish." Others, determined to serve in the army even if not in uniform, went as waiters, cooks, hostlers, teamsters and laborers generally. Many of the Providence Negroes who had drilled with the rejected company, attached themselves as servants to Rhode Island regiments and batteries. An Ohio Negro wrote to the Toledo *Blade* offering himself as "cook, waiter, or in any other way." Less than ten months after hostilities broke out, there were five hundred teamsters with the Union troops in Kansas.

One Negro said nothing about his race and hoped for the best. Joseph T. Wilson, subsequently to win fame as a chronicler of the Negro soldier, managed to join up for three days. He had enlisted in a New York regiment in company with two Spaniards, the three of them having arrived from Valparaiso, Chile, and gone straight to the recruiting office. Sworn in, they were sent to one of the islands in the harbor. On the third day the barracks cook, an aged Negro, recognized Wilson and greeted him effusively. Before the recruit could "give the cook a hint," a summons came. The officer of the day, to whom the incident had been reported, sent for the cook. Wilson did not remain in suspense long. Within a few hours he was escorted to the launch by a guard of honor, landed in New York, and honorably discharged.

A Negro in a Kansas company who managed to enlist before his color was ascertained was not handled as delicately as Wilson. When Company G of the First Regiment of Kansas Volunteers discovered a Negro in their midst, thirty-five of them sent a letter to the commanding general that he be removed. "We have no objection to endure all the privations we may be called upon to endure," stated their petition, "but to have one of the company, or even one of the regiment, pointed out as a 'nigger' while on dress parade or guard, is more than we like to be called upon to bear."

The Negro's eagerness to strike a blow even though he was denied the wearing of the blue was vividly illustrated by the *Waring* incident, a heroic deed whose bloody details held a gruesome fascination for readers throughout the North. The incident was the hard-to-believe story of a Negro, William Tillman, who came home as captain of a ship in which he went out as steward.

The *S. J. Waring* was a vessel of 300 tons bound in early July for Montevideo with an assorted cargo. She was scarcely 150 miles out from Sandy Hook when she was captured on July 7 by the daring Confederate privateer, *Jeff Davis*. The *Jeff Davis*, "the number of whose prizes and the value of whose merchandise captured have no parallel since the *Saucy Jack*," was one of a dozen privateers authorized by letters of marque issued by the Confederacy. The captured *Waring* was declared a prize of the Confederate States of America, and was relieved of a portion of her cargo, particularly foodstuffs. Her captain and four of her crew were also taken aboard the privateer. Not removed from the captured schooner were four persons — two seamen, William Stedding and Donald McLeod, a passenger, and William Tillman, the twenty-seven-year-old, "strongly built" steward, of "unmixed blood."

In place of the five men who were removed, the *Jeff Davis* substituted a prize crew of five — a captain, Montague Amiel, two mates and two sailors. The *Waring* thereupon was pointed south, its destination Charleston.

The prize ship was within a hundred miles of that port when Tillman decided to carry out a plan of action he had devised. He had been indignant at the lowering of the Stars and Stripes and its cutting up to make it into a Confederate flag. He had reason, moreover, to believe that once at Charleston he would be sold into slavery, even though he had been born free. "I am not going to Charleston a live man," he confided to William Stedding, "they must take me there, if at all, dead." After agreeing to assist him, Stedding was let in on the plan.

On July 16 within a half hour of midnight, Tillman, hatchet in hand, approached the captain's cabin where the ship's master and the first mate were slumbering. Each was killed quickly by a vigorous blow on the skull. The second mate, sleeping on the poop deck, was next. As Tillman stole up to him, the mate was just on the point of drowsily getting up from his reclining position "with little expectation that he was about being launched into eternity." With Stedding's help, Tillman threw the three bodies overboard. The three killings and the disposal of the bodies took only seven and a half minutes.

Tillman summoned the two remaining privateer sailors and told them that henceforth they would take orders from him. One he put in irons, the other agreed to assist in working the vessel.

The *Waring* arrived at New York on Sunday, July 21, and immediately became the object of great curiosity. Thousands wished to see the bloody hatchet. Crowds followed Tillman; indeed, as the *Tribune* phrased it, he "created such an interest in the public mind that Mr. Barnum has induced him to receive visitors at the Museum for the next few days." The underwriters, although they could not capitalize on Tillman's popular appeal like the master showman, P. T. Barnum, were nonetheless overjoyed; the ship and its cargo were valued at over $100,000. Tillman eventually received $6000 prize money.

Tillman's exploit was hailed by the friends of the Negro. "To this colored man was the nation indebted for the first vindication of its honor at sea," announced Horace Greeley's *Tribune*. Another New York journal wrote that "it goes far to console us for the sad reverse of our arms at Bull Run," and added that Tillman put to shame "those who question the Negro's capacity for the enjoyment and defense of liberty."

Before popular excitement over the *Waring* incident had died down, the name of another Negro sea hero was in the public prints. This was Jacob Garrick, a twenty-five-year-old steward of the *Enchantress*, a vessel which had cleared from Boston on June 29, bound for Cuban ports with an assorted cargo. On the day preceding the capture of the *Waring*, the prowling *Jeff Davis* seized the *Enchantress*. In this instance, however, the entire crew of the captured vessel, except Garrick, was removed. A prize crew took over the ship, and forthwith steered it toward Charleston. The captain of the prize crew had taken the precaution of providing himself with the clearance papers of the *Enchantress*, with the intention of representing his crew as the original crew if stopped by a Union man-of-war. This precaution proved wise, but the prize crew had not reckoned with Garrick.

For on July 22 the U.S.S. *Albatross*, of the Atlantic Blockading Squadron, caught sight of the *Enchantress*, and hailed her. As the *Albatross* approached, Garrick was ordered to the forecastle. "I said I would rather stay in the galley," reported Garrick in the testimony he gave in court, a portion of which follows. "I went in the galley and watched the steamer coming. When the steamer saw us tack ship, she hauled right up for us. . . . The steamer hoisted the American flag, and we hoisted our American flag. The steamer kept coming on. When the steamer got pretty close to us, I heard a hail, 'What schooner is that?' The reply was 'the *Enchantress*.' 'Where bound to?' 'St. Jago de Cuba.' As soon as that was said, I jumped out of the galley and jumped overboard."

Q. "How far was the steamer from you?"
A. "About across this room — within speaking distance."

Q. "What did you do when you jumped in the water?"

A. "I sang out, 'a captured vessel of the privateer *Jeff Davis*, and they are taking her into Charleston.' I sang it out so they could hear me on board the steamer."

The concluding details are supplied by the laconic log of the *Albatross* for July 22. "Came up with a schooner at 1:45. Hailed schooner, when a Negro jumped over board, exclaiming, 'Save me captain, she's bound for Charleston.' Turned our guns on her and ordered her to heave to, and sent a boat aboard with Lieutenant Neville picking up the Negro on the way. Boat returned at 2, with schooner's crew of five men. . . . Put the crew in double irons and sent Master's Mate Wendell and five men to take charge of her, with the Negro who belonged to the schooner when captured."

The *Waring* and *Enchantress* incidents strengthened the belief of the Negroes that the time would come when their services would be welcomed. They did not have to be readers of history to sense that war is an uprooter of old beliefs, a disturber of long-held notions, a crucible in which new things are fashioned. Robert Purvis, keeping watch in late May at the deathbed of his eldest son, sent word to his fellows: "I apprehend that a realizing sense of the services which colored people have rendered, and can render again, will yet be reached by the people of this country."

❖

Not dissimilar from the patriotic response of the Northern Negro was that of the 182,000 free Negroes in the eleven states flying the Stars and Bars. Southern Negroes too came forward in a general eagerness to be of service.

Many of the offers were without strings — their makers indicated a willingness to assist in whatever capacity assigned. Many such responses came from Virginia's nearly 60,000 free Negroes.

The Old Dominion had scarcely voted to secede when seventy Lynchburg Negroes tendered their services. A week later a group from Richmond, having volunteered for "the work of defense, or any other capacity required," were directed to report "to the Captain of the Woodis Riflemen." In Amelia County, Chesterfield and Petersburg, free Negroes volunteered to do any work assigned to them.

When Negroes specified the type of service they would care to perform, it was generally the work of defense. Petersburg Negroes were among the first to take such action. One morning in late April 1861 they gathered in the courthouse square, preparatory to leaving for Norfolk to work on the fortifications. They listened to white speakers including former mayor John Dodson who presented them with a Confederate flag, assuring them that when they returned they would "reap a rich reward of praise, and merit, from a thankful people." Charles Tinsley, a bricklayer and a "corner workman," acted as spokesman for the Negroes. His remarks in acceptance of the flag were brief: "We are willing to aid Virginia's cause to the utmost of our ability. . . . There is not an unwilling heart among us, not a hand but will tell in the work before us; and we promise unhesitating obedience to all orders that may be given us."

At Hampton three hundred Negroes solicited employment on the batteries. "Indeed," wrote a Norfolk correspondent of the Petersburg *Express*, "the entire fortifications of the harbor might be constructed by the voluntary labors of Negroes, who would claim no higher reward than the privilege of being allowed to contribute their share toward the defense of the State. . . ."

Ten days after South Carolina left the Union, one hundred and fifty-three Charleston Negroes volunteered to erect redoubts and coastal defenses. They were put to work at once. At Savannah, fifty-five free Negroes offered their services in defense of the state at any point and for any length of time. In the closing week of March 1861, Bowman Seals of Clayton,

Alabama, addressed a letter "To His Excellency, the President of the Confederate States," reporting that he was a good marksman and a practical mechanic "with physical powers not much impaired." He did not ask any "office or emolument," but only that the President of "this favored republic . . . shall assign me some duty that may make me serviceable in its defense."

Some Negroes gave money or goods. Richard Kennard of Petersburg gave a hundred dollars. Jordan Chase of Vicksburg, too old for physical exertion, having borne arms in the War of 1812, gave a horse for the Confederate cavalry and authorized the government to draw on him for five hundred dollars. Thomy Lafon, New Orleans real estate broker, donated five hundred dollars to the Confederate defense fund. An Alabama Negro presented a state regiment with one hundred bushels of sweet potatoes. Among the contributors to the ninety dollars raised in the small town of Helena, South Carolina, for soldier relief were a number of Negroes "who were as anxious to add their mite as anyone." At Charleston a little Negro girl sent a "free-will offering of 25¢" for the gunboat fund sponsored by the women of the city. Blind Tom, "the little African prodigy" gave concerts in the summer of 1861 for the sick and wounded of the Confederate Army. Confederate war bonds found Negro subscribers.

The offers coming from Negroes were not confined to noncombatant services. There were numerous instances of a single person volunteering to bear arms, such as that of a Memphis Negro who agreed to equip himself at his own expense, requesting only that his family and property be protected during his absence.

Most offers for military duty came however, as in the North, from groups. Even before Virginia had decided to join her sisters to the south, seventy Negroes in Lynchburg volunteered for fighting in defense of the state. Late in April, sixty Richmond Negroes, bearing the Confederate flag, asked to be enlisted. In Tennessee a Negro company at Nashville sent word of its availability and willingness. Two companies of Negroes at Fort Smith, Arkansas, held drilling exercises even though they had no arms; if they were not called, it would be through no fault of theirs.

In Mobile the Creole Negroes were anxious to go to war, reported G. Huggins Cleveland, who promised that he could raise "a battalion of regiment." These Negroes were of French-Negro or Spanish-Negro origin, and had been guaranteed citizenship rights in 1803 in the treaty with France by which Louisiana was acquired. "If such a battalion can be received," wrote Cleveland, "I can raise it in a few days."

By far the most successful effort to form military units was that of the Negroes in New Orleans. Having bespoken, at a monster mass meeting on April 28, their readiness "to take arms at a moment's notice and fight shoulder to shoulder with other citizens," they organized two regiments of "Native Guards." These companies were joined with the state militia, and paraded with other Louisiana troops on November 23, 1861. As they passed in review before Governor Thomas O. Moore, these Negro soldiers made a favorable impression; they had been well drilled and they were smartly uniformed. Well-to-do Creole Negroes, they carried themselves with a military bearing; as they informed a commanding general on a later occasion, they came of a fighting race: "Our fathers were brought here as slaves because they were captured in war, and in hand to hand fights, too. Pardon me, General, but the only cowardly blood we have got in our veins is the white blood."

Why did these free Negroes throughout the South offer their services as combatants and otherwise to the Confederacy, a government which had committed itself to Negro bondage, and whose collapse would almost certainly unshackle the slave?

To begin with, these Negro volunteers placed the cause of their respective commonwealth above every other public duty. Invariably their offers were to their state of locality, rather than to the central government. A strong sense of local patriotism pervaded the ante-bellum South, and it cut across the color line. Negroes thought of themselves as Virginians, North Carolinians, Louisianians, and so forth, and they behaved as citizens of their state. Like thousands of white Southerners who personally hated slavery and felt that it was doomed with the coming of the war but who nevertheless defended the Confederacy, these free Negroes had a sense of community responsibility which impelled them to throw their lot with their neighbors.

There were other motives. Some of the free Negroes welcomed the prospect of defense jobs at good wages in war-swollen industries. As they viewed things, it need not be "a rich man's war and a poor man's fight."

Some who volunteered had a belief that if the free Negro came forward to do his bit, there would be no more hostile legislation against him. A grateful state would show its appreciation in a concrete way. And every colored parent could share the sentiment expressed by the New Orleans Negro who in the spring of 1862 entertained Union officers at a seven-course banquet, with solid silver service: "No matter where I fight, I only wish to spend what I have, and fight as long as I can, if only my boy may stand in the street equal to a white boy when the war is over."

State and local officials found it possible to accept a few of the offers for the building of fortifications. But, except in New Orleans, there was no acceptance for bearing arms. In August 1861 the Chief of the Bureau of War informed W. S. Turner, of Little Rock, Arkansas, that the War Department gratefully declined his request to recruit Negro soldiers. In his gracious letter, Chief Albert T. Bledsoe granted that there was "high authority" for such a step inasmuch as "Washington himself recommended the enlistment of two Negro regiments." But at the present time, added Bledsoe, "there is a superabundance of our own color," and for them the supply of arms was inadequate.

As for the two Louisiana regiments of Negroes enlisted under the Confederate flag, they were never given an order to fire a gun. As late as March 1862, Governor Moore had asked them to stand by and maintain their organization pending further orders. A month later when the intrepid Union admiral, David G. Farragut, successfully ran the gantlet of the two forts guarding the approaches to New Orleans, the Confederate troops hastily evacuated the city. But the "Native Guards" were left behind. At their post on Esplanade Street they had, as per official instructions a month earlier, held themselves "prepared for such orders as may be transmitted to them." But no such orders ever came.

This failure to enlist the free Negro did stem in part, as Bledsoe said, from a lack of arms. In the early weeks thousands of enthusiastic whites had come forward. "The anxiety among our citizens," boasted Howell Cobb, chairman at the Montgomery convention which established the Confederacy, "is not as to who shall *go* to the wars, *but who shall stay at home.*" Moreover many Southerners, like their foes in the North, expected the war to be over in no time — one glorious victory would end it all.

But the basic failure to fully use the services of the free Negro was simply that such a use posed a cruel dilemma. Horace Greeley's paper had published many of the offers made by free Negroes, and the *Tribune* pointed a barb: these responses "should call a blush to the cheek of every secessionist who reflects that the ultra pro-slavery interest in Virginia has for years endeavored to pass an act subjecting every free Negro to slavery or exile." But ruling classes have remarkable propensities for self-exculpation, and the South's planter aristocracy was certainly no exception. To them it was not so much a matter of conscience.

It was the slave: again here was the difficulty. To in any way officially raise the status of the free Negro would have repercussions in the form of additional slave discontent. Now that war had come, the dangers of slave insurrections were thought to be immeasurably increased. Uppermost in the mind of every slaveholder was the question: What now will be the conduct of the slaves?

But those white Southerners who hoped that the war would bring no change in the attitude and behavior of the slave were brothers to the ostrich. "War," wrote Basil L. Gildersleeve, a volunteer aide on the staff of Confederate Major General John Brown Gordon, "is an omelet that cannot be made without breaking eggs, not only eggs in *esse*, but eggs in *posse*." That which befell slavery, to which attention is now directed, is a case in point.

"Well, Ebony, what do you do these times?"
"Ah, Massa," said he, with a significant twinkle of
the eye, raising a hand to one ear, "I harks!"

CHAPTER III

No More Driver's Lash

ALEXANDER HAMILTON STEPHENS was not a man of few words. On the contrary, he was in the habit of expressing himself often and at length. He was not a married man. A lawyer of long standing (he was only twenty-two when he passed the Georgia bar), his was a profession whose business was the use of language. Moreover, if he attracted attention it would be through voice or pen for he was not physically prepossessing. Stoop-shouldered and wrinkle-faced, he had never weighed over ninety-six pounds — "if he were laid out in his coffin, he needn't look any different."

As a public speaker and as a writer "Little Aleck" was a powerful figure in the South. But of all his hundreds of thousands of printed words, his innumerable orations, and his thousands of personal letters — and he thought nothing of writing twenty in one evening — the one passage for which he is remembered was a line in a speech delivered at Savannah on March 21, 1861. He had just come from Montgomery where on February 11, his forty-ninth birthday, he had been inaugurated as Vice-President of the Confederacy.

Now, the enormous crowd at Savannah's Athenaeum, overflowing into the streets, listened as he predicted a bright future for the new nation. The founding fathers at Philadelphia in 1787, said he, had erred in establishing the United States on the assumption of the equality of races. The South's new government — and here is the notorious passage — "is founded upon exactly the opposite ideas; its foundations are laid, its cornerstone rests, upon the great truth that the Negro is not equal to the white man; subordination to the superior race is his natural and moral condition." This stone which the first builders had rejected was the chief stone of the new Confederate edifice.

In the North the Negro and his supporters would see to it that this "cornerstone" statement would be even more widely publicized than Robert Toombs's boast that he would call the roll of his slaves on Bunker Hill in Boston. But Stephens's words had been loudly applauded by the Savannah audience, and as he pointed out in the same speech, the Confederate constitution put at rest "all the agitating questions relating to our peculiar institution." Unlike the national constitution it showed no squeamishness in using the word slavery: "We have sought by no euphony to hide its name," wrote Robert H. Smith of Alabama. Under the Confederate constitution the central government and the territorial governments were required to recognize and protect slavery. State governors were required to "deliver up" runaways who fled within their borders, and each state pledged to the citizens of other states the right of "transit and sojourn with their slaves and other property." The foreign slave trade (except with the slaveholding states of the United States) was prohibited.

The Confederate constitution protected slavery from legislative enactment; now it remained to protect slavery from the slave. For war had come and slavery required perfect peace. The white South was nervous, with a feeling akin to that of sitting on a keg of gunpowder. But white Southerners did not wait for an internal explosion; they immediately proceeded to set up controls — methods of preventing uprisings and thwarting escapes.

Obviously a close watch must be kept on the free Negro. State laws were passed for the dual purpose of keeping down the number of free Negroes and reducing their contacts with the slave. To prevent an increase in the free Negro populations, some states prohibited slave manumissions except by action of the legislature. To reduce contacts between the two groups, the free Negro was not permitted to own or to hire slaves.

In directly controlling the slave population the most widely used method was that of policing. The cane and cotton estates had their plantation guards whose duty it was to patrol the roads after darkness had fallen, accosting all Negroes and demanding that they produce their passes. Semimilitary in nature, often mounted, these police were outfitted by the planters and recognized by the state authorities. In the towns the use of passports became mandatory. Time after time in a single day, slaves were challenged to show a passport, properly made out by their owner or some other responsible party. And when evening shadows fell, the curfew and the night patrol emptied the streets of black feet.

Voluntary policing was not always dependable, hence every state passed laws requiring state patrols to tighten their surveillance of slave activities. In some states, Florida for example, each county was divided into beats, and local citizens were assigned to duty. As a rule, exemptions from patrol duty were turned down, and fines and imprisonment faced those who shirked it. The patrols made their rounds at night, arresting and examining Negroes, and dispersing gatherings of more than four or five.

The system of civilian patrols broke down when white men became scarce. One substitute was the state militia. In some commonwealths these reserves were required to perform patrol duty. Occasionally the Confederate Army would supply a detachment of light cavalry for police duty in those sections exposed to the ever-advancing Yankee troops.

In the control of the slave, Southern white women played a key role. They assisted the clergy in fostering programs of religious training; as Dr. Charles Colcock Jones announced before the General Assembly of the Presbyterian Church, meeting in Augusta eight months after the war broke out, "The importance of the instruction of Negroes under our present circumstances cannot be too highly estimated."

To allay discontent, the plantation mistresses did all they could in encouraging the simple pleasures and recreations of slave life — the Saturday night dances, the 'possum hunts, the group singing, and the annual barbecue after the "laying by" of the crops. Mistresses did not neglect slave weddings as a means of winning loyalty. Occasionally they permitted the ceremony to be held in the halls of the mansion, and they assisted in bedecking the bride and preparing the wedding feast. A plantation in Eufaula, Alabama, was the scene of such a ceremony:

> With flowers scattered all around, our laps and hands full, we twined the wreath for the Negro girl, the bride elect of the evening. When twilight had deepened into darkness, the bride was called to make ready for the marriage. When fully robed in her wedding garment, she was inspected by every member of the household and judged to be quite *au fait*. But Winnie pulled off her own watch and chain, together with her bracelets, and with these further adorned the bride.

While insuring against any curtailment of slave privileges, mistresses also sought to minimize the privations brought on by the war. Less meat — pork and beef particularly — was available, but there was no reduction in the total amount of food. Some items of diet appeared more often in the "allowance day" rations — molasses, sorghum, sweet potatoes and vegetables generally. For with cotton production restricted, plantation labor was diverted to the cultivation of food crops.

More serious than the shortage of meat was that of clothing. The cast-aside garments of other days were salvaged and curtains were transformed into dresses, as mistresses sought to provide their slaves with the yearly clothing allotment. Spinning wheels and looms, their layers of dust wiped off, were brought down from attics, and soon one could hear everywhere the incessant whirr, hum and clang of domestic garment-making. There was, nevertheless, a shortage of clothing, but as it bore more heavily on the whites than on the slave, the latter could make no unfavorable contrast between his garb and that of the ruling class.

More widely practiced than control through kindness was control through fear. Slaves were told that the Yankees were horned — Beelzebub incarnate — and that no mercy would be shown to their victims, innocent or guilty. It was dinned in the Negroes that "the Yankees make the severest and most cruel masters of slaves of any people on the face of the Globe." Captured blacks would be put in the front line of battle, cannon fodder for sure. Or, they might be harnessed like horses and cut by the long whip if they pulled their loads too haltingly. It had happened, said the Norfolk *Day Book*, in a little piece titled, "How the Yankees Treat Negroes." Colored men at Old Point "are put in harness like so many oxen, and beneath the lash of a cruel and unmerciful overseer, are forced to do the work of mules, and haul large quantities of stone to the different works now being built." Slaves were told that the avaricious Yankees, with their ever-itching palms, would sell them to Cuba. The Cuba propaganda was most useful — "There is not a rebel master," wrote Edward L. Pierce in February 1862, "from the Potomac to the Gulf who has not repeatedly made this assurance to his slaves."

Another method of controlling the slave was by removal. As soon as the war broke out many planters withdrew their slaves from the towns. But this was small scale. More drastic steps were necessary when the Union troops began their invasion of Southern soil. Plantations exposed to Yankee raids were abandoned, their owners hastening to the interior with their able-bodied slaves. Southern roads after 1861 were swarming with Negroes being transferred to safer spots. This movement, "running the Negroes," as it was called, became a familiar spectacle. "These caravans of refugees were interesting sights," writes Bell Wiley, "Negro women, their heads wrapped in gaudy bandanas perched high on wagons loaded with chairs, tables, and bedding; stalwart Negro men trudging beside the slow-moving vans; dust-covered, bare-footed pickaninnies, to whom the journey was more of a frolic than a flight, now running along beside the wagon, now stealing a ride on the 'perch-pole.' . . ."

Another form of slave control was through impressment. Six of the states authorized their governors to enroll slaves for non-combatant military service — primarily constructing fortifications and embattlements. Impressment officers were required to notify slaveowners of the numbers and occupations of the blacks whose services they sought. If more than twenty were needed, the state would pay the wages of an overseer. The occupational skill of the worker determined the amount paid to his master. The Virginia slave-rolls for 1861–1862 show that a water boy was paid 25¢ a day, a common laborer averaged 50¢ a day, a carpenter $1.30, a bricklayer $1.37, and "Sam, Horse and Cart," $2.00 a day.

The Confederate army was also authorized to impress slaves. General J. Bankhead Magruder, commanding the Army of the Peninsula, ordered the printing of a form announcement, dated September 7, 1861, at Williamsburg, notifying the slaveowners that he had received full authority from the Secretary of War to impress slaves into service, and called upon the owners to send one half of their slaves to the nearest wharf to be conveyed to Williamsburg: "They will send with their slaves the necessary implements of labor — spades, shovels, picks, grubbing-tools, and axes. The Negroes will be allowed 50¢ a day and plenty of provisions; the money to be paid by the quartermaster to their masters."

The use of impressed labor was of enormous advantage to the South. It enabled her to put a large portion of her white population under arms. From the very beginning of hostilities the military labor of the slave made itself felt. At the first battle of Bull Run in July 1861 "slave-built batteries repulsed the finest army ever organized on the American Continent," ran the angry comment of the Chicago *Tribune*. "General McDowell threads his way through roads and defiles obstructed by Negroes, and plunges into a honeycomb of batteries erected by Negroes, suffers a stunning defeat and loses his command."

The *Tribune* was vexed because the North had refused to enlist Negroes, and its editors believed that a bit of comparison might serve a useful purpose. But there could be no doubt of the key role of the slave's brawn and job skills in the war potential of the Confederacy. The military labor of the slave was not limited to working on the defenses. As an army cook the Negro was preferred to the white man, even if the black chef "did boil his shirts and greasy trousers in the kettle in which he cooked our food, made soup, tea and coffee," thus giving the fare a somewhat ambiguous flavor. Negroes were the teamsters, and they loaded and unloaded the wagons and railroad cars. Thousands moved on the battle fronts as hospital attendants and body servants. Indeed, when the labor of slave women and children behind the lines was added to that of these black men, the combined efforts of four million slaves "offset at least eight million of Northern whites," according to a contemporary estimate by a ranking general. In comparing the productivity of Northern workers with that of the slaves, it must be remembered that there was no ten-hour day in Dixie.

⚜

The various methods of controlling the slave could be fully effective only if the slave himself co-operated. Therefore the "morale" of the bondman — his own attitude and conduct — furnished the staple of conversation in the Confederacy. Now that the flower of Southern manhood was bound for the battle fronts, would the slaves resort to fire, plunder and murder, led by a hundred Nat Turners or black John Browns, like Ate "come hot from hell"? Or would the slave simply do as he was told in the unquestioning obedience that befits his humble state?

When it became apparent that there would be no general, large-scale uprisings and outbreaks, the white South, with great relief, began to boast of the "loyalty" of the slaves. Their faithfulness was proclaimed from the housetops. A good bit of wishful thinking entered in — without this belief and hope concerning the Negro's quiet deportment, the future would have been fearful to contemplate. Slave loyalty, therefore, quickly became the accepted "line": useful in the South to reassure the nervous, and serviceable in the North as a propaganda counterpoise to the abolitionist assertion that slavery was a tinderbox awaiting only the slightest spark to set off a conflagration. Thus the South publicized stories of slave loyalty and devotion.

Some of these tales reflected the wishful thinking of the whites more than anything else. For it was questionable to assume that a chattel, anxious to please, meant everything he said. While in the presence of the ruling class, slaves said many things with their lips, their words little more than tinkling cymbals. A white Southerner deceived himself if, as did a New Orleanian, he believed that all slaves were loyal because he "heard a dining-room servant of one of our citizens, who is as black as Erebus, say to his mistress, 'Missus, don't you think us 'Mericans can whip them Yankees if they does come down here?'"

Undoubtedly, however, many of the recitals of slave loyalty had the ring of truth. Instances there were such as that of a slave on Hilton Head Island, South Carolina, who rounded up the horses on one of the batteries, got them on a flat, and floated them down to Savannah, accomplishing this feat after the battery had been abandoned to the approaching Union forces. And doubtless there were two slaves in Mobile who took $400 of the Confederate loan, and one in New Orleans who subscribed $200. And at

Talladega, Alabama, "Mrs. Averitt's Negroes have taken up a collection of $53.20 to relieve the wants of the soldiers." And in Petersburg "an old hackman came to his master, with tears in his eyes, asking that he accept all his savings, $100, to help equip the volunteers." And in Richmond there was a slave preacher who publicly prayed for the Confederate Army.

Individual instances of slave loyalty might be multiplied, but it is perhaps safe to say that slaves who were faithful were those who had a close personal relationship with whites. On the battle fronts the body servant who had grown up in the family proved his devotion time and again. Such fidelity was less likely from a hired body servant, but the latter might easily develop an affection for one whose personal effects he handled — clothes, shoes and weapons — and for whom he foraged, cooked, barbered and nursed.

On the plantation some house servants likewise tended to be loyal. They it was who sewed the family silver in the mattress, and who buried the heirlooms, and who shrilly rebuked the marauding Yankee "bummers." Within the big house the bonds of affection which had grown up over the years withstood the shock of war; in fact, when a family faced serious trouble, the house slaves did their work with greater efficiency. Such, for example, was the case of the Dabney plantation, "Burleigh," in Hinds County, Mississippi, where the slaves "went about their duties more conscientiously than before," wrote Susan Dabney Smedes. But here it must be noted that the Thomas Dabneys were the kind of owners who would never hire out or sell a slave, who encouraged every field hand on the plantation to come and chat with them, and who taught their sixteen children that slaves were flesh and blood like themselves.

And in reaching any conclusion about slave loyalty, it must be remembered that the slaves were a forgiving lot, and often their sympathy for a stricken owner was mistaken for a love of bondage. Life had taught Negroes to pity. Themselves familiar with bereavement, slaves could be sincerely solicitous and well behaved in the presence of a grief-laden mistress. Themselves no strangers to sorrow, they might well walk with hushed tread and sober mien in the half-vacant mansion where a Susan Leigh Blackford lamented her absent spouse: "I well remember now those lonely evenings; after my two children were asleep I would picture him that was dearer to me than life lying stark upon some lonely battlefield or wounded on a stretcher. There can be no sorrow like that — it was the sorrow of death itself."

Whatever the degree of slave loyalty, it invariably went hand-in-hand with a desire to be free. The conduct of the slave might be orderly and restrained, particularly in the opening stages of the war and in the interior regions far removed from military action, but the magic word "freedom" was whispered in every cotton field and canebrake. Perhaps a few favored house servants might shy at cutting loose from mistress, and perhaps a few elderly slaves might fear starvation if thrown on their own resources. But to all others the distant rumble of battle meant deliverance, and in the roar of the big guns they heard the blast of advent blow.

That their freedom was the object of the war was a dominating conviction. For they were a believing people — religion was an ever-present dimension of experience — and to them the war was a fulfillment of Old Testament prophecy. They did not doubt that a new dispensation was at hand. Their folk songs had always reflected, in some guise or another, this longing for freedom. And now that the day of reckoning was at hand, they sang with new fervor the old spiritual:

> We'll fight for liberty,
> We'll fight for liberty,
> We'll fight for liberty,
> When de Lord will call us home.

Slaves at Georgetown were thrown in jail for voicing this song in 1861. But in the same state before the year was over, the Sea Island Negroes were singing out a verse which had a one-way meaning only:

> No more driver's lash for me
> No more, no more:
> No more driver's lash for me
> Many tousand go.

Since in their thinking the mission of the war was human freedom, the slaves strove to keep themselves fully informed. "I never found one at Hampton or Monroe who did not perfectly understand the issue of the war," wrote a New York *World* correspondent. Every victory for the Federal forces and every defeat for the boys in gray was noted with absorbing interest. Slaves might feign ignorance for they had learned that it was not always prudent to reveal how much they knew. "Not by one word or look can we detect any change in the demeanor of these Negro servants," wrote Mary Boykin Chesnut during the bombardment of Fort Sumter. "Lawrence sits at our door, as sleepy and as respectful and as profoundly indifferent. So are they all. But," added she — for she was not given to self-deception — "they carry it too far."

At every stage of the war the slaves knew something of the existing state of affairs. "The Negroes of the South had a great deal of surreptitious knowledge, and her bondsmen were a conclave of unrecognized free masons," wrote James Guthrie. Another Negro writer, Booker T. Washington, made a similar observation: "Though I was a mere child during the preparation for the Civil War and during the war itself, I now recall the many late-at-night whispered discussions that I heard my mother and other slaves on the plantation indulge in. These discussions showed that they understood the situation, and that they kept themselves informed of events by what was termed the 'grapevine telegraph.'"

Slaves had ways of finding out. Some of them crawled under houses and kept recumbently quiet while they eavesdropped on the white folks. So as to overhear after-dinner conversations, black boys climbed trees and hid themselves under the heavy moss just a little before the master and his guests rose from the table and came out to sit on the piazza for a slow cigar. One waiting-maid whose master and mistress spelled out things they did not wish her to know, performed the prodigious feat of carrying all the spellings in her head, to be interpreted later by some Negro who was literate.

Because they were relatively well informed the slaves did not rise up en masse and smite, pillage and burn. "A thousand torches would have disbanded the Southern Army," wrote Henry W. Grady, postwar editor of the Atlanta *Constitution*, "but there was not one." For the blacks knew that they were being watched very closely. This constant surveillance robbed them of their main chance of staging successful revolts. Every slave uprising had depended for its success upon the element of surprise and sudden thrust. Whenever these were lacking, failure ensued even though the planning was as careful as that of Denmark Vesey, hanged in Charleston in 1822 for plotting a slave revolt, and the leadership as courageous. And now that war had come the white South, as has been indicated, had taken every precaution against being surprised in the rear.

Another reason for the small number of slave uprisings was the almost total arming of the white South. A beleaguered country, the Confederacy bristled with every gun and mortar she could build or run through the Union blockading squadron. A garrison state, Dixie was armed to the teeth.

The slaves knew something else that made them think twice before going on a rampage. Word had come to them that some Union generals were not allowing slaves to come into their lines and that others had served notice that they would use the military to quell any slave insurrection. A final deterring influence against violence was the advice of the old men. Patriarchs with great prestige, they counseled a policy of watchful waiting. "I tells 'em they must be quiet," said one ancient of days. "I says to 'em, keep yer eyes wide open and pray for the good time comin'." These elders too were well informed, but theirs was a special brand of knowledge vouchsafed only to those who walked by faith.

✦

The desire of the slaves for freedom was evidenced by the way in which they received the Union troops. In the invaded areas the story was always the same; whether it was Virginia or Florida, whether it was the summer of 1861 or the spring of 1865. In Alabama "the first Federal troops were almost smothered by welcoming blacks." When Pensacola fell, the Union naval and military officials expected to be met by the municipal authorities with the keys to the city. But when the *Harriet Lane* docked and the Union forces landed, their only welcomers, wrote Admiral David D. Porter, were "a crowd of ragged Negroes grinning from ear to ear and turning somersaults to show their delight. Amid their squalor and ignorance shone out a true affection for the old flag."

When the Union ships, after running past the forts which guarded the entrance to the Mississippi, sailed up the river to New Orleans, not a single white person cheered the fleet as it turned bend after bend in the ninety mile trip. "The blacks alone," wrote Chaplain Hepworth, "welcomed us with vociferous shouts and frantic gestures." As the Union forces marched into the South's largest city in early May 1862, New Orleans Negroes waved hats and branches and shouted gleefully. Captain DeForest took particular note of the conduct of one of them: "One old mauma, who spoke English, capered vigorously on the levee, screaming, "Bress de Lawd! I knows dat ar flag. I knew it would come. Praise de Lawd!"

In Georgetown, the response followed the pattern: "Bress

de Lord! Tanks be to Almighty God, the Yanks is come! De day of jubilee hab arribed!" shouted the slaves, and insisted on hugging those soldiers nearest the sidewalk. When the Union troops strode into Norfolk in May 1862, they found the Negroes out in full force and "in their most smiling holiday attire." At Port Royal one of the welcoming Negroes kept repeating, "De Lord would bress these d——d Yankees," never having heard the Northerners designated in any other way and anxious to give them their full title in his prayer.

When the Union forces entered the Teche country in Louisiana, a young trooper, puzzled by the great joy of one bowed, wrinkled and white-thatched slave, could not refrain from asking, "Uncle, freedom will do you no good; you are just on the edge of the grave." "I knows dat, master," replied he of the walking cane. "I knows dat well enough, but I've got my boys; and I bless you all, kase you give im free."

In Rapides Parish, the Louisiana planter John H. Ransdell had an aging experience with the coming of the Federals. A close friend of Governor Moore, he had undertaken to supervise his plantation. Wrote he in sorrow to the governor: "The arrival of the advance of the Yankees alone turned the Negroes crazy. For the space of a week they had a perfect jubilee. Every morning I could see beeves being driven up from the woods to the quarters — and the number they killed of them, to say nothing of sheep and hogs, it is impossible to tell. The hogs are mostly yours. . . ."

Some of the cheering and shouting for the Union troops came from the slaves' appreciation of the dramatic. With the Northern armies came pageantry and excitement — uniformed men on prancing horses from far-off places, conquerors playing martial airs ("Prettiest thing I ever saw when the Yankees was travelling was the drums and the kettledrums and them horses. It was the prettiest sight I ever saw."). Some of the cheering was for the prospect of making a trip to the master's larder and to his wardrobe, and appropriating a portion of that which the slaves believed was rightfully theirs. Some of the cheering was for the opportunity of "loading every scow and boat they could lay their hands on," as a Union naval officer said of a group of Beaufort Negroes. But in all the welcoming to the Union forces, the dominant impulse was the desire, now apparently come true, to be free.

This desire was so strong in tens of thousands of slaves that they decided not to wait for the coming of the Federals. Freedom might be a bit too long in finding its way into strange places. They would, they concluded, take the matter in their own hands and help themselves to freedom. In what direction should they journey? Seek ye your freedom where it may be found. Perhaps it could be found where the Union flag fluttered. It was worth risking. It was worth giving up the familiar surroundings and the deep local attachments, and worth the wrench of separation from loved ones. Yes, and it was worth a leap into the perilous unknown.

And thus began a series of mass migrations, by individuals, by families, and by small groups, unparalleled in American annals for daring, sacrifice and heroism. It was an exodus whose Moses was multiple, an Odyssey whose Ulysses was legion. It was, wrote observer John Eaton, a movement "like the oncoming of cities."

"Aunty," said an anxious mother in the hearing of her little ones, "you would not go and leave the children, would you?"

"I love the children very much, mistress, but it is a great ting to be independent."

C H A P T E R   I V

I Can't Stay Behind

UNCLE BILLY was up in years and his time wasn't long, and for a slave his lot was not bad. His dwelling place, the Oakley plantation, was located in the beautiful little town of Upperville, Virginia, at the foot of the Blue Ridge Mountains. Over the years Uncle Billy had won the confidence of his white folks so that he carried the house keys and the keys to the storeroom. He it was who had been entrusted to pack the silver and bury it out of reach of the grasping Yankees. He it was whom the mistress sent to inform the Union officers "that we were a household of unprotected ladies." Seemingly, Uncle Billy would have been content to spend his remaining brief span in sunning in the summer and rocking by the fireside when the hoarfrost glistened on the ground.

But although his yoke was easy and he didn't have long to stay here, the old slave decided one day that he would make the most of what he yet might spend. What action he took is indicated in the opening line of a letter which the young miss of the household wrote to her intended husband: "The first news that greeted us this morning before we were out of bed was that Uncle Billy, the servant we trusted most, had gone off to the Yankees."

The white folks at Oakley could not understand how they

had been deceived in their faithful servant. But they did not know that something had been planted in Uncle Billy's breast that was deeper than his affection for them, and stronger than old-age security. It was simply that Uncle Billy loved liberty more than home.

This was a lesson that many a planter learned one bleak morning as his wife or daughter fumed over the unfamiliar kitchen stove, getting up a belated breakfast, or one day when he sent his slave after his clothes and after a few hours, then a few days, the slave was still after them. But the lesson was evident to those who faced facts. For within two weeks after hostilities broke out, Negro slaves began to sift within the lines of the Federal troops. Without the slightest regard for the rights of property, the slaves initiated a movement which a contemporary newspaper headlined as a "Stampede from the Patriarchal Relation."

The movement began in Virginia late in May 1861, and by a singular circumstance the first group of runaways to seek the shelter of the Northern troops made their appearance at a spot, Fortress Monroe, already become historic because of Negroes. The fortress, at that time one of the strongest fortifications on two continents, lay at the tip of the peninsula between the James and the York rivers. Fortress Monroe stood, therefore, on the same peninsula and within a few miles of the place where, according to "Master John Rolfe," on an August day in 1619, "came a Dutch man of warre that sold us twenty Negars." Thus the site where slaves were first introduced into the English colonies was destined to witness the setting in motion of their mass liberation.

As was the case nearly two centuries and a half earlier, the opening scene was quiet enough. On the night of May 23, 1861, three runaway slaves paddled soundlessly up to Fortress Monroe and presented themselves to the picket guard. They said they had come across the Chesapeake Bay from Sewall's Point where they had been sent by their master to work on the construction of a Confederate battery. The fugitives were given shelter for the night; the next morning they were brought before the general in command of the Department of Virginia, Benjamin F. Butler.

As a military man Ben Butler did not cut much of a figure, but he was not without his talents. In civil life he had been the most successful criminal lawyer in Massachusetts, being "more fertile in expedients" than any other legal light in the state. He was essentially a lawyer in epaulettes, and now with the case of these three Negroes he was prepared to call into play his special abilities. After listening to their story, he directed that they be fed, and then put to work in building a new bakery within the fort.

The next day John B. Cary, a major in the Confederate Army, made his way across the bridge, carrying a flag of truce, and requested an audience with the commanding officer. Brought before Butler, Cary claimed that the three Negroes should be surrendered under the Fugitive Slave Law. From Butler's official report this important interview was accurately reconstructed by James Parton, the most successful biographer of his generation.

MAJOR CARY: I am informed that three Negroes, belonging to Colonel Mallory, have escaped into your lines. I am Colonel Mallory's agent and have charge of his property. What do you intend to do with regard to these Negroes?

GENERAL BUTLER: I propose to retain them.

MAJOR CARY: Do you mean, then, to set aside your constitutional obligations?

GENERAL BUTLER: I mean to abide by the decision of Virginia, as expressed in her ordinance of secession. I am under no constitutional obligations to a foreign country, which Virginia now claims to be.

MAJOR CARY: But you say, we *can't* secede, and so you cannot consistently detain the Negroes.

GENERAL BUTLER: But you say you *have* seceded, and so you cannot consistently claim them. I shall detain the Ne-

groes as contraband of war. You are using them on the batteries. It is merely a question whether they shall be used
for or against the government. Nevertheless, although I
greatly need the labor that has providentially fallen into my
hands, if Colonel Mallory will come into the fort and take
the oath of allegiance to the United States, he shall have his
Negroes, and I will endeavor to hire them from him.

MAJOR CARY: Colonel Mallory is absent.

The younger officer made his way back to the Confederate
lines to report the failure of his mission.

It is probable that Butler was not the first to use the word
"contraband" as applied to a human being, but that this distinction belonged to a reporter from the New York *Tribune* who
used it in a dispatch from the fortress on the day prior to Butler's
interview with the Confederate flag-bearer. But the general
claimed the honor — "A poor thing, sir, but mine own," quoted
he, in *Butler's Book*, and it immediately came to be associated with
his name.

Regardless of ownership, the designation was at once recognized
as a stroke of genius. It was quickly used in all official communications; the North was squeamish about calling the runaways free
men, but it had no objection to calling them contraband. "Never
was a word so speedily adapted by so many people in so short
a time," wrote Union officer Charles Cooper Nott. Butler's own
military aide, the young and brilliant Yale graduate, Theodore
Winthrop, summed up the general sentiment throughout the
North: "An epigram abolished slavery in the United States."

The news of Butler's action quickly became known to the
slaves in the vicinity of the fortress. A thousand local calls went
out via the "underground telephone." The joyful word was
whispered that the time was at hand for the downtrodden "to
come up out of Egypt." And forthwith there was a concerted
effort to reach "freedom fort." Two days after Cary's request
was rejected, eight Negroes came to the fortress gates; on the

following day fifty-nine of all ages showed up. On May 27 — three days after the interview — Butler reported that $60,000 worth of slave property had come within the fortress walls.

Throughout the length of the peninsula, Negroes were on the lookout for opportunities to escape. Since tidewater Virginia, the area of earliest Union control, was a network of streams, many of the first fugitives made their way to freedom by water transport. Some simply put their meager bundles in a scow and drifted down the river with the current. On one occasion a group of twenty-five Negroes escaped from Yorktown and worked their way down the James River at night. Negroes from the Rappahannock River country often took possession of oyster and fishing boats and under cover of darkness pushed down the river, on guard to elude the vigilant coastal patrol.

Many a determined Negro, unable to lay his hands on anything that would float, proceeded to fashion a homemade canoe. Some of these craft were made of grass, twisted into skeins of rope and bound round with other grass to hold them together. These skeins would then be plaited like a door mat. Three pieces of pine board would be inserted in the floor of the canoe to prevent it from collapsing. Other canoes, those of the dugout variety, were made of a hollowed log large enough for one person.

For those escaping by water a Union warship was just as good an asylum as a fort. Negroes from Sewall's Point, across Hampton Roads from Fortress Monroe, commonly secreted boats and paddles and waited for the first dark night to make for the watchboat of the Federal blockading squadron. Five Negroes seized a yawl at Matthias Point one night while the sentry was dozing, and after lugging it two miles to escape the shore guard, put out to sea. Sighting the U.S.S. *Young Rover*, blockading the York River, the yawl hoisted a flag of truce. The five seafarers gladly clutched the line thrown out to them — none of them was an experienced boatman and they had tasted quite a bit of Neptune's salts before being picked up.

The U.S.S. *Kingfisher*, blockading off St. Marks in the Florida waters, had a similar experience to the *Young Rover's*. It sighted a boat whose total sail consisted of an old flannel blanket. At the masthead fluttered a faded coat, meant presumably as a flag of truce. In the boat were six contrabands, scantily clad and half famished, having lived for several days on wild hog, herbs and roots.

That large numbers of Negroes were taking refuge on Union vessels was well known to the Secretary of the Navy. Constantly he received from the flag officer of the North Atlantic Blockading Squadron dispatches which began like these:

"We picked up a canoe with three colored men in it."

"I beg leave to report that 15 contrabands made their escape from Sewall's Point last night and were picked up by one of our tugs."

"This morning 19 contrabands, as they are popularly called, came over to us from Middletown, Hyde County, North Carolina."

By land as by sea, the fugitives were resourceful in planning and carrying out their escapes. To foil the nose of bloodhounds and prevent them from picking up the trail, runaways applied turpentine to their shoes and bathed their feet in it. Onions too were put to use in destroying scent; even contrabands who preferred to travel light would carry a small bag of onions which they would rub over the entire body each time they waded across a creek or swamp.

A few daring souls had themselves sealed up and shipped as freight, following the example of the celebrated Henry "Box" Brown of the early fifties. Thus in the interior of South Carolina, William and Anne Summerson permitted themselves to be headed up in rice casks and conveyed in a wagon to Charleston and through the city streets to the shore.

Forging passes was a favorite trick. One Negro traveled 500 miles, making out his own passes the whole way. Another slave,

Nathaniel Evans, body servant to an officer in the Sixth Alabama Infantry, forged an officer's servant's pass to leave Richmond. With it he struck eastward to the Pamunkey River where the Confederate cavalry was rebuilding the bridge burned by Union troops. Needing another pass, he made out one for Caroline County and was allowed to proceed. At the county courthouse he went to the basement and scribbled another pass to Fredericksburg. From there he finally came across the Federal picket lines thirteen miles outside the city.

There was no stopping the Negroes when the Yankees were nearby. Patrols were vigilant, but their success was limited. A slaveowner at Hampstead, Virginia, after a night of patrol duty, returned home in the morning to find that his own bondmen had taken French leave. John T. Washington filed with the commanding general a rueful report of his loss:

> That he was one of the patrol last night, 6th instant, starting on duty about 10 P.M., with six or seven others, and that upon his return home the following morning, about sunrise, he discovered that five of his Negro men had packed up their clothing and absconded, and from some tracks he discovered, thinks they moved in the direction of Fredericksburg.
> Upon making inquiries he found that Mr. John Hill Stuart had missed two of his Negro men, Dr. A. B. Hooe two of his, Mr. Custis Grymes two of his, Mr. H. M. Tennent two of his, and Mrs. Virginia Washington two of hers.

At Hampstead as elsewhere the slaves ran away in considerable numbers despite the heavy risks. They might elude the patrol unit only to run across a Rebel picket with a quick trigger finger. Those who took to the woods could not know how many days or weeks they would have to remain under cover. Those who escaped by sea ran the danger of having the boat, generally an overloaded craft, swamped by water or upset by wind.

But to win freedom they were "nerved to face every danger, to suffer every loss, to sacrifice every feeling," as eyewitness

Charles Nordhoff remarked. To the securing of their liberty they brought skill, forecast and courage. It was a common mistake to assume that slavery was no climate for heroes. Having lived under the pressure of stress and tension since their cradle days, blacks had become immunized to danger.

❖

The number of Negroes coming into the Yankee lines inevitably mounted as the Northern armies pushed further into the Confederate heartland. No sooner did the Union forces march into a town or steam up to a wharf than the problem of the abandoned Negroes loomed up — to be further aggravated within twenty-four hours by the swelling numbers of escaping slaves seeking the protection of the Stars and Stripes. How to handle these fugitives became the most insistent problem faced by the Lincoln administration. There was no bypassing the issue. Clever Ben Butler had adroitly handled the first refugees, but they were slaves who had been working on rebel fortifications and who belonged to a Confederate officer. However, Butler's contraband theory did not apply to slaves of loyal owners or to women and children.

The whole matter was delicate, and neither the White House nor the War Office cared to take any firm measures. Apparently in official circles it was thought best to sit tight until that position became too uncomfortable. The rank and file soldier would follow orders but he too scarcely knew what to make of these uninvited camp followers. Billy Yank had not shouldered a gun to fight for the rights of black men, and even those soldiers who abhorred slavery were loath to interfere with an institution whose existence was legal, if regrettable.

What should be done with the contrabands? Nothing but evasions came from Simon Cameron; the Secretary of War appeared to be at sea. A proposal came to his desk from James Redpath, general agent of the Haitian Bureau of Emigration. It would be a good plan, wrote Redpath, to establish a central station to which all contrabands would be sent. Redpath offered to provide every such Negro with a comfortable home and farm in Haiti. Cameron was not sure of his own mind. He would, he promised Redpath, give the idea careful consideration "as soon as I can find a leisure moment to give it thought."

Cameron's wishy-washy course meant just one thing: every commander, lacking clear instructions, acted as he chose. In the opening months of the war before the Northern manpower losses became heavy, and before the large-scale invasion of the South, a majority of the generals were cool toward the runaways. Commonly they ordered subordinate officers to crush any attempted slave uprising. The most prominent of the early Union generals, George B. McClellan, commanding the Department of the Ohio, sent orders dated May 26, 1861, to colonels at Marietta, Bellaire and Wheeling, requesting them to "suppress all attempts at Negro insurrection." The following day he issued a proclamation to the "People of Western Virginia," assuring them that "not only will we abstain from interfering with your slaves, but we will, on the contrary, with an iron hand, crush any attempt at insurrection on their part." A week later Major General Robert Patterson issued a similar proclamation to the troops of the Department of Pennsylvania, ordering that "should occasion offer, at once suppress servile insurrection."

Sending slaves back to their masters was another common practice. Within three weeks after the war broke out, the commander of the Department of the West, William S. Harney, was carefully returning runaways. Colonel D. S. Miles, with a command in northern Virginia, ordered a subordinate officer to "send back to the farm the Negroes his troops had brought away." When six Cape Henry Negroes took refuge on the blockading vessel *Quaker City*, Flag Officer Silas H. Stringham had them delivered to the authorities at Norfolk. It was a common occurrence for Confederates to come to some camps under a flag of truce and to seize their runaways.

After the Union defeat at Bull Run, attributed in part to the Confederate military defenses constructed by slaves, Congress decided that the administration needed a little prodding. In early July the House passed a resolution declaring that it was no part of the duty of soldiers of the United States to capture and return fugitives. Four weeks later, on August 6, 1861, the national legislature took definite action. It passed a law which declared that all slaves were forfeited whose masters had permitted them to be used in the military or naval service of the Confederacy. These slaves were not freed — the country was not quite ready to go that far — their exact status awaited the future action of Congress or the courts.

This action of Congress strengthened the hand of the small band of Union officers who from the beginning had been in favor of freeing the slaves. These commanders now declared that they would return no fugitives unless ordered to do so. James H. Lane, the homespun hero of the Kansas voters and soldiers, vowed that his brigade would "not be constituted into Negro-catchers."

Other Kansas regiments shared Jim Lane's attitude; invariably their camps were safe asylums for runaways. An officer who attempted to return a slave would have invited mutiny in the ranks. Kansas soldiers had a standard procedure whenever a slaveholder appeared. A master who prowled around one of their camps looking for his runaways or seeking an order to take them home, would hear a number of shots being fired. In alarm, the slaveholder would ask what the shooting was for. He would be advised that there was a good deal of careless firing going on in the barracks and that it would not be prudent to tarry.

One antislavery officer, a colonel of a Massachusetts regiment, exercised a rule-of-thumb justice that invariably worked in the slave's favor. When a master came to the colonel's headquarters and asserted title to a Negro harbored in the camp, the colonel put both the claimant and the claimed outside the lines at the same time, leaving the outcome to their fleetness of foot.

Another abolitionist sympathizer, Colonel Josiah W. Bissell, commanding the "Engineer Regiment of the West," was a bit more subtle. Confronted one day by a western Missouri master who wished to search for his slave, Bissell had him shown through the camp. As the slaveowner got ready to enter one small tent, he was tapped on the shoulder and told that the tent's occupant, Captain Hill, was sick with symptoms of smallpox. The master drew back, and shortly afterward left the camp empty-handed. When he was out of sight, a brown-skinned "Captain Hill" emerged from the tent, showing every sign of a miraculous recovery.

The antislavery commander whose action drew national attention was the dashing and colorful John C. Frémont. As "the Pathfinder," Frémont had captured the popular imagination as an explorer. As the Republican candidate for the Presidency in 1856, he had polled a sizable vote as the standard-bearer of a party then only two years old. Placed in command of the Department of the West in July 1861, Frémont had faced trying difficulties in coping with Rebel guerrillas who wrecked trains, destroyed bridges and raided farms.

Believing that the situation called for a bold stroke, Frémont on August 30 declared martial law in Missouri. Under martial law, continued the edict, the property of all Rebels was thereby confiscated and their slaves were freed. Frémont thereupon set up a commission to issue deeds of manumission to slaves. The significance of Frémont's action was immediately apparent: his proclamation would shift the war's emphasis from preserving the Union to that of liberating the slaves.

There was jubilation in antislavery circles; now the abolitionists could warm up to the war. The author of *Uncle Tom's Cabin* took time from the writing of two novels simultaneously to dash off a word to the faithful: "The hour had come, and the man!" wrote Mrs. Stowe in brother Henry Ward Beecher's *Independent*. "The hero of the golden gate who opened the doors of that splendid new California world has long been predestined in the traditions of the slave as their coming Liberator." Another potent voice among the abolitionist literati, Frances Ellen Watkins Harper, hoped that the boldness of Frémont's stand would "inspire others to look the real cause of war in the face and inspire the government with uncompromising earnestness to remove the festering cause."

This abolitionist point of view was not shared by President Lincoln. He sent a characteristically courteous message informing Frémont that the proclamation would "alarm our Southern Union friends," and "perhaps ruin our fair prospects for Kentucky. The Chief Magistrate suggested that Frémont modify the proclamation to conform to the August 6 act of Congress, which limited the freeing of slaves to those who were used in insurrectionary purposes by the rebels. When the stubborn general refused to retract, Lincoln cleared the air by ordering the proclamation modified in the manner he had suggested.

Lincoln's repudiation of Frémont brought a barrage of criticism. The White House mail pouch was bulky with protesting letters. Added to these personal missives were the public denunciations appearing in the abolitionist press. John Greenleaf Whittier assured the general that he had acted "a brave man's part"; William Lloyd Garrison, usually sympathetic with the administration, thundered that Lincoln was guilty of a serious dereliction of duty, and Theodore Tilton was gloomily sure that "the retreat from Bull Run was hardly a greater disaster to the cause of the Union."

Much of the criticism was wide of the mark; Lincoln was on sound ground. Confiscating and liberating slaves were matters to be handled by the President and the Congress rather than by the off-the-cuff edict of a commander in the field, who could not be expected to weigh the wider significance of a sweeping proclamation. But however misguided, the hostility to Lincoln's action revealed one fact: the people of the North were beginning to come around to the abolitionist viewpoint that the cost of secession was abolition.

Further evidence of this sentiment was the rising volume of censure directed against generals who excluded slaves from their lines. Frederick Douglass struck a responsive chord when he spoke of Union soldiers "who made themselves more active in kicking colored men out of their camps than in shooting rebels." The widely publicized General Order No. 3 issued by H. W. Halleck, Commander of the Military Department of the West, denying fugitives admission into his lines, was warmly debated in the House. Halleck barely escaped a vote of censure, despite the respect for his military lore.

After the attack on "Old Brains," other officers were more careful about the "general orders" they issued concerning the Negro. Some of them continued to permit loyal masters to enter their camps in search of runaways, notably William Tecumseh Sherman in the Department of the Cumberland, Joseph Hooker, commanding in the Upper Potomac, and Don Carlos Buell in the Department of the Ohio. But the "military slave hunt," as George Washington Williams called it, gradually slowed down. If the War Office was reluctant to provide instructions, the generals more and more would take their cue from public opinion. Thus in early January 1862, when Ambrose E. Burnside was embarking to conduct an operation in the inland waters of Pamlico Sound, he carried an order from the ranking general, George B. McClellan, which read, "Say as little as possible about the Negro."

❖

At the time McClellan ordered Major General Burnside to soft-pedal the Negro question, the Union flag had been planted in tidewater Virginia, and in the coastal region of the Carolinas.

In these regions the slaves took immediate advantage of the coming of the Federals. Daily they flocked into the lines. In the counties of Accomac and Northampton on Virginia's eastern shore, "an almost stampede of slaves" took place in consequence of Union invasion. "The colored population is getting up and dusting," reported a war correspondent at Monterey. The fall of the South Carolina Sea Island in the waning weeks of 1861 opened another floodgate to runaways.

Formed by intersections of the creeks and arms of the Atlantic, the Sea Islands were strategically invaluable as a depot for coal and other supplies needed by the South Atlantic blockading fleet. Of the numerous islands the largest were Hilton Head, at which the army located its headquarters, Port Royal, St. Helena, Edisto and Ladies. On Port Royal, halfway up the Beaufort River, stood the town of that name, which had been a watering place for wealthy planters. When Beaufort fell, and Lieutenant David Ammen landed, he found that except for one man, the white population had fled in small boats to Charleston, using inside routes.

During the winter of 1861–1862 the Union forces extended southward their toe hold on the Atlantic coast. Tybee Island at the mouth of the Savannah River was occupied, and the Florida coastal towns of Fernandina and St. Augustine laid down their arms. Into the surrendered towns of the Sea Islands and Florida — created into a military Department of the South — poured streams of slaves.

Particularly was the Port Royal region a mecca for runaways. At Coosaw Island, just above St. Helena, they came in such numbers as to "assume formidable proportions." On the mainland at Grahamville, near the Charleston and Savannah Railroad, forty-eight escaped from a single plantation in one week, reaching Hilton Head after nearly a hundred perilous hours of hiding by day and threading their way through the waters at night. At Beaufort every boat that came in from any direction brought with it a cargo of fugitives.

One cold January day, Elizabeth H. Botume observed one hundred and fifty runaways from interior Georgia huddled at the Beaufort wharf. They were hungry; for days their only food had been a little hominy and some uncooked rice mixed with a few nuts. The fortunate ones were scantily clothed; the others were stark naked. "How do you do?" they were asked. "Thank God, I live!" said one. Another mumbled, "Us ain't no wusser than us been."

At Beaufort, Charles Nordhoff watched incredulously one morning as a flat-bottomed boat pulled up to the wharf and disgorged seventy-six colored persons. On a Sunday midnight in December 1861 a group of Negroes reached Great Tybee Island and asked the squadron to give them shelter. The leader of the group was a tall, well-built, young pilot, Isaac Tatnall, who when questioned repudiated any blood relationship to Confederate Commodore Josiah Tatnall.

Perhaps as many as 15,000 Negroes from middle Georgia escaped to the coast during the first nine months of Union occupation. On August 5, 1862, a Committee of Citizens of Liberty County, Georgia, wrote a what-are-you-going-to-do-about-it letter to Confederate Brigadier General H. W. Mercer informing him that a low estimate of the number of slaves "absconded and enticed from our sea-board would reach 20,000, valued at from $12,000,000 to $15,000,000." The Reverend Mansfield French estimated on September 15, 1861, that "15,000 blacks in the Southern Department have escaped to the Flag."

Of these thousands of escapes the most spectacular was that of Robert Smalls and his party. Unparalleled for audacity, Smalls's feat was carefully planned and brilliantly carried out. What Smalls did was to take a Confederate steamer and run it out of the Charleston harbor. He delivered it to the Union Navy, saying, "I thought the *Planter* might be of some use to Uncle Abe."

Stockily built and in his early twenties, Smalls had worked on boats in the Charleston waters for more than ten years. Since early April 1862, he had been on the *Planter*. Formerly a cotton boat capable of carrying 1400 bales, the *Planter* had been converted into an armed vessel. Her captain and the two mates were white; the rest of the crew were Negroes.

Determined to escape from Charleston, Smalls hit upon the idea of making his getaway in the open. He thought through the details. The escaping party would number sixteen, of whom seven would be women and children — Smalls's wife, three children and sister, and the wife and child of his brother John, the first engineer. They would put out to sea casually, as though the *Planter* were making a routine run out to sea to reconnoiter. The whole party agreed that if something went wrong and they were pursued without hope of escape, they would scuttle the ship, and if it sank too slowly they would then join hands together and jump to a watery grave. Their plans perfected, they had to wait for a night when the three white officers would all decide to sleep ashore.

One Monday such a night finally came. On May 12, 1862, the three whites went home to get a good night's sleep. Smalls's party boarded the ship in the crisp early morning, and in pin-drop quiet the women and children were led below deck. At 3 A.M. Smalls lit the fire under the boilers; twenty-five minutes later he cast off the hawsers which moored the *Planter* to the wharf. As the ship glided slowly from the wharf, Smalls hoisted the Confederate and palmetto flags. At headquarters one of the shore sentries remarked to another that the *Planter* was being "put to work right early this morning." Yes, nodded the other, without interest.

Now to run the gantlet of the many fortifications in the Charleston harbor. Now for the great deception. Resisting the temptation to dash at full speed, Smalls guided the *Planter* at its customary pace. As the ship passed each harbor post, Smalls pulled the lanyard on the steam whistle and gave the proper salute. Finally they approached the last hurdle, Fort Sumter itself.

Perhaps someone at the fort would want to exchange a word with one of the officers. Perhaps someone had a bit of advice to give.

Abreast of Sumter, Smalls stood in the pilot house "with his arms folded, after the order of Captain Relay, commander of the boat, and his head covered with the huge straw hat which Captain Relay commonly wore on such occasions." Smalls sounded the countersign with the whistle, three shrill sounds and one hissing sound. The sentinel sang out to the Corporal of the Guard, "The *Planter*, flag ship for General Ripley giving the prescribed signal." The next second seemed like an eternity to the ship's crew; then they heard the words, "Pass the *Planter*, flag ship for General Ripley." The sentry shouted a personal word, "Blow the d — d Yankees to hell, and bring one of them in." "Aye, Aye," came the answer.

The fugitive ship proceeded at a regular pace until she had passed beyond the line of fire of the harbor guns. Then she got up steam, lowered the Southern flags, and hoisted a bed sheet as a flag of truce.

The bed sheet was not run up a moment too soon. The *Planter* had come within the range of the Union fleet blockading the harbor, and the lookout on the *Onward* bawled out that a strange vessel was approaching. As the *Onward's* crew stood manning the guns and on the point of sending a volley of shot, the captain caught sight of the flag of truce. The gunners relaxed. The captain sent out a prize crew which came aboard and greeted Smalls, and there in the main ship channel of the Charleston harbor, the ownership of the *Planter* was transferred from the Confederate States of America to the Union Navy.

So spectacular was Smalls's exploit that the commanding officer of the South Atlantic blockading squadron immediately sent a full report to the Secretary of the Navy. Flag Officer Samuel F. Du Pont's report described the *Planter* as an armed despatch and transportation steamer attached to the engineer department at

Charleston. "The armament of the steamer is a thirty-two pounder, on pivot, and a fine twenty-four howitzer. She has, besides, on her deck, four other guns, one seven inch, rifled, which were to be taken on the following morning to a new fort on the middle ground."

Du Pont recommended that Smalls and his associates be given prize money for the *Planter*. Such a measure was at once introduced in the Senate. That body, with unusual speed, passed a bill authorizing the Secretary of War to have the *Planter* appraised, and when her value was ascertained to give one half to Smalls and the other men. Before the month of May was over, the House had passed the measure and Lincoln had signed it.

❖

The flood of Negroes coming into the Federal lines in the Sea Islands had its parallel in the western theater. Three months after the occupation of the Port Royal region, the key city of Nashville ran up the white flag. In the same month, February 1862, the hitherto obscure Ulysses S. Grant seized the strategic Confederate fortified enclosures, Fort Henry on the Tennessee River and Fort Donelson eleven miles to the east, on the Cumberland. With the fall of these west Tennessee strongholds the "back door" of the Confederacy was sprung open, and Union armies would soon be on the march into the heartland.

Six weeks after Grant had delivered his famous "unconditional and immediate surrender" terms to Simon Buckner at Donelson, the Confederacy received another stunning blow. The proud Crescent City fell, and on May 1, 1862, unhappy New Orleanians watched in tight-lipped silence as Ben Butler rode from the levee to the St. Charles Hotel, there to establish his headquarters as commander of the Department of the Gulf.

Grant and Butler had one problem in common — the contrabands. In desperation the conqueror of the Tennessee forts wrote to ranking general Halleck, asking what was to be done about the Negroes who were "coming in by wagon loads." Butler's problem was even more acute since in many of the Louisiana parishes the slaves outnumbered the whites two to one. "The marching of a Union column into one of the sugar parishes," wrote Parton, "was like thrusting a walking stick into an ant-hill." At the other end of the Mississippi the problem was the same; every day at least one hundred slaves were leaving Missouri for Kansas.

Butler was a resourceful man, used to handling hard problems. New Orleans was the most difficult spot to govern in all "Rebeldom," but Butler proved to be its match — except for the contrabands. Their numbers were large; their employment was uncertain, and their legal status was undetermined. Six weeks after he took over at New Orleans, Butler requested the Secretary of War to send instructions about the runaway slaves.

Fortunately by the summer of 1862 Washington was beginning to unwind itself. In March, Congress passed an act forbidding officers to assist in capturing runaways. An officer found guilty of flouting this law would be dismissed from the service.

The government was taking off its gloves, but not fast enough for one Union general. The war had converted Major General Hunter into an abolitionist, and "Black Dave," as his soldiers called him, was as much feared by his officers as by the enemy. Placed in command of the Department of the South on the last day of March 1862, he immediately began passing out certificates of freedom to all slaves who had been employed in assisting the Confederacy. On April 12 he issued a declaration freeing the slaves at Fort Pulaski and on Cockspur Island. Four weeks later he dropped the bombshell. He declared martial law in the Department of the South, and in the next breath he asserted that since slavery and martial law could not exist side by side in a free country, all persons hitherto held as slaves were forever free.

The proclamation was received with great joy by the Sea Island

Negroes and their white friends. Mrs. A. M. French, one of the more expressive of the Yankee teachers, clapped her hands and praised the Lord. An old colored coachman was standing nearby, and Mrs. French, a little puzzled by his composed manner concerning such excitable news, questioned him:

"How do you feel?"

"Most beautiful, missis; onspeakable!"

"But you don't say Hallelujah as I do?"

"I am burning inward, madam."

Lincoln learned about the order when he read it in the newspaper. If he did not burn inwardly, he was at least hot under the collar. Secretary of the Treasury Salmon P. Chase advised him to let the proclamation stand. Lincoln was of another mind, despite his personal friendship for Hunter. "No commanding general," he replied, "shall do such a thing on my responsibility without consulting me." Hunter, said Lincoln, was "a little too previous."

This time the country agreed with the President. Moreover, Congress was moving along. On July 17, 1862, it passed an important measure — the Confiscation Act — which declared free the slaves of all who were in rebellion.

Quickly in slave circles was the news spread of this great step toward "the loosening of all bonds." The journalist Charles Coffin reported on a question he put to a young Negro:

"Are you a slave, Dick?"

"I was a slave, but I's free now, I's 'fiscated."

The "stampede from the patriarchal relation" gained new momentum. The popular spiritual, "I can't stay behind, my Lord, I can't stay behind," took on a new meaning. For the blacks were on the move toward freedom — the old and the young, the sick and the dying, of all colors, sizes, and conditions. An old man might be observed trudging along with an ailing wife on his back, followed a few steps behind by a teen-age boy hand-in-hand with his blind daddy, guiding his steps. Mothers waded through water, a baby in one hand and a bedquilt and a frying pan in the other. They bore the pelting rain without complaint — their eyes were on tomorrow. And no matter what the future held, of one thing they were certain: the manacles had been struck from their limbs forever; the crack of the whip had been heard for the last time, and the word "master" would no longer be uttered.

These fugitives brought to the Union Armies serious problems of disease and disorder. But they brought something else. They brought brawny arms, broad backs, and trained skills for labor; they brought an unrivaled knowledge of the South's waterways and land configurations, and they brought an eagerness to put these services to use in the fight for freedom.

And they were put to use, as we may see.

CHAPTER V

Rehearsal for Freedom

A CONTRABAND NEGRO, George Scott, set in motion the first pitched battle of the Civil War. Scott was one of the earliest arrivals at Fortress Monroe. He had escaped from a plantation near Yorktown and while making his way cautiously to "freedom fort," he discovered that the Confederates had established themselves at two points between the fortress and Yorktown. At these outposts, reported Scott, they had thrown up fortifications.

Scott's story had the ring of truth, but it was advisable to check. Thereupon Major Winthrop took Scott with him and together they reconnoitered the roads leading to the enemy positions. Winthrop soon found out that Scott's report was accurate: at Big Bethel and Little Bethel (the names of two churches), the enemy had erected fortifications.

Winthrop and Scott made several additional scouting trips. On one of them Scott crawled so near the Rebel lines that he had to spend twenty-four hours hugging the ground until he thought he saw an opportunity to withdraw without being detected. As he crawled out of the bushes, a picket caught a glimpse of his shadowy figure, and Scott returned to Fortress Monroe with a bullet through the sleeve of his jacket.

As a result of these "spying out" trips, Major Winthrop became convinced that the Confederate commander, J. Bankhead Magruder, was planning a surprise attack designed to seize Newport News and Hampton. Such a move, if successful, would isolate Fortress Monroe. The young major reported his findings and his opinions to the commanding general.

Ben Butler listened carefully and made up his mind to strike the first blow. To his subordinate officers he sent word of his plan to attack Big Bethel and Little Bethel, and he asked for any suggestions. Brigadier General E. W. Pierce submitted several recommendations, and one of them indicates that he knew about Scott's services as informant and scout. George Scott, said Pierce, was to be furnished with a gun.

The encounter at Big Bethel did not go well for Yankee arms. The plan was to move one column up from Newport News and another up from Hampton and, in a pincers movement, converge upon the enemy. It would be necessary to take the Confederate troops by surprise since their position along the bank of the Back River was a strong one. But nothing went right for the Union forces. The Southerners were on the alert. Moreover, one of the Union columns opened fire on the other, mistaking it for the enemy. One of the death casualties was Major Winthrop.

The Bethels remained in Southern hands, but it is noteworthy that in the war's first battle of any military scope, a contraband should have played a role of some consequence. Scott, however, was simply the forerunner of a host of escaped slaves who brought with them valuable information. Possibly, as Herbert Aptheker states, "the greatest single source of military and naval intelligence, particularly on the tactical level, for the Federal government during the war was the Negro." It is certain that what the contrabands had seen and what they had overheard constituted an encyclopedia of the South.

The Old Dominion was the opening theater of battle operations, and it was here that the army began its extensive use of the Negro as a source of military intelligence. General John E. Wool, who succeeded Butler at Fortress Monroe in August 1861, ordered that every runaway be brought to his headquarters for examination. It was from a "Virginia Volunteer" that General Wool first learned that the Confederate troops near Bethel had evacuated that site and had withdrawn to Yorktown. During the same month, December 1861, six contrabands who escaped from Yorktown in a canoe informed Wool that Magruder had 20,000 troops under his command, made up of six regiments from Louisiana, three from North Carolina, two from Georgia, two from Alabama, one from Tennessee and the balance from Virginia.

Some of this information Wool considered of sufficient importance to transmit to the general in chief. Wool, for example, on November 11, 1861, sent to General McClellan a report which he had received from his assistant adjutant general. The report, which Wool dispatched without an hour's delay, reveals the powers of observation of an unnamed contraband:

> GENERAL: I learned the following from ——, colored, who with five others, came from Nansemond River last night on a small boat: He says that there are two batteries on the Nansemond River about one and one half miles apart — the first about four miles from the mouth — both on the left bank. Each mounts four guns, about 24 pounders. The first is shaped thus: V V V V. The first is garrisoned by forty of the Isle of Wight regiment, the second by eight. One gun in each fort will traverse; the chassis of the others are immovable. Both open in the rear, very flimsy and trifling affairs. River about three miles wide opposite the batteries. Can land midway between them. . . . The Petersburg cavalry is at Chuchatuck. There are thirteen regiments of South Carolina troops at the old brick church near Smithfield. . . . At Suffolk there are 10,000 Georgia troops. They have been coming in for the past three weeks in small detachments.

Like many other generals, McClellan had at first turned thumbs down on the runaways. But as soon as these commanders got a taste of battle, their concern for their divisions produced a marked change in their views. They were wise enough to know that a slave might bring news that would save a whole army.

McClellan's indebtedness to Negroes was great. "The most reliable information he can get," reported *Harper's Weekly* on
December 7, 1861, "comes from fugitive slaves." Exactly so,
echoed the New York *Times* in describing "Little Mac's" operations on the Virginia peninsula in the summer of 1862:

> Some of the most valuable information McClellan has re-
> ceived in regard to the position, movement and plans of the
> enemy, the topography of the country and the inclination
> of certain inhabitants has been obtained through contra-
> bands. Spies and traitors have been detected and brought to
> the attention of the authorities.

Most of McClellan's information from former slaves was dug
up by the great Allan Pinkerton, founder of the National Detective Agency. Pinkerton was given the rank of a major and in
order to prevent his identity from becoming known, his commission was made out to "E. J. Allen." Every contraband who came
into the lines of the Army of the Potomac was turned over to
him. After a question-and-answer session, Pinkerton jotted down
his findings. At the end of the day he drew up a written report
of what he had gleaned from the runaways. This report was immediately placed before the commanding general.

One contraband who entered the Union lines in Virginia caused
as much excitement as though a Rebel general had been bagged.
He was President Jefferson Davis's coachman, William A. Jackson, who came into the Union camp at Fredericksburg on May 3,
1862. "Black as a Congo Negro," Jackson was a thirty-one-year-
old slave whose master hired him out by the year.

When it became known that Jeff Davis's coachman was in
camp, he was immediately surrounded. Everyone, it seemed,
wanted to talk to him. "Generals, colonels and majors flocked
around him in great numbers." The commanding officer, Irvin
McDowell, sent for him, "and immediately telegraphed his information to Washington." McDowell and others who talked
with Jackson found him quite alert. He could read and write,

"and converses in a manner which shows that he had been used to good society."

The army officials did not divulge anything that Jackson had told them. But Jackson himself gave out some bits of information to the public. According to him, there had been heated discussions between Davis and General Joseph E. Johnston over the retreat from Manassas. The President constantly complained, said Jackson, "that while he was making plans for holding positions, his generals were making plans to evacuate them." When news came of a military defeat, continued the coachman, Davis stretched out on the floor in front of the fire and dozed there murmuring in his troubled sleep about plans and campaigns. The government property, added the fugitive, was all packed up ready to be moved to Danville should Richmond be further imperiled.

Another Negro who brought news from the besieged capital was Nathaniel Evans, who escaped in August 1862. He reported that Richmond was a hospital. The city's defenses he described in some detail. Although many earthworks had been thrown up, said he, the following were the only forts that were mounted:

> One on each side of the Williamsburg road, mounting three guns each, one on the Brook turnpike, mounting two guns, one on Fulton's hill, mounting two guns, one on the Mountain road, with three guns, three in Manchester, with two guns each, one at Strawberry Hill, with two guns, and two at Mechanicsville, mounting two guns each.

This type of specific information was highly prized. At the nation's capital, General Abner Doubleday, commanding the Military Defenses North of the Potomac, ordered that no fugitives be excluded from the lines, and that they be treated as persons and not as chattels. The reason was simple. "The General is of the opinion that they bring much valuable information which cannot be obtained from other sources," wrote his Acting Assistant Adjutant General, E. P. Halstead. "They are acquainted with all the roads, paths, fords and other natural features of the country, and they make excellent guides. They also know, and frequently have exposed, the haunts of Secession spies and traitors, and the existence of rebel organizations."

Union officers in other theaters could almost repeat Halstead's words verbatim. General John M. Schofield, commanding in northern Missouri, made effective use of information supplied by Negroes. On one occasion the Rebel guerrillas had burned most of the railroad bridges, and it was necessary to teach them a lesson. Learning their whereabouts from contrabands, Schofield seized six of their leaders. Tried by court-martial, they were found guilty and shot.

A spot check across the Confederacy would have revealed a "cloud of witnesses" who could testify to the value of information from the "black dispatch." Reported General Rush C. Hawkins in August 1861, then in command of Forts Hatteras and Clark, guarding the best sea entrances to North Carolina: "Since the capture of the two forts contraband began to arrive, often bringing with them news of important military activity in several directions." Said a Union colonel at Nashville to the war correspondent of the Cincinnati *Gazette*, "If I want to find out anything hereabouts, I hunt up a Negro; and if he knows or can find out, I'm sure to get all I want." At New Orleans General Ben Butler's orders were "that whoever else might be excluded from headquarters, no Negro should ever be."

At Chickamauga — "the great battle of the West" — where the two bloodiest days of the war were fought, the Union forces had the advantage of information obtained from Negro sources. Confederate General Braxton Bragg, "whose information service was not of the best," was thus at a marked disadvantage. Daniel H. Hill, lieutenant general hurriedly sent from North Carolina to assist Bragg, succinctly stated the situation. Bragg, wrote he, "knew only that he was encircled by foes, without knowing who they were, what was their strength, and what were their plans.

His enemy had a great advantage over him in this respect. The Negroes knew the country well . . ."

Another military service rendered by fugitive slaves was that of scout and spy. Accustomed to travel at night, Negroes "were as thoroughly acclimated as the black snakes and alligators that bask in these Southern waters," wrote a newspaperman from above the Ohio. One of these scouts was "Uncle Jim" Williams, who ran away from his master and joined the Ninety-fifth Illinois as cook. Under cover of canebrakes and bushes he led a scouting party of forty Yanks at Carroll Parish, Louisiana, the home of his former master, Benjamin Barber. The party routed a Confederate contingent of two hundred and fifty, taking them by surprise. Thirty-one prisoners returned with the expedition.

In the spring of 1862 an escaped slave, William Kinnegy, went to Kinston, North Carolina, to take a good look at the Rebel encampments. He returned to New Bern with the information and with his wife and four children. For his services as guide, another North Carolina Negro, Samuel Williams, was presented with a certificate signed by S. H. Mix, colonel of the Third New York Cavalry, which read:

> Samuel Williams, colored man, served the United States Government, as guide to my regiment out of Newbern, N. C., in the direction of Trenton, on the morning of the 15th of May, and performed effective service for us at the imminent risk and peril of his life, guiding my men faithfully until his horse was shot down under him, and he was compelled to take refuge in a swamp.

Fugitive slaves also proved valuable as spies. One of Allan Pinkerton's most trusted operatives in the Army of the Potomac was John Scobell, a Mississippi-born Negro who had learned his letters. When Scobell first came into the lines he was brought before Pinkerton for the customary questioning. The fugitive gave such a detailed and knowing account of what he had seen that Pinkerton decided on the spot to use him as a spy.

On one occasion Scobell and ace spy Timothy Webster, working as a team, succeeded in obtaining some valuable papers for
which Pinkerton had sent them. But they were in Confederate
territory at Leonardsville, Virginia, and they were wondering how
they could get the papers to Washington without their returning,
for they had other assignments. Scobell finally hit upon a solution. He took Webster to a run-down building on the outskirts
of the town, and there he rapped three times. The door swung
back into pitch darkness, and Scobell whistled shrilly. The following interview, wrote Pinkerton, took place:

"Who comes?"

"Friends of Uncle Abe," was the reply.

"What do you desire?"

"Light and loyalty!" came the response.

Thereupon an overhead trap door was lifted, a rope ladder
was lowered, and the two spies climbed up. They found themselves in a large loft and by the dim light they estimated that
about forty men, all Negroes, were present. It was a lodge meeting of the Loyal League, whose purpose was to speed runaway
slaves on their journeys, and to furnish information to Union
commanders concerning the movement of the rebels.

The president of the group welcomed the visitors, and then addressed the group, describing the activities of the various other
lodges he had visited. A tall well-built man of about thirty-five,
the president looked as if he might be reliable and resourceful.
When Webster and Scobell asked him to deliver the confidential
papers to Pinkerton at Washington, he readily consented. Webster sewed the documents in the lining of the messenger's coat,
and the two spies bade him Godspeed.

A few days later the documents were delivered into Pinkerton's
own hands. Said the country's greatest detective, "The papers
were of a highly important nature, and conveyed information to
the rebel authorities which would have been dangerous had they
reached their ultimate destination."

On another occasion Scobell worked with Hattie Lawton, a twenty-five-year-old beauty whom no one would have suspected of being a spy. In April 1862 Mrs. Lawton and Scobell, carrying forged identification papers, located themselves in Richmond itself. They met every morning. Mrs. Lawton passed as a lady of leisure languidly riding about the city and its environs, and Scobell passed as her faithful colored attendant. From the joint observations of these trained spies, Pinkerton learned much. This information he transmitted to the military high command.

Sometimes Scobell worked solo. On one occasion he made a two weeks' trip which took him into five towns in Confederate-held Virginia. Striking southward from Washington on a line paralleling the Potomac River, he covered Dumfries and then went to Fredericksburg. From that strategically important stronghold, so expertly fortified by Lee's engineers, Scobell returned northward. Crossing the Occoquan River, he successively spied at Manassas, Centerville and Leesburg. A versatile man, he worked as a laborer on the earthworks at Manassas, a cook at Centerville, and a peddler of delicacies at Confederate camps. For his daring and for his services, Scobell well deserves a place on the honor roll of Civil War spies.

Charles Coffin, accompanying the Thirteenth Massachusetts, describes the activities of another spy whose information was transmitted direct to Washington. This runaway from a Winchester master came into the Yankee lines on the Upper Potomac. It was quickly discovered that he was shrewd and cautious.

The commanding officer asked him if he would go back and ascertain the whereabouts of Stonewall Jackson. Upon his ready assent, he was supplied with things hard to get in the Confederacy — needles and thread, packages of medicine and other articles of light weight. With these he passed the Rebel pickets without trouble. "Been out to get 'em for massa," was his answer whenever he was challenged. In this manner he repeatedly circulated within the Confederate lines, all eyes and ears.

When Louisville was threatened in the fall of 1862, colored Henry Blake furnished valuable information to the command of Don Carlos Buell. Blake, who lived at Glasgow, nearly a hundred miles below Louisville, spent his nights spying on Confederate positions and reporting his findings to Unionists who, in turn, forwarded the information to the Union lines. One night Blake learned from a slave girl that her master was going to confer with one of Bragg's lieutenants. Blake concealed himself in the room and overheard the discussion of plans. This information he sent to the Federal Army through one of the white Unionists so numerous in Lower Kentucky. When Blake's activities became known by the Confederates, a reward of $1000 was offered for him.

At New Bern, wrote Vincent Colyer, the army constantly employed "upwards of fifty" as spies, scouts and guides. These former slaves went into rebel lines in Kinston, Goldsboro, Trenton, Onslow, Swansboro, Tarboro and points along the Roanoke River. Frequently they went as far as 300 miles within Confederate-held territory, visiting camps and posts and bringing back important information. A contraband boy, Charley, made three visits to Kinston, where the Southerners had established a military post. The distance from New Bern to Kinston was forty-five miles, thirty of them within the Rebel lines. One of Charley's reports told of a quiet withdrawal of a large portion of the enemy forces. The Union command immediately investigated and found that Charley's statements were based on facts.

Admiral David D. Porter relates an unusual incident in which the Southerners made use of a Negro spy. In turn, Porter used a contraband as counterintelligence. The episode occurred in April 1863.

In that month the Confederates decided that the Union flotilla off Vicksburg could be captured by a land force moving through the swamps surrounding the approaches to the city. Ten troublesome mortar vessels were the particular prizes sought by the Confederates. On the morning of the planned assault, the Confederates sent out a Negro spy. Admiral Porter, inspecting the Union defenses, saw the Negro emerging from the woods and ordered two patrolmen to seize him.

Giving his name as Brutus Munroe, the Negro said he was a pastor, "a anarkist an' orthodox up to de hub." He was "a anarkist," he patiently explained to Porter, because he believed "all about the ark an' de animiles wot went in." Trying to draw him out, Porter asked which President he prayed for. "I prays for 'em bof, sar — Massa Linkum an' Massa Davis — for dey bof stans in need ob prayer." Pressed as to which side he was on, Brutus replied, "I am just now on de Lawd's side."

Convinced that Brutus was "a first-class romancer," and noting that during the conversation his eyes "were wandering in every direction," Porter ordered him seized and confined to a cabin with a sentry over him.

Hitting upon a plan, the Union officers selected a contraband to whom they gave instructions, and then tumbled him in with Brutus. The pretended prisoner soon broke into tears, wailing that "dey done gwine ter shoot me tomorrow. . . ." Brutus ordered him not to boo-hoo so, for, whispered he, if the Unionists didn't shoot him "befo' fo' 'clock dis arternoon," they would never have another chance.

Suddenly the contraband was taken violently ill, and had to be carried on deck. When he told his story, the Union officers were certain that a Confederate attack was scheduled at four o'clock. Two hours before the expected assault, all was ready. The mortars were loaded with the amount of powder, half a pound, required to land shells just inside the woods; one watch was placed at the guns; the other stood by.

Shortly after three o'clock the advancing enemy, their coming having been signaled by two sentries, came in sight. A sharp volley of musketry greeted their unbelieving ears. Simultaneously the Union steamers opened fire with shells and shrapnel, firing steadily for twenty minutes.

The Rebels retreated hastily. Going into the woods, a Union reconnoitering party found knapsacks, caps, shoes and muskets which the fleeing men in gray had abandoned. Upright in the swamp was a pair of officer's long boots, "with the toes pointing toward Vicksburg."

"The Confederates troubled us no more," reported Admiral Porter. Subsequently he learned from the captured Confederate commandant of Fort Jackson that the Southerners supposed that spy Brutus had betrayed them.

❖

The United States Navy did not lag behind the sister service in making use of information from fugitive-slave sources. To the Union war vessels the contrabands thronged, their small boats sidling crabwise up to the ships of both the North and the South Atlantic Blockading Squadrons. Once aboard they divulged information, much of it of consequence.

Sometimes their statements led to the capture of Confederate-held ships. "Four fine-looking Negroes, contraband of war, slaves of Lancaster County, Virginia," to use Commander O. S. Glisson's description, were picked up in Hampton Roads at dawn on August 21, 1861. They reported that the brig *Monticello* was lying at a wharf twenty miles up the Rappahannock. Acting Flag Officer Glisson at once ordered the *Daylight*, under Captain Samuel Lockwood, to go up the river. Lockwood found the brig at the spot indicated by the runaways, boarded her and took possession. At Wilmington in late December 1861, a group of slaves were picked up by the *Amanda*. According to a newspaper correspondent they "gave valuable services and trustworthy information as to the construction and location of certain war vessels."

Another gunboat blockading off Wilmington, the U.S.S. *Penobscot*, picked up a group of fugitives from coastal North Carolina. They reported that at Little River Inlet, two Confederate schooners were lying in a stream, preparing to make a dash for the open sea. Believing the story, the Union commander dispatched five boats and seventy-five men, ordering them to attack the blockade-runners. The Yankee assaulting party steamed up to Little River Inlet at daybreak. The crews of the schooners were ashore and together with the inhabitants of the small settlement, they were completely taken by surprise. Hastily snatching anything at hand, civilians and sailors fled into the woods. Unmolested the Union forces came aboard the two 100-ton Confederate vessels, which were located precisely where the contrabands had indicated. Finding it impossible to carry away the ships' cargoes, they put everything to the torch. Up in smoke went 250 barrels of turpentine, 100 bales of cotton, a considerable quantity of rosin, and a large supply of priceless salt badly needed in the Confederacy. The destruction over, the Yankee boats left without a single casualty.

Naval officers in the Sea Island region probably received more information from fugitives than did any other commanders in the watershed from Cape Hatteras to Cape Florida. With Port Royal as a base, the South Atlantic fleet busied itself throughout 1862 establishing beachheads on the defenseless or lightly defended bays and inlets up and down the seaboard.

When runaways brought news that there was a Rebel contingent of five hundred at Rockville, a handsome village overlooking the Edisto River, Commander Percival Drayton himself led an expedition of marines and armed boat crews. When they landed on the morning of December 18, 1861, they found a deserted village. Pushing inland a mile they discovered an abandoned encampment from which the Rebels had hastened when they spotted the Union forces entering the creek.

"I have the honor to communicate some information from colored man Brutus who accompanied me from Tybee this morning. He is quite familiar with the rivers and creeks between Savannah City and Tybee Island." Thus opens a dispatch marked "Confidential," sent on December 30, 1861, by Quincy A. Gillmore, Chief of the Engineer Corps and addressed to T. W. Sherman, commanding the Department of the South. Gillmore then went into particulars, and concluded thus, "I must say that I place great reliance on Brutus' statement, for everything he said of Big Tybee Inlet, was verified with remarkable accuracy by my examination."

The first news that the important Florida seacoast town of Fernandina was abandoned came from a Negro. For several days, in February 1862, Flag Officer Du Pont had been making arrangements for an attack on that city. Finally on March 2 he had everything as he wanted it. A formidable fleet had been assembled off St. Andrews Inlet, twenty miles north of the entrance to Fernandina by sea. The attacking fleet had already formed in line, with eleven warships in the lead positions followed in order by an armed cutter, an armed transport and six army transports.

It was at that moment that a contraband in a small boat was picked up. He was hurried to the *Mohican* and brought into the presence of the admiral. The Confederates had fled Fernandina, he told Du Pont, and were at that moment preparing to abandon Amelia Island, carrying with them such munitions as they could. Du Pont took action at once. From the flagship he immediately dispatched the following "Memorandum for Captain Lardner":

A contraband brings news that the enemy is abandoning Fernandina. The flag-officer wishes Captain Lardner to cut off the retreat by sea, if any is attempted within his reach, and to command the southern end of Amelia Island with his guns, the railroad included, if possible.

Possibly no naval intelligence from a Negro was more important than that supplied by Robert Smalls. "His information," wrote Du Pont to Welles, "has been most interesting, and portions of it of the utmost importance." The facts furnished by Smalls were so noteworthy that the Secretary of the Navy, in his annual report to President Lincoln, made it a point to describe them as follows:

> From information derived chiefly from the contraband Pilot, Robert Small, who has escaped from Charleston, Flag Officer Du Pont, after proper reconnaissance, directed Commander Marchand to cross the bar with several gun-boats and occupy Stono. The river was occupied as far as Legarville, and examinations extended further to ascertain the position of the enemy's batteries. The seizure of Stono Inlet and river secured an important base for military operations, and was virtually a turning of the forces in the Charleston harbor.

Supplying information was not the only naval service rendered by escaped slaves. Thousands saw active duty on board ships of war. The naval expedition which sailed from Fortress Monroe in August 1861 to seize the Hatteras forts carried Virginia contrabands who served as cooks, coal heavers and firemen. Fourteen of them were assigned to work one of the afterguns on the upper deck of the *Minnesota*. In bombarding the Confederate fortifications, "no gun in the fleet was more steady than theirs." A war correspondent from the Boston *Journal* sent word, "Let me say that the Negro worked well." Colored men shared in the victor's pride as the Stars and Stripes was again planted on the soil of the Carolinas.

Because droves of runaways were hailing warships and asking to be taken aboard, the navy found it necessary to adopt a policy. Hence on September 25, 1861, a month after the assault on the Hatteras forts, Welles authorized Flag Officer L. M. Goldsborough "to enlist them for naval service, when their services can be made useful, under the same terms and regulations as apply to other enlistments."

Welles met no opposition whatsoever in taking this step. For the navy was relatively free of color prejudice. Negroes had never been barred from joining, although by general understanding among recruiting officers the number of Negro enlistments had been limited to 5 per cent of the service. But as a group, white seamen were unprejudiced. "They mess with their colored ship-mates," wrote a newspaper reporter from Beaufort, "toil, suffer, rejoice, sing, and divide prizes together, without showing the least difference." Before the autumn of 1862 (on August 26), Admiral Du Pont was informing Welles that he was employing "many contrabands in the working parties and boats of the squad-ron," and that he had recently placed ninety from Georgetown on the *Vermont*.

Many Southern Negroes served as pilots whatever may have been their official ratings. Particularly in the South Carolina and Georgia sheets of water were Negro pilots commonly put to use by flag officers. Navigating these sinuous channels required the skill and knowledge that came only from years of experience. Contrabands like Isaac Tatnall, who was "conversant with every inlet between Savannah and Brunswick," were indispensable to Union mariners. More important to the naval command than the guns of the *Planter* was Smalls's intimate knowledge of the intricacies of the Sea Island coastal waters. Negro pilots were invaluable in the month-long siege of ancient Fort Macon, in the Beaufort, North Carolina harbor, almost the very last of the Con-federate-held Atlantic ports to run up the white flag. It is not surprising that in June 1863 Admiral Du Pont informed Welles that he had made use of certain contraband pilots and had author-ized payments of thirty and forty dollars a month to them. "May I hope," concluded the flag officer, "that this course meets your approval. They are skillful and competent."

❦

"Will the people of African descent work for a living?" This was a question raised widely in the North as word came of the droves of slaves who were escaping into the Federal lines. Union

Army officers could give a convincing answer. For during the war there were more than 200,000 Negro civilians in the service of the Northern armies as laborers, cooks, teamsters and servants. One of the great contributions of the contraband was his labor. With a song on his lips to make the work seem like play, he performed heavy tasks with cheerfulness and good humor.

From the sound of the opening gun, the army made use of Negro muscle and brawn. The first three contrabands at Fortress Monroe, Colonel Mallory's slaves, were put to use constructing a bakehouse for the army. One of the chief reasons for Butler's refusal to surrender them to Mallory's agent was the need for their labor at the fortress.

When in July 1861 Butler decided to erect a line of breastworks, contrabands were selected for the job. The task of supervising them fell to Edward L. Pierce, a private in Company L of the Third Massachusetts. No better selection could have been made. By profession a lawyer, Pierce was a man of broad understanding and wide learning. A friend of Senator Charles Sumner and Secretary of the Treasury Chase, he was accustomed to move in circles of influence. Patriotic impulse had led him to enlist as a three months' private upon Lincoln's first call for volunteers.

On being detailed to supervise the contrabands, Pierce sent out a notice that a meeting would be held on July 8. When the Negroes had assembled, Pierce gave a short and friendly inspirational talk such as few of them had ever heard before. He then made a record of their names and ages and the names of their former masters. They were next provided with tools and assigned to specific jobs. Pierce set their hours of labor, considerately giving them a recess during the three hottest hours of the day. From the commissary, he procured their rations — salt beef or pork, hard bread, beans, rice, coffee, sugar, soap and candles, and on Sunday fresh meat. Private Pierce thus set in operation the first Union use of contraband labor on military fortifications.

The Negroes worked with a will; there was not a single instance of shirking. General John E. Wool, Butler's successor at the fortress, established their pay at ten dollars a month and subsistence. By the end of September "they were paying their way admirably." Their withdrawal, reported a newspaperman, "would seriously embarrass operations on the docks and in making and working the railroads."

The experiment had been a success, and the War Department hesitated no longer. On September 20, 1861, Wool received a telegram from Washington: "Send to General McClellan at this place all Negro men capable of performing labor, accompanied by their families." The Secretary of War added an unnecessary sentence of explanation: "They can be usefully employed in the military works in this vicinity."

Wherever Union arms extended their sway, whether in the Atlantic seacoast regions, down the center through the Confederate grand line, or along the thousand-mile stretch of the Lower Mississippi, the contrabands proved as useful as in tidewater Virginia or invasion-jittery Washington. Northern generals who marched into Rebel territory soon found that they were compelled by military necessity to welcome runaways to their camps. "Whenever a Negro appeared with a shovel in his hands," wrote the Negro soldier-historian, George Washington Williams, "a white soldier took his gun and returned to the ranks."

Negro labor was indispensable in the Carolinas. General Burnside, on March 30, 1862, appointed Vincent Colyer as "Superintendent of the Poor for the Department of North Carolina," and authorized him to employ as many Negroes as he could, up to 5000. "I never could get enough," wrote Colyer. Working as an agent of the Brooklyn Y.M.C.A., Colyer was another in the illustrious roster of whites who were anxious to assist the Negro in the transition from slavery to freedom. Under his supervision the contrabands threw up three earthwork forts in four months, one at New Bern, one at Washington, and one at Roanoke Island. The New Bern fort was successfully used on two occasions to repulse Confederate attempts to retake the city. As stevedores at New Bern, the fugitives loaded the discharged cargoes for three hundred ships over a span of four months.

Colyer learned, as did Union commanders throughout the South, that the Negroes were excellent foragers. The Federal armies, fighting and marching in enemy territory, frequently found it necessary to supply their food from the countryside. Foraging was a system of informal requisitioning of someone else's goods. Sometimes the taking was done without so much as by-your-leave; in other instances, such as in the cases of the grand marches of William Tecumseh Sherman, the owners were given a certificate acknowledging the rather obvious fact that the Union Army had requisitioned their foodstuffs. Foraging expeditions were dangerous since a foraging party was in essence a sort of advance guard into enemy-held territory.

Negro foragers at New Bern brought in boatloads of pine and wood for army hospitals. They were ever on the alert for hidden supplies of baled cotton, which was indispensable for the protection of gunboats. A contraband informed Colyer that he had discovered a large pile of cotton concealed under a thicket of shrubs and small trees. "If you can give me a flat boat and some men, we can get the cotton," said Charlie. General Burnside provided a boat and a detail of one hundred soldiers. With Charlie and twenty other Negroes the expedition located the hiding place, uncovered the bales and loaded them on the steamer. A day later they returned to New Bern with a load of cotton the cash value of which was estimated at $26,000. Negro foragers were thorough, leaving little behind. They stripped cornfields, corralled horses and mules, rounded up pigs and calves, milked cows, dug for potatoes and climbed for fruit.

Frequently the foragers worked as one of the units in a wagon train. In all theaters of war Negro contrabands were used in the wagon trains. In addition to serving as forage men in these army transports, Negroes were employed as wagon masters, assistant wagon masters, teamsters, wheelwrights and blacksmiths. Commanders in the Kansas brigades preferred Negro teamsters, and some officers would use no others.

Had the fleeing Confederates been able to take all of the Negroes with them, they would have given a crippling blow to the military operations of the Department of the South. In the Sea Islands, the Quartermaster Corps employed more than 1000 contrabands by the summer of 1862. That department had been paying them $8.oo a month and rations. But so eagerly were their services sought by the other military departments that the Quartermaster Corps had to raise their salary to hold them. "The Negroes are working industriously," wrote Rufus Saxton, Brigadier General of Volunteers, to Secretary of War Edwin M. Stanton, in July 1862. "The system of voluntary labor works admirably."

In the Department of Tennessee, the labor of the thousands of contrabands was supervised by John Eaton, chaplain in an Ohio regiment. Appointed General Superintendent of Contrabands by commanding officer, U. S. Grant, Eaton set to work with the same zeal and spirit shown by Pierce at Fortress Monroe and Colyer at New Bern. With a deep interest in their welfare, Eaton organized the contrabands into suitable units for working and then assigned them their jobs.

The Secretary of War soon sent a dispatch to General Grant ordering that the "refugee Negroes" be used in the Quartermaster department, also as teamsters, as laborers in building forts and roads and in picking and "removing" cotton. During the winter of 1862–1863 Eaton put the Negroes to work piling up the wood stores so necessary for military and naval operations along the Mississippi.

The commanding officer of the Army of the Mississippi, William S. Rosecrans, made a particularly effective military use of a group of contrabands. When his troops advanced into Northern Alabama in the summer of 1862, slaves flocked to the camps in great numbers. Rosecrans hit upon the plan of organizing all the able-bodied men into a corps to do fatigue duty. To Captain W. B. Gaw, one of the assistant engineers on his staff, Rosecrans gave the task of organizing the corps, with authority to draw on the Commissary and Quartermaster departments.

Captain Gaw questioned the Negroes and was surprised to learn that over one quarter of them were skilled laborers. He divided them into three groups — one group he supplied with tools for carpentry, masonry and blacksmithing, the second group he gave axes and broadaxes, and those in group three were given spades, shovels, pickaxes and mattocks. Late in August this corps was put to work in constructing bridges and fortifications on the roads approaching the town of Iuka, Mississippi. From the hour of their first efforts, Rosecrans had reason to be "elated" over the experiment.

On September 10 these three groups of laborers moved from Iuka and worked all that night, preparing the roads and bridges over which the troops were to pass in the morning. Three days later the Negroes reached Corinth and at once commenced working on the town's inner defenses. In less than three weeks they had constructed "six redans, with gabion revetments, each mounting six guns; and in the same time felled the timber covering at least 300 acres, to give a clear range for the play of the work of the guns." A war correspondent reported that this feat of labor "saved our defeat of Corinth."

✣

The great services that the contrabands performed for the armed forces were highly praised by the Northern Negroes and their abolitionist allies. These reformers had contended all along that the slave was ready for freedom, and now, with an I-told-you-so air, they pointed to the record. Unquestionably the contrabands constituted a potent military and naval resource. Fugitive slaves had shown that they would run great risks to serve the Union cause. They had shown that they could adapt themselves to a free-labor economy — that they would work without being herded together in the ancient gang system under the constant threat of the driver's whip. They had shown that no sacrifice was too great to be free, and that they regarded manhood as their rightful possession.

With this increased ammunition furnished them by the performance of the contrabands, the abolitionists and the Northern Negroes were ready to intensify the agitation for Negro soldiers and equal rights for all.

CHAPTER VI

A High Day in Zion

THE DAY IS FINE — for Boston, that is, and it has been possible for people with top-boots and rubbers to cross the street without drowning," wrote the New York *Times* reporter, who had waded "through slush and mush" to reach Alston Hall, where he sat huddled in his overcoat.

The occasion which brought the shivering newsman to Boston in January 1862 was the twenty-ninth anniversary meeting of the Massachusetts Anti-Slavery Society, the oldest abolitionist organization in the country. Out-of-town dailies were not in the habit of covering the Society's meetings, but in attendance at this convention were reporters from sixteen of the most widely circulated journals in the North. "Peculiar circumstances," ran the *Times's* explanation, "have arisen to give anti-slavery societies an importance which hitherto has not been theirs, and which justifies the most wide circulation of their sayings, doings, prophecies and lamentations."

Reporters covering their first antislavery convention were given a close-up of the "high brass" of Bay State abolitionism and their camp followers. Presiding over the session was a middle-aged, sturdily built man with a domed brow, clear complexion, slightly hooked nose and thin, firm lips. William Lloyd Garrison's eyes seemed to twinkle behind his gold-rimmed glasses, as though things were going as he would have them. Now that war had come, Garrison tended to slow down, and was gradually becoming a reformer emeritus. His mantle fell naturally to his long-time associate, Wendell Phillips, whose zeal for humanity and justice was still white-hot. It was Phillips who captivated the thousands with an unrivaled eloquence, and if his arguments lacked anything in logic, the beauty of his diction and the grace of his delivery made ample amends in the opinion of his partisan audiences.

In evidence at the convention were the Negro followers of Garrison and Phillips. Charles Lenox Remond made his customary speech, lengthy and pessimistic, but eloquent and absorbing. Thin-faced and dark-skinned, Remond enjoyed the distinction of having been the first Negro to take the field as a professional abolitionist lecturer. Prominent also as a speaker was John S. Rock, a late-comer among the Garrisonians. Rock had practiced medicine and dentistry before becoming a lawyer. Hopeful of being admitted to the bar of the Supreme Court, he was impatiently waiting for Chief Justice Taney to shed his robe: "I suppose," wrote Rock to a friend, "the old man lives out of spite."

Attending the sessions, although not down for formal addresses, were Negroes William C. Nell and Lewis Hayden. A sometime journalist, Nell had won fame in abolitionist quarters for his *Colored Patriots of the American Revolution*, published in 1855, the first sustained attempt at history-writing by an American Negro. At the moment the impoverished Nell was seeking employment in the post office, but the law was still on the books that "no other than a free white person shall be employed in carrying the mails." Hayden was a janitor at the State House. His residence at 66 Phillips Street was a gathering place for the antislavery cohorts. It was there that Theodore Parker, of sainted abolitionist memory, had married the fugitive slaves, William and Ellen Craft; it was there that John Brown had lodged during his last trip to Boston. Hayden had been the first to suggest to John A. Andrew that he run for governor; on Thanksgiving Day in 1862 Governor Andrew was to come down from Beacon Hill and have turkey dinner at the Haydens'.

Visiting reporters attending this convention were doubtless a little surprised at the outspoken language. But the abolitionists never bridled their tongues in flaying the slaveholders, and to them a kind master was still one who never put wires in his cowhides. Some of the newspapermen may have been shocked when Stephen S. Foster said that he had deterred many young men from entering the army, or when Henry C. Wright proposed a resolution that "we regard the preservation of Liberty and the abolition of slavery as of more importance than the preservation of the Constitution and the Government of the United States."

Despite these vigorous utterances and the general severity of tone of all the addresses, not a single boo or hiss was heard during the entire two days of meetings. Such calm was unprecedented. Only a year earlier, abolitionist meetings had everywhere been broken up. But all that belonged to a day that had passed. "The sessions," said the man from the Boston *Post*, "lack the animation which made them so spicy and interesting in former years." Hitherto abolitionist gatherings had been enlivened by interruptions from the floor, but in these sessions there had only been one such interruption, and that of a mild nature. One speaker in discussing compensated emancipation had asked, "What is a fair compensation for a slavemaster?" A voice from the gallery had replied, "The State Prison."

Otherwise, everything passed off pleasantly — no hissing, hootings, catcalls, spitballs, eggs or tomatoes. The women who brought their long needles were able, for the first time, to stick to their knitting — they waited in vain for the customary explosions. Women who had brought their Whittiers found the proceedings so placid that they were able for once to concentrate on the singing verse of one of the few abolitionist poets whose lines were not metrically faulty.

Such decorum was hardly satisfying to the true abolitionist — he missed "the fierce mob's hounding down." As Garrison had said, "Every demonstration of violence helps the cause of freedom onward." An abolitionist speaker was accustomed to rising to his feet, listening to a loud chorus of boos, and then sitting down to rest until the noise had subsided sufficiently for him to be heard if he shouted. So habituated was Phillips to stormy sessions that once when a Cincinnati mob stoned him, he said of the incident, "I really imagined I was back in Boston."

The peace and quiet prevailing at this convention of the most radical abolitionist society in the country revealed one thing clearly. The force of circumstances was impelling the country toward the goal of slave emancipation. The abolitionists, who had repeatedly insisted that slavery would go out in a sea of blood, were being regarded as latter-day prophets as abolitionism slowly but definitely became the higher patriotism.

The mob no longer thirsted for Phillips's blood and he was no longer regarded as the abomination of desolation. Northern newspapers now printed in full his speeches which a year before had been dismissed as incoherent ravings and farrago. Early in 1862 Phillips had nearly two hundred invitations to lecture and many of them came from towns and cities where he had not been welcome previously. "The cause is striding forward with seven-leagued boots," wrote Theodore Tilton to Garrison in April 1862. "If you do not hurry and grow old," continued Tilton in a rollicking mood, "you may see slavery abolished before you have a gray hair on the top of your head."

As the war took on a decidedly antislavery complexion the abolitionist movement gradually lost its distinctive character and merged into the total war effort. Adopting a united-front approach, the abolitionists joined hands with other groups who favored freeing the slave. Thus Boston abolitionists supported the Emancipation League, organized in December 1861, to create a sentiment in favor of abolition by means of public addresses, and the circulating of facts and figures. Similarly New York abolitionists, such as Theodore Tilton, George B. Cheever and Oliver Johnson, joined forces with William Cullen Bryant and Willam

Curtis Noyes who in the same month, December 1861, started gathering signatures for a monster petition to the President and to Congress, urging them to adopt such measures "as will ensure emancipation to all the people throughout the whole land."

This new united-front approach meant the virtual disappearance of the organized antislavery movement. However, most of the former abolitionists had no trouble in finding outlet for their reform energies. New occasions, wrote James Russell Lowell (a former colleague who had unforgivably succumbed to the cloistered environs of Harvard), teach new duties. Harriet Tubman was for the moment attempting to incorporate a "Fugitives' Aid Society for St. Catherine's, Canada West," an organization that would give legal protection to the runaways settled in Her Majesty's dominions. William Wells Brown was also in the Canadian provinces. As an agent for the Haitian Emigration Bureau, he was having only a soso response in soliciting voyagers to the land of the palm.

With few exceptions, every abolitionist found a niche in some war-related effort. Tall, angular Sojourner Truth was beating the drums — If she were ten years younger, she confided to a Steuben County, Illinois, audience, she "would fly to the battle field and nurse and cook, and if it came to a pinch, put in a blow now and then." She was still supporting herself by selling photographs of herself on which she inscribed, "I sell the shadder to support the substance."

Practically every woman abolitionist supported the Women's National Loyal League in its goal to obtain a million signatures petitioning Congress to pass an amendment abolishing slavery. Susan B. Anthony was one of the founders of the League, but of all the suffragettes she was the unhappiest that the women's rights movement had to be stymied for the duration. In both 1861 and 1862 the National Women's Rights Convention had to be postponed. The strong-minded Miss Anthony really had little patience with the Civil War and was anxious to have it over with so that she could concentrate her fire on that form of slavery in which "woman is owned and possessed by man."

One of the woman abolitionists who wholeheartedly supported the war and was anxious to do her bit was Julia Ward Howe, composer of the greatest song to come out of the war, "The Battle Hymn of the Republic." First put to paper in the early hours of a gray November morning in 1861, and destined to be "sung, chanted, recited and used in exhortation and prayer on the field of battle," the anthem was rooted in Mrs. Howe's firm belief that the Northern cause was just. Its religious tone came from her daily reading of the Bible. It was written for the air of the John Brown song, and it is significant that John Brown had been a friend of Mrs. Howe's reformer husband and had been a guest at their house.

Other abolitionists lent their distinctive talents to the war effort. The singing Hutchinsons, a musically self-trained family famous for their rendition of abolitionist songs, secured a pass from the Secretary of War to cross the Potomac and visit army camps. Their purpose, as an admirer put it, was to "cheer the ruggedness of Winter with the spontaneous, unbought carol of their simple, heartfelt songs."

While they were giving a concert at a camp in northern Virginia, the soldiers listened absently, undoubtedly wishing for something a bit more spicy. Finally the Hutchinsons launched into a recent composition of Whittier's, "We Wait Beneath the Furnace Blast," whose inspiration and melody was Martin Luther's famous hymn, "A Mighty Fortress." Whittier's lines were antislavery and the Hutchinsons sang them with gusto. They were not destined to complete the number. They were pouring their voices into the stanza

> In vain the bells of war shall ring
> Of triumphs and revenges,
> While still is spared the evil thing
> That severs and estranges.

But blest the ear
That yet shall hear
The jubilant bell
That rings the knell
Of slavery forever!

when a loud hiss came from a soldier in the audience. The major ordered the hissing stopped or he would put the hisser out. "You had better come and put me out," was the reply from the ranks. In the excitement that followed the concert was not resumed.

The next day the chaplain who had scheduled the Hutchinsons was summoned by Philip Kearny and put on the carpet. General Kearny also sent for the singers and reprimanded them for not submitting their program in advance. A day later the Hutchinsons received a letter from commanding officer McClellan revoking their permit and pass and requesting them to depart within twenty-four hours.

The abolitionists bitterly assailed McClellan whom they already disliked, but this temporary set-back did not disturb them deeply. Their principal energies were devoted to the arming of the Negro. They publicized the military and naval services of the contrabands as geographers, provisioners and spies. Digging fortifications, said they, was as much a military duty as shooting. Moreover, men who worked in the face of enemy fire should have arms to protect themselves. Abolitionists ridiculed the nice distinctions by which contrabands were allowed to wheel a gun into position but not to point it, and to ram a cartridge but not touch off the gun.

To refute the charge that the Negro was wanting in soldierly qualities and that bondage had crushed out his manliness, the reformers referred to the record. Since the Revolution of 1775, recited they, the Negro had shed his blood on every battlefield and on every naval vessel. The abolitionists urged everyone to read the pamphlet by George Livermore, *An Historical Research Respecting the Opinions of the Founders of the Republic on Ne-*

groes as Slaves, as Citizens and as Soldiers. Livermore had read
this paper at a meeting of the Massachusetts Historical Society,
and as a public service the Society published the monograph at
its own expense. Livermore pointed out, as William C. Nell had
likewise done, that large numbers of Negroes, free and slave, had
served with distinction in the Revolutionary armies. "We wish,"
exclaimed the *Liberator*, "that Livermore's booklet could find
a place in every household in the North."

For those who preferred their facts in capsule doses, the abolitionists issued a *A Short Catechism*, with questions and answers
such as:

> When Major Pitcairn of the British army leaped on the
> redoubt at Bunker Hill, shouting, "The day is ours," and
> striking terror in the colonial troops, who sealed his lips and
> laid the invader in the dust? Peter Salem, a Negro.
> For whom did the principal officers in the Battle of Bunker
> Hill petition the General Court for some special token of
> approbation, describing him as "a brave and gallant soldier"?
> Salem Poor, a Negro.
> Which is pronounced the best fought battle of the Revo-
> lution? The Battle of Rhode Island. But it was saved to us
> by a Negro regiment that three times repelled the Hessians
> with a devastating fire.

This kind of information had its value, but public opinion
responded less to history's scroll than to current reality. Fortunately for the abolitionists, one of the obvious realities foreshad-
owing the use of Negro soldiers was the dawning realization that
the war was turning out to be more than a parade at arms. By
February 1862 more than 60,000 boys in blue were sick every
day, and the death rate by disease amounted to twenty-seven
regiments a year. As army hospitals became overcrowded with
hapless victims of ague and malaria, the North began to rethink
the question of the Negro soldier. "Shall we love the Negro so
much," inquired a New York daily, "that we lay down our lives
to save his?"

As the country pondered this poser, the army, to the great satisfaction of the abolitionists, began to take its first halting steps toward arming the colored man.

✥

In the middle of October 1861 as General Thomas W. Sherman was about to embark for the Port Royal region, he received from the War Department a list of instructions concerning the contrabands. However, one matter was left to his own discretion. If "special circumstances seem to require it," Sherman was authorized to employ the contrabands in any capacity whatsoever, "with such organization (in squads, companies, or otherwise) as you may deem most beneficial to the service, this however, not being a general arming of them for the service."

In essence this gave the commanding general carte blanche to create Negro military units in limited numbers. "The order to Sherman," exulted one editor, "is better than a great victory in the field." Said Wendell Phillips, "The hint is enough for the dullest brain."

General Sherman, however, did not take the hint. In fact, he almost went to the other extreme. As soon as he had effected a landing on the seacoast, he announced to the people of South Carolina that his mission was one of peace and good will, and he assured them that he would not interfere with their "local institution." In Sherman's judgment no "special circumstances" were ever to arise which seemed to require arming the Negro.

Two months after his instructions to Sherman, the Secretary of War took a step which hastened his dismissal from the cabinet. By December 1861 Simon Cameron had come under the influence of a group of Republican politicians who were bent on dominating Congress and the President. These "Radicals," so-called, planned to punish the South severely, and they naturally favored the arming of the blacks. Seeking the political support of this clique because he was already under fire for mismanaging war contracts, Cameron decided to reverse his position on Negro soldiers.

In his annual report to the President, Cameron asserted that it was the right, and might become the duty, of the government to arm the slaves. Before the report had been put in Lincoln's hands, Cameron rushed copies out to the postmasters of the larger cities. Lincoln was as vexed as he ever permitted himself to become. He immediately ordered that the mailed copies be recalled by telegraph and that the offending paragraphs be revised. Cameron had no choice. His revised statement simply said that the slaves were a military resource and as such should not be returned to their masters.

Too shrewd to put himself in open opposition to the powerful Radicals and the abolitionists, Lincoln waited a month before easing Cameron out of the cabinet and packing him off to the distant Court of the Romanoffs. His successor in the war office was Edwin M. Stanton. The new secretary was a friend of Charles Sumner, and the abolitionists and Negroes were not at all displeased with the change.

Within five months after Stanton was sworn in, he was officially requested by the House to explain the recruiting policies of one of his generals. The officer was David Hunter, who without express authorization had proceeded to recruit the first regiment of Negroes in the Civil War. Hunter had been recently rebuked by Lincoln for the order proclaiming martial law, but the general was not easily discouraged. When he succeeded T. W. Sherman as commanding officer in the Department of the South, Hunter took full advantage of the instructions given to Sherman the preceding October. He lost no time in organizing a Negro regiment.

His first step was to send for Abram Murchison, a minister with great influence among Hilton Head Negroes. Hunter asked the preacher's opinion on the feeling of the Negroes toward military service. Murchison was enthusiastic and offered to call a meeting to find out whether his sentiments were shared by the other Negro men. Such a meeting was called on April 7, 1862. Murchison made a short talk, emphasizing the Negro's responsibility to support the government and repel "Secests." The administration, continued he, was thinking of offering them an opportunity to bear arms. The explanations over, Murchison asked those who wished to enlist to stand. Every man rose.

Murchison then invited each man to come forward and have his name entered on the list as a volunteer soldier. The old men and the boys were rejected, and the remaining 105 were enrolled. The next day 25 more names were handed in, and within a week the roll totaled 150.

With these Murchison recruits as a nucleus, Hunter quickly proceeded to organize the "First South Carolina Volunteer Regiment." Thereupon the commander duly forwarded to army headquarters a report of the mustering in of the black infantry, and his action soon became generally known throughout the North.

It was then that the House of Representatives sent its request to Stanton. Upon motion of Congressman C. A. Wickliffe of Kentucky the House passed a resolution inquiring of the Secretary of War whether Hunter had organized a regiment of Negroes, whether the War Department had authorized the step and whether Hunter had been supplied with equipment and arms for them. Stanton, with an air of injured innocence, forwarded Wickliffe's resolutions to Hunter with a request for an answer.

Late one Sunday evening, a perspiring messenger delivered into Hunter's hands the dispatch from Stanton. The general began to smile as soon as he read the first few lines. He was elated at the prospect of setting forth his views; in high spirits he told his adjutant general that he "would not part with the document in his hand for fifty thousand dollars." Anxious to get his reply on a steamer sailing the next morning, Hunter did not lose a minute in getting to his desk. His answer suggests that he may have missed his calling, for without doubt it was a masterpiece. It was ironic and forceful.

Its opening lines set the tone. Hunter said that he had organized no "fugitive slaves," but that he had, however, organized "a fine regiment of persons whose late masters are fugitive rebels," and that the loyal persons comprising this regiment were anxious to go in pursuit of "their fugacious and traitorous proprietors." His authority for organizing the regiment, continued the general, was based on the instructions given to T. W. Sherman in October and turned over to him. These instructions had placed no restrictions on color or nature of service and he had taken them at face value. Hunter concluded by asserting that the arming of the Negroes was a success and that he hoped by the end of the year to have under enlistment from 48,000 to 50,000.

As soon as Stanton received the letter and noted its contents, he rushed it to the House. It pleased him to transmit a reply which left his own skirts unsullied. Moreover, Hunter's saucy tone would perhaps discourage Congressmen from asking embarrassing questions in the future.

When the letter was delivered to the House, the Speaker ordered it read. Few communications have ever called forth more laughter in the halls of Congress — as the clerk read it aloud he could scarcely keep a straight face, and the Republican members of the House completely abandoned decorum. The fuming Wickliffe and his Kentucky colleagues did not share the boisterous merriment. They proposed a resolution condemning Hunter for discourteous language and for insulting the dignity of Congress. But their resolution had little support and was never acted upon.

Hunter hoped that his letter would smoke out Lincoln and Stanton and force them to uphold his stand. But the administration was not yet quite done with muddle. Hunter was neither ordered to disband his troops nor given any further means to organize them. When on August 4 he appealed for commissions for the officers and pay for the men, he might as well have spoken to the wind.

Hunter decided that enough was enough. His Negro soldiers had served without pay for three months and there was no immediate prospect that the regiment would be officially mustered in. Hence on August 10 he gave up the experiment and the troops were disbanded except for one company.

This company, however, was destined to be the first group of Negro soldiers to be given an offensive assignment. Under Sergeant Trowbridge it was detailed on August 5 to garrison St. Simon's Island off the coast of Georgia. As the company prepared to debark, Commodore Goldsborough asked Trowbridge to take the men and flush up a band of rebel guerrillas. "If you should capture them," added Goldsborough, "it will be a great thing for you."

Trowbridge and his company landed only to find that the Negroes on the island had already undertaken that mission. Led by a contraband not inappropriately named John Brown, this group had armed itself and had set out in pursuit of the rebels. The latter had astutely withdrawn to a swampy region which could be entered single file only. Hiding behind a log, the rebels waited. John Brown was first to approach, and when he came within six feet of the log he was shot dead. A brief skirmish followed. Then the Negroes retreated and the guerrillas did likewise. This was perhaps the first armed encounter on land in which colored men took part. It is significant that this action was taken by Negroes entirely on their own initiative — it was an action planned and carried out by former slaves.

Trowbridge and his Negro soldiers assisted by a posse of sailors took over the task of searching for the nest of guerrillas. They scoured the island all during the hot and sticky day. The assignment was dangerous, but not a man held back. The Rebels, however, were not to be found. They had concealed themselves behind a dense thicket of palmettos from which they eventually escaped by boat.

The guerrillas reached the mainland tattered and dirty from head to foot. They did not quickly forget their experience. Wrote Rebel leader Miles Hazzard to a friend, "If you wish to know hell before your time, go to St. Simon's and be hunted ten days by niggers."

The Trowbridge company remained at St. Simon's for two months doing picket duty. But the island was untroubled by the enemy. The men, however, were growing more ragged — there had been no new supply of uniforms, and they had received no pay. But they were proud of being the last of "Hunter's regiment." And by their fidelity, Hunter's efforts were not barren. His organizing and arming of a slave regiment dramatized an issue that now would never down. Lincoln and the War Department could not ignore the storm of public indignation which followed the disbanding of the regiment.

Another general who tried to jump the gun on the using of Negro troops was Jim Lane, of Kansas. Lane had received a commission as brigadier general of volunteers with authority to raise troops in Kansas. On August 6, 1862, Lane sent word to the astonished Stanton, "I am receiving Negroes under the late act of Congress." Lane referred to an act passed three weeks earlier which authorized the President to receive "persons of African descent" into any military or naval service for which they might be found competent.

No one could put this law into operation except the President, but a man of action like Lane was not to be held up by what he regarded as a mere formality. He took out advertisements in the newspapers, reprinting the law of July 17, 1862, and urging Negroes to come to Leavenworth and sign up with him. A sharply worded note came from the War Department on August 23: Negro troops could only be raised upon the express authority of the President, said Stanton's letter, and no such executive authority had been given to raise troops in Kansas.

General Lane did not abandon his plans — he was also a United States Senator and ran little risk in defying Stanton — but the order from Washington undoubtedly threw a damper on any large-scale recruiting of Negroes. Nonetheless Lane persisted. By the end of October, he had organized two regiments of Negroes. The First Regiment of Kansas Colored Volunteers drilled daily at Camp "Jim Lane" near Wyandotte. They were supplied with gray pants, blue jackets, and forage caps. Their camp was "very clean and orderly." The Second Kansas Colored Volunteers drilled at Mound City.

The Negro recruits soon found out that there was more to soldiering than drill. On the night of October 7 they had a brush with a band of guerrillas in Clay County, Missouri. Neither side suffered any casualties in this engagement, which marked the first time in the war that Northern Negroes saw action as soldiers.

Their first blood was shed in a battle three weeks later at the Osage River in Bates County, Missouri. The object of the First Kansas Colored was to clear out a rendezvous of Rebel guerrillas on what was called the Island, a long, marshy strip lying in the Osage. Landing on the island on October 27, they found themselves opposed to a force of about six hundred men. In the hand-to-hand struggle which ensued, the First Regiment fought courageously. One of their number, Six-Killer, a Cherokee Negro, fell with half a dozen wounds "after shooting two men, bayonetting a third and laying a fourth *hors de combat* with the butt of his gun." Another wounded volunteer, Sergeant Edward Lowrie, was reloading his gun when three men on horseback ordered him to surrender. As an answer he knocked one of them off his horse with a stunning blow from his rifle, and as the other two charged, he felled them also with the butt of his gun. One fourteen-year-old Negro, Manuel Dobson, received a ball through each arm. "What I narrate," wrote the New York *Times* war correspondent who described this Battle of Island Mounds, "I saw myself."

Shortly after the skirmish, William Truman, one of the Rebel leaders, informed a group at Butler "that the black devils fought like tigers . . . and that not one would surrender, though they had tried to take a prisoner." The Rebels soon withdrew to the southeast to join guerrilla chieftain William Clarke Quantrill, the scourge of Unionists in Kansas and Missouri.

Despite these passages at arms, the Kansas colored regiments were still not mustered in. Washington said nothing about them nor did anything about them. Colonel James M. Williams told the unpaid troops they would be furloughed on November 21 unless the military authorities took action by that time. Another Kansas officer who favored Negro troops, Colonel R. J. Hinton, urged them early in December to wait a little longer.

Just as South Carolina had its Hunter, and Kansas its Lane, so Louisiana had its general who was impatient to put a musket in the hands of the Negro. Brigadier General John W. Phelps, a West Pointer, was a loosely built, six-footer, gruff and driving, but popular with his men. A Vermonter, he was a fervid abolitionist and therefore disliked Southerners not because they were Rebels, but because they were slaveholders.

In command of the Union forces at Carrollton, Louisiana, Phelps on June 16, 1862, wrote to the ranking officer in the Department of the Gulf, Ben Butler, suggesting that fifty regiments of contrabands be enlisted. This step, said Phelps, would prepare them for freedom and would also "prevent the necessity of retrenching our liberties, as we should do by a large army exclusively of whites." Butler pigeonholed the letter.

Six weeks later, having received no reply, Phelps unburdened himself again. He could, wrote he, raise three regiments in a short time if he were provided with the proper facilities. "I have now upwards of 300 Africans organized into five companies who are ready and willing to show their devotion to our cause . . ." Only a Cain could reject such an offer. As a final suggestion, Phelps added that West Pointers just graduating could be sent to drill the recruits, and that the line officers could come from the sergeants, corporals and privates already in the service.

Butler dared not ignore this second letter since it was apparent that Phelps, unless checked, would proceed on his own hook to raise the three regiments. Butler wrote to Phelps the next day, calling a halt. He was quite willing to accept the Negro as a laborer, ran his communication, but not as a soldier. He ordered that the contrabands be used in cutting away the timber "between your lines and the lake," in order to "perfect the fortifications."

Butler's letter was friendly in tone — he had a fondness for Phelps, regarding him as "a crank upon the slavery question solely." But there was no mollifying the brigadier general. He at once wrote out his resignation, and with it a frosty letter stating his unwillingness to become a slave driver, "having no qualifications in that way." Butler asked the trusted commander to reconsider resigning, but Phelps was unbending.

Three weeks later Butler had a change of heart concerning Negro soldiers. There had been military action at Baton Rouge on August 5 and Butler had again pressed Stanton to send reenforcements. The general was given to understand that none could be spared. On August 14 Butler informed the Secretary of War that the Union forces at New Orleans were threatened by an attack and that "I shall call on Africa to intervene, and I do not think I shall call in vain."

Butler thereupon sent for twenty of the colored officers who had been enrolled under the Confederate flag as recently as the preceding April. The ensuing discussion was frank and to the point. Butler asked free Negroes if they would like to be organized as part of the United States Army. There was a unanimous chorus of "yes." Butler has reconstructed his conversation with their spokesman, "a Negro nearly as dark," said he, "as the ace of spades":

"General," he asked, "shall we be officers as we were before?"

"Yes, every one of you who is fit to be an officer shall be, and all line officers shall be colored men."

"How soon do you want us to be ready?"

"How soon can you give me two regiments of a thousand men each?"

"In ten days."

"But," I said, "I want you to answer me one question. My officers, most of them, believe that Negroes won't fight."

"Oh, but we will," came from the whole of them.

On August 22 Butler issued a general order authorizing the enlistment of free Negroes "to defend the Flag of their native country, as their fathers did under Jackson at Chalmette, against Packenham and his myrmidons, carrying the black flag of 'beauty and booty.'" Recruiting offices were established and notices were carried in *L'Union*, the French-English newspaper published by New Orleans Negroes. Prospective volunteers were promised that they would receive $38 in advance and be paid $13 to $22 a month, with arms and equipment free. Their families would receive army rations, and at the end of the war each soldier would receive $100 or 160 acres of land.

Negroes flocked to the enlistment offices. At one hotel on September 1 a war correspondent was told by his waiter, a tall light-skinned man of about twenty-three, "Colonel, I'll bid you good-by tomorrow, as I shall have to join my regiment." Many who were runaway slaves represented themselves as "free Negroes," and no recruiting officer ever inquired whether a volunteer was or had been a slave.

The first regiment filled its quota in two weeks. On September 27, 1862, this group of free Negroes was mustered in as the "First Regiment Louisiana Native Guards," thus becoming the first Negro soldiers mustered as a unit into the United States Army during the Civil War. The Native Guards were proud of their regiment and were fond of calling themselves the "Chasseurs d'Afrique."

In enlisting these recruits, Butler had acted on his own authority.

Eleven weeks after his first call for volunteers, having heard nothing from the sphinxes in Washington, Butler decided to bring the matter to a head. On November 7 the general wrote to Commander-in-Chief Halleck calling attention to the existence of the colored regiments. Then came the clincher: "Though I have had many communications from the War Dept. and the General Comm'd'r-in-Chief," wrote Butler, "no communication approving that organization has been received. I must therefore take it to be approved, but would prefer distinct orders on this subject."

The first assignment given to the Native Guards was in the Lafourche district, guarding the bridges, railroads and important bayous. "They have done well," wrote Treasury Agent G. S. Denison on November 14, 1862, "and have accomplished all that has been given them to do." On January 1, 1863, eight companies were sent to Forts Jackson and St. Phillip, the famed fortifications barring the Mississippi River approaches to New Orleans. On the same date two companies, A and D, were sent to Fort Macombe, on the Chef Menteur Pass, connecting Lakes Borgne and Pontchartrain.

With the enlisting of the Native Guards, a signal step was taken that soon spread to South Carolina and Kansas. Three weeks after General Hunter disbanded his Negro troops, the War Department authorized his successor, Brigadier General Rufus Saxton, to "receive into the services of the United States such number of volunteers of African descent as you may deem expedient, not exceeding five thousand. . . ."

As soon as Saxton reached Beaufort he wrote to Thomas Wentworth Higginson offering him the colonelcy of the regiment. Higginson, captain in the Fifty-first Massachusetts, received the letter while dining with his lieutenants at the barracks. Had he received an invitation to take command of a regiment of Kalmuck Tartars, wrote Higginson later, it would not have been more unexpected. But he was not long in making his decision. As an active and militant worker in the abolitionist cause, Higginson had come in contact with Negroes and knew "by experience, the qualities of their race." He thereupon resigned his Massachusetts commission and for weal or woe became an officer in a black regiment.

With Hunter's disbanded troops as a nucleus, the First South Carolina Volunteers was mustered in on November 7, 1862. Eight days later, Sergeant Trowbridge's St. Simon's Island group, having learned the good news, was mustered in as Company A. Thus came into existence the first official regiment made up of former slaves; strictly speaking, the first of all the Negro regiments with official military status.

The regiment saw action six days after mustering. Two hun-. dred and forty of them were assigned on a foraging expedition to obtain a supply of boards and planks. Their destination was a Rebel-held small island in the Doboy River, east of the town of Darien, Georgia. After landing, they discovered that before reaching the mills they would have to cross a causeway. As they went forward, a sharp burst of shot came from a concealed enemy. In the skirmish which followed, the Rebels withdrew. For two days and two nights, one troop detail guarded the causeway while another loaded the transports, the *Darlington* and the *Ben Deford*. Two hundred thousand feet of superior lumber and hundreds of circular and other makes of saws were placed in the ships' holds. With this cargo the two transports, accompanied by the gunboat *Madgie*, returned to Beaufort.

The conduct of the soldiers was noteworthy since two hundred of the two hundred and forty had never handled a gun before, and forty of them had been in the regiment for only two weeks. Their exploit was the occasion of much satisfaction among the Sea Island Negroes. Old Aunt Phyllis on St. Helena laughed and chuckled over the encounter, her account of which is a bit exaggerated: "Dey fought and fought and shot down de 'Secesh,' and ne'er a white man among 'em but two captains."

It is understandable that Sea Islanders took pride in the behavior

of the troops in this first organized action of regular Negro soldiers in the war. Their assignment, of course, had not been in the
tradition of the grand strategy and great campaigns. But in the
large-scale military operations the individual foot soldier was but
a pawn, a body, an expendable. In these smaller engagements, so
many of which fell to the lot of colored troops, the individual
soldier was more on his own, his sense of participation was keener,
and his relative importance far greater.

On January 13, 1862, not long after the mustering in of the
South Carolina contrabands, the First Kansas Colored Regiment
was mustered in, with the indefatigable James M. Williams as its
colonel. Thus to Kansas went the distinction of organizing the
first colored regiment in the North, although many of the men
who filled the ranks were runaways from Missouri.

These first steps in enlisting the Negro as a soldier were viewed
with gratification by the abolitionists and their colored co-
workers. There was still much to be done in spurring the administration to recruit Northern Negroes, and in proclaiming
emancipation for the slaves. The reformers, therefore, did not
propose to rest on their oars. In the meantime they found another vital way in which they could help their cause.

✤

"We have come to do anti-slavery work, and we think it noble
work and we mean to do it earnestly." Dated April 17, 1862, and
written in the Sea Islands, so runs this entry from the diary of the
noble-spirited and enthusiastic Laura M. Towne. Of abolitionist
background, it was inevitable that Miss Towne and hundreds like
her would come to the South in the wake of the Union Armies.

For as the Confederates retreated they not only stripped the
plantations of produce and equipment — they also made it a
policy to remove as many able-bodied male slaves as possible and
to leave behind all others. Confederate commanders advised mas-

ters that "old and decrepit" slaves would be a liability all around. Hence when the Yankees arrived, they were usually met by a Negro population made up of a goodly number of the aged and the infirm.

The plight of these thousands of destitute former slaves aroused a profound sympathy in the North. Throughout the free states citizens opened their purses and sent "contraband boxes," generally clothes and shoes. Philanthropic associations, church groups, independent clubs and individual donors were caught up in a wave of benevolent enthusiasm to aid the freedmen by sending "bundles for blacks."

Clothes, bedding, sewing materials, garden seeds, farm implements and medicines were needed and were sent. But just as important, teachers and missionaries were essential in this great crusade. To hundreds of abolitionists and church people in whom the humanitarian impulse beat strongly, this seemed like a call from on high.

The first of these missionaries to the freedmen, Lewis C. Lockwood, was sent to Fortress Monroe in the fall of 1861. The Reverend Mr. Lockwood went under the auspices of the American Missionary Association, an independent nonsectarian organization which had been founded in 1846 to combat "the sins of caste, polygamy and slaveholding." Destined to write a glorious page in the history of better race relations, the Association was the outgrowth of an "Amistad Committee," which had been founded in 1839 for the defense of a group of Africans who had seized the slave ship upon which they were being held captive. The Association's treasurer, Lewis Tappan, a well-known figure in abolitionist and reform circles, had written to General Butler on August 3, expressing concern over the plight of the contrabands and suggesting that they be sent to the North.

Butler replied within forty-eight hours. He promised that the fugitives would not be returned to slavery. Moreover, he saw no reason to send the contrabands North since "this part of the state is but little more cultivated than in the days of Powhattan." Encouraged by the general's prompt and courteous reply, Tappan and his colleagues decided to send a missionary without delay. The Association commissioned Lockwood to go to the fortress and to minister to the moral, physical and religious interests of its Negro inhabitants.

Lockwood arrived at the fortress on September 4 and was greatly heartened by the cordial welcome he received from the freedmen. Less than two weeks later, on September 16, he sent back an inspiring message:

> Thank and praise the Lord! Yesterday was a high day in Zion. 9½ A.M. opened a Sabbath school in ex-President Tyler's house near Hampton.

Two days later, at the request of twenty students, Lockwood started a day school at a small brown house in the town of Hampton. The teacher of this one-room school was Mary S. Peake, a Negro woman whose father was English. Mrs. Peake had always been free and had received her education from private tutors at her home in Alexandria.

Of frail physique and in poor health, Mrs. Peake nonetheless was not content to stop after meeting with the children in the day; dominated by the idea of helping others, she soon began to hold evening classes for adults. A character-building teacher, Mrs. Peake mixed her instruction with prayer and hymns. It was her belief that the teacher of a mission school "should educate the children for eternity as well as for time." For her efforts she would accept no money. She was fully rewarded, she told Lockwood, "in having the privilege of doing good in this way."

Mrs. Peake's success led quickly to the organizing of day schools in nearby neighborhoods. On September 24, a week after the first meeting of Mrs. Peake's class, a "good" school had been set up at Fortress Monroe, wrote Lockwood, "under the instruction of Mrs. Bailey, assisted by Miss Jennings, and James, a bright boy who acts as monitor. They are all colored persons, and Mrs. Bailey is a free woman."

Lockwood continued his labors at Fortress Monroe for thirteen months. Before his departure the community was a beehive of schools and churches. Seven thousand eager pupils were enrolled in the day and night schools, and 5000 came on Sundays for Bible lessons. "This is not a day of small things," wrote Lockwood in prayerful thanksgiving, "but already a day of great things."

In the Sea Islands a similar dawn was breaking. In the middle of January 1862, Salmon P. Chase sent an investigator down to Port Royal to make recommendations concerning the freedmen. Although the Secretary of the Treasury was stiff and formal in person-to-person contacts, he was held in high esteem by Negroes. As a fledgling lawyer in Ohio, Chase had defended so many runaways that he had become known as "the attorney-general of fugitive slaves." For his zeal in defending runaway Samuel Watson, Chase had been given a punch bowl by the Negroes of Cincinnati and when Chase was governor he used the bowl on all official occasions. (Since he never served anything in it other than straight lemonade, the sight of Chase's celebrated punch bowl had become something of tribulation to lovers of the social glass.)

Chase selected his friend and associate, Edward L. Pierce, to go down to the Sea Islands and look into the contraband situation. Pierce had already distinguished himself for his brief but effective job with the Negroes at Fortress Monroe. After spending nearly a month in the Port Royal region, Pierce submitted a report recommending that carefully selected superintendents and teachers be screened for service among the 8000 Negroes inhabiting those parts of the seacoast then held by Union forces.

Within a week after Pierce's report, the commanding officer of the Department of the South, Thomas W. Sherman, issued a general order appealing to the philanthropic North for aid. One of his sentences pinpointed the need: "A system of culture and instruction must be combined with one providing for their physical wants." He was dividing the territory into districts, explained Sherman, and for each of these districts competent instructors would be needed. "Never was there a nobler or more fitting opportunity," declared the general.

News of Sherman's order winged its way to every corner of the North. Immediately thereafter freedmen's aid societies were formed, mushrooming particularly in former abolitionist centers. Boston organized a relief society on February 7; two weeks later New York followed suit, and on March 5, the citizens of Philadelphia, after a monster mass meeting, organized the Port Royal Relief Committee. The forerunners of numerous others, the societies in these three cities undertook the dual task of providing material relief — clothes and supplies — and the recruiting and paying of teachers.

The first group of teachers, fifty-three strong, sailed from New York one cold, drizzly March morning, the rain freezing as it fell. Before boarding the steamer, they had taken the oath of allegiance. Pierce, now government agent in charge of Port Royal plantations and contrabands, accompanied this "Gideon's band." En route during the five-day trip, he briefed the forty-one men and twelve women. "You go to elevate, to purify, and fit them for the duties of American citizens." To have an influence on them, explained Pierce, "you must first convince them that yours is a brother's hand and heart."

It was in this spirit that Pierce's small pacific band landed on the shores of South Carolina. Undoubtedly a few had come seeking adventure or romance, and some of them looked like "broken-down schoolmasters or ministers." But almost without exception they were enthusiastic and they were prepared to make personal sacrifices. Taking quarters in the abandoned houses of the South Carolina gentry, they quickly set up schoolhouses in cotton barns, tents and old sheds. By May 8 — two months after their arrival — eight schools were in operation.

After a year's effort the freedmen's relief associations had established thirty schools in the Sea Islands. An average of 2000 pupils reported daily and were instructed in the elementary branches of study — reading, writing, spelling, geography and arithmetic. Over the same twelvemonth the relief agencies distributed 35,829 books and pamphlets, 91,834 garments, 5895 yards of cloth and $3000 worth of farming implements and seeds.

The seacoast Negroes were genuinely appreciative of the efforts of their friends from the North. As J. Miller McKim prepared to leave the islands after a visit as an agent of the Philadelphia association, he was approached by an old man who took his hand and said earnestly, "Tell 'em tank 'em; tell 'em God bless 'em." Then, as if straining for an appropriate climax, the old man added, "Give 'em my compliments."

Further up the coast, in North Carolina, the schooling of Negroes was first started in the New Bern region. Vincent Colyer, the Superintendent of the Poor, was the guiding spirit. On the first night his school opened, in February 1862, more than six hundred eager Negroes reported for enrollment at the two colored churches designated as schoolrooms. Their teachers were the chaplain and a few of the college graduates of the Twenty-fifth Massachusetts.

Colyer's work was significant not only in bringing the alphabet to Negroes in a Southern state in which hitherto it had been a criminal offense to teach them to read: his concern extended to the poor whites. They were taught in the daytime hours, and like the Negroes, they showed a keen desire to master the mysteries of the printed word. It is noteworthy that the humanitarian efforts to assist the Negroes often embraced the poor whites, and that popular education for whites in the South, as well as for Negroes, owed its origin to the pioneer labors of men like Colyer and philanthropic agencies such as the American Missionary Association.

A month after Colyer opened his schools at New Bern, a similar effort was launched in the nation's capital. Late in March 1862, the National Freedmen's Relief Association of the District of Columbia came into existence, its goal to relieve the immediate wants of the freedmen and to bring them under moral and religious influences. In May the Association established two evening schools — one at Alexandria and one in Washington, D. C., both taught by convalescent soldiers. The Sunday services were conducted by such prominent Negro clergymen as Bishop Daniel A. Payne of the African Methodist Episcopal Church. Soon other associations sent teachers — the American Tract Society, and the Boston and Philadelphia groups.

Another freedmen's relief association that came into existence in March 1862 was the Kansas Emancipation League. A school for fugitive Negroes had been started in Lawrence at the courthouse late in 1861. Classes were held in the evenings since the Negroes worked during the daytime hours. Here, as was common elsewhere, the teachers were volunteers and they received no salary.

The Kansas Emancipation League appointed William D. Matthews as superintendent of contrabands, and established branches throughout the state. The League had a broad program. In addition to relieving the immediate wants of the freedmen and organizing schools, the League proposed to assist the Negro to stand on his own feet. The freedmen were urged to establish savings fund clubs and land associations, and to spread out into the farming counties where their labor was particularly needed.

Further down the Mississippi, educational efforts on behalf of the Negro showed a marked lag. In the West, except for Kansas, the freedmen's associations were not able to begin any effective work until the fall of 1863. This somewhat retarded beginning resulted from the presence of the slaveowners. For in the West, particularly along the Mississippi, the planters did not flee en masse. Thousands of them remained on their property, swallowed their pride, and took the oath of allegiance, professing themselves loyal to the government at Washington. These "loyal" slaveholders could scarcely be expected to put out the welcome mat for agents of the freedmen's aid societies.

Those plantations from which the masters had fled were leased to private speculators whose ruling desire was to get rich quick — men whom James E. Yeatman characterized as "adventurers, camp followers, and army sharks." While such devotees of the Almighty Dollar did not share the slaveholders' intense hostility to "book-learning" for Negroes, they would not lift a finger to provide instruction for their Negro hired hands.

Against this hostility of the planters and indifference of the lessees, John Eaton, supervisor of contrabands in Mississippi, Tennessee and Arkansas, threw his great energies. He worked almost singlehandedly until late in the summer of 1863 when the freedmen's associations were finally permitted to send their teachers in. Of these many organizations — the American Missionary Association, the Western Freedmen's Aid Commission, the Freedmen's Aid Society of Cincinnati, the Northwestern Freedmen's Aid Society of Chicago, the Assembly of the United Presbyterian Church, the United Brethren in Christ and the Western Sanitary Commission — perhaps the most active was the last named. The Lower Mississippi Valley its field of operations, the Western Sanitary Commission did a notable piece of work in procuring and sending relief to the blacks, and in preparing them for the responsibilities of free men.

In Louisiana the schooling of the freedmen got under way more slowly than anywhere else. Here, too, the resident planters had taken the oath of allegiance with their fingers crossed. Any move for Negro education could count on their opposition. There were a few individuals with a broad philanthropy who did what they could, such as Chaplain George H. Hepworth whose actions were governed by the philosophy that "there are some born to rule but they are not all white; there are some born to serve but they are not all black." But it was not until August 1863 that any significant beginning was made in Louisiana toward teaching the freedmen. In that month, General N. P. Banks, commanding the Department of the Gulf, appointed a Commission of Enrollment and charged its three members with, among other responsibilities, the schooling of colored persons.

No survey of the pioneer efforts to assist the freedmen would be complete without mentioning the role of the Negro as donor and giver, for colored people were participants in these early efforts, North and South, to assist the freedmen. Philadelphia Negroes held benefits and church suppers for contrabands. At a mass meeting held in Bethel church and attended by most of the Quaker City's colored clergy, a resolution was passed pledging to fugitives "the protection of our homes and firesides, a part of our personal property, even to the last crumb."

Shiloh church, in New York, held an entertainment on December 13, 1861, in the church basement for funds to help the freedmen at Fortress Monroe. Under a banner inscribed, "The Glory of a United People," which streamed above the rostrum, the congregation raised $61.50, and collected a huge box of clothes. In Boston the colored people gave an entertainment for the benefit of the Kansas contrabands. Two locally well-known elocutionists, Louisa DeMortie and Susa Cluer, gave dramatic and poetic readings.

In Washington the colored citizens organized a Contraband Relief Association to assist fugitives coming to the city. The Association was headed by Elizabeth Keckley, whom Mrs. Abraham Lincoln had engaged as dressmaker and seamstress the day after her husband's inauguration, and who had become Mrs. Lincoln's only intimate friend in Washington. Mrs. Keckley was a former slave who by her needle had raised $1200 to purchase her freedom and that of her son George, destined soon to die in combat on a Missouri battlefield. Mrs. Keckley was a queenly-looking, graceful mulatto, with hair already turning beautifully white. A woman of tact and poise who looked on the bright side of things, she was an emotional balance wheel to the high-strung and explosive

Mary Todd Lincoln. Moreover, she knew just how to individually fashion Mrs. Lincoln's evening gowns so as to reveal her firm neck and round shoulders while slenderizing her somewhat dumpy lines.

As founder and president of the Contraband Relief Association, Mrs. Keckley's first collection was a $200 donation from Mrs. Lincoln. When the latter went to Boston to visit her son Robert at Harvard, she took "Lizabeth" as her companion. Mrs. Keckley made the most of the occasion. She talked with patron saint Wendell Phillips and held a mass meeting at Boston's Twelfth Baptist Church. She then organized a branch society, headed by the wives of clergymen Leonard A. Grimes and J. Sella Martin. Boston colored women were to send more than eighty large boxes for the Washington poor and needy.

Returning by way of New York, Mrs. Keckley held a meeting at Henry Highland Garnet's Shiloh church. She also laid her project before the steward of the Metropolitan Hotel and succeeded in raising "quite a sum of money" from the Negro dining-room waiters. Frederick Douglass gave $200 from his own pocket. Mrs. Keckley sent her appeal across the seas. From the Sheffield Anti-Slavery Society she received $24; the Birmingham Negro's Friend Society sent $83; the "Friends at Bristol" raised $176; the Aberdeen Ladies' Society forwarded $40, and the Anti-Slavery Society of Edinburgh sent $48.

Another Washington society, the National Freedmen's Relief Association, hired a Negro, Edward M. Thomas, as its agent. The Association reported him as being intelligent and well informed: "He rendered valuable service in the execution of our plans." In its first annual report the Association deemed it "proper to say a word of praise for the free colored citizens of the District, and throughout the country generally, for the interest and zeal which they have manifested in behalf of their less fortunate brethren, contributing largely to their comfort from their own slender stores."

Freedmen along the Mississippi did not wait for outside aid in setting up schools. When James E. Yeatman, President of the Western Sanitary Commission, made his trip to the towns along the river, he was surprised to find that in Natchez there were three schools run by colored women. He had an even more astonishing experience in a single rural locality where he ran across a beehive of schools conducted by Negroes. This is his description:

> There is at Groshon's plantation a school taught by Rose Anna, a colored girl. She has between forty and fifty scholars. Uncle Jack, a colored man, at the Goodrich place, is teaching a school of eighty-one scholars. Uncle Tom, a colored man at the Savage plantation, has a school of thirty scholars. He is infirm, and teaches them remaining himself in bed. Wm. McCutchen, a colored man, has commenced a school on the Currie place. He has sixty-three scholars . . . He has but one arm, having lost the other by a cotton gin.

✤

The abolitionists did a thorough job in hammering on the theme of emancipation and in ministering to the needs of the freedmen. But as the summer of 1862 wore on, the friends of the slave realized anew that their progress would have been much greater if it were not for the tall, rawboned man in the White House. Congress had picked up speed in the right direction, the armed services under Stanton and Welles had become receptive to the idea of blacks in uniform, and the masses of people had generously responded to the appeals on behalf of the freedmen.

But the laggard Lincoln, in the judgment of the emancipationists, was apparently trying to put down the rebellion without hurting the rebels. In their opinion such an attempt "wouldn't scour," to borrow a Presidential turn of phrase. The reformers did not doubt Mr. Lincoln's integrity (although he was, as Wendell Phillips put it, "Kentucky honest," which was of course not quite the same thing as "Massachusetts honest"). The reformers did not doubt Lincoln's good intentions. His face was turned toward Zion, but he seemed to move on leaden feet.

However, the Negroes and their reformist friends did not have much longer to drum their fingers impatiently. For the autumn of 1862 was only twenty-four-hours old when on September 22 the "tortoise President" showed unmistakable signs of walking a little faster.

Whenever I hear anyone arguing for slavery, I have a strong impulse to see it tried on him personally.

A. LINCOLN

CHAPTER VII

The Tortoise Gets a Move On

A M I NOT A MAN and a brother?" This question was widely quoted by abolitionists for over fifty years. The slogan had been coined by free Negroes at the turn of the century, and when the organized abolition movement got under way in the 1830's, it had been adopted semiofficially. It appeared on the letterheads of the antislavery societies, generally below a drawing of a dark-skinned, half-clad, muscular slave, holding up his manacled hands, a beseeching look on his face. Those who had grown weary of the rub-a-dub abolitionist agitation and of the eternal Negro question had proposed dropping from this watchword a single letter — the first "r" in "brother."

If there was anyone in the country to whom the Negro was a bother, it was Abraham Lincoln during his first two years as President. Mr. Lincoln was not a fretful man. When he did not know what to do, writes William E. Barton, he did not do anything. But the Negro question — the arming of the colored man and the freeing of the slave — would not yield to a policy of inactivity, no matter how masterly.

"Old Abe had a tough job," as young Archibald Rutledge's Confederate father told him years afterward. The Negro question made Lincoln's job particularly difficult. He had to contend with such Congressional champions of the black man as rough-and-tumble Ben Wade in the Senate, blunt and ruthless, and Thaddeus

Stevens in the House, an aged Pennsylvania ironmonger with a steel-willed, relentless hatred of the "slavocracy." Lincoln also had to deal with such antislavery generals as Frémont, Hunter and Phelps, and to listen to unsolicited advice from such scolding editors as Horace Greeley and Theodore Tilton. From the public platforms Wendell Phillips thundered his invectives, and Frederick Douglass unleashed his denunciations of the "slow coach at Washington."

The clergy did not tarry in joining this uncelestial choir. Two of Lincoln's chief pulpit castigators were George B. Cheever, pastor of the Church of the Puritans, and Henry Ward Beecher at Plymouth church in nearby Brooklyn. It was bewhiskered Dr. Cheever who urged his congregation to "fight against slavery until Hell freezes, and then continue the battle on the ice." It was the handsome Beecher with his flair for the dramatic who had brought into the pulpit the chains that had bound John Brown, seized the clanking irons and stamped upon them, and who on a June Sabbath in 1861 had led into the pulpit a beautiful young slave woman robed in spotless white who needed $800 to purchase her freedom.

And of course this anvil chorus did not exhaust the roster of Lincoln critics. From the Confederacy nothing could be expected but abuse, and some of the early criticism from overseas was scarcely more temperate. On the home front Lincoln had to cope with "malice domestic" from Southern sympathizers such as "Copperheads" Fernando Wood and Clement Vallandigham, whose fifth-column activities reached the proportions of a "hidden war." In his cabinet the President had a gallery of prima donnas whose early attitudes toward their prairie-lawyer chief (who had gone to school only "by littles," and who wore a rusty, ill-fitting swallow-tailed coat and "high-water" trousers) was a form of implied reproof. And after the White House doors closed at midnight and Lincoln ascended to his bedchamber, he still found no escape from censure, for lo, Mrs. Lincoln was there.

Lincoln had not expected to avoid a severe raking over the coals on the slavery issue. The problem was a most vexatious one, as he had found out from the day he first journeyed to Vandalia in 1834 to take a seat in the Illinois state legislature. Twenty years later, in October 1854, in an address at Peoria, he had admitted that "If all earthly power were given me, I should not know what to do with the existing institution." In the next year (August 15, 1855) he made a similar confession to George Robertson:

> Our political problem now is, "Can we as a nation continue together — forever — half slave and half free? The problem is too mighty for me — may God, in his mercy, superintend the solution."

Lincoln made clear his own personal feelings: he was naturally and sentimentally opposed to human bondage. When he was twenty-eight years old and on the threshold of his political career, he stated, in a resolution introduced in the Illinois legislature, that "slavery is founded on both injustice and bad policy." As a member of the Thirtieth Congress, which sat from 1847 to 1849, he had consistently opposed the spread of slavery in the territories. In a letter to his friend Joshua F. Speed on August 24, 1855, Lincoln unburdened himself:

> I confess I hate to see the poor creatures hunted down and caught and carried back to their stripes and unrequited toil; but I bite my lips and keep quiet. In 1841 you and I had together a tedious low-water trip on a steamboat from Louisville to St. Louis. You may remember, as I well do, that from Louisville to the mouth of the Ohio there were on board ten or a dozen slaves shackled together with irons. That sight was a continued torment to me, and I see something like it every time I touch the Ohio or any other slave border.

Lincoln's natural tendency to sympathize with the slaves was strengthened by his own personal experiences with Negroes. At

Springfield one of the first persons he came to know was William de Fleurville, "Billy the Barber," a Haitian by birth. Lincoln had first met Fleurville at New Salem in the fall of 1831 as the penniless young barber was footing his way to Springfield. Taking him to Rutledge Tavern, Lincoln explained his unhappy plight to the guests. That night Billy got several customers, and he was in good spirits the next morning as he left for Springfield. Here he opened the town's first barbershop in 1832.

Fleurville's shop was the informal social center for the men of the community; it was "Lincoln's second home," before his marriage in 1842. Frequently he would leave his law books there; he would have nobody in Springfield shave him except Billy. The youthful Lincoln, then a Whig in the lower house of the state legislature, liked to stand before the stove in Billy's shop and swap tall stories. A thrifty man, Fleurville engaged Lincoln to handle his real estate investments. "Billy will blame me if I don't get things fixed up," wrote Lincoln in September 1852 as he sought to obtain a writ for the conveyance of certain lots in Bloomington which Fleurville had purchased. When Lincoln left Springfield as President-elect in February 1861, one of his most sorrowful leave-takings was at the old barbershop, where Billy cut his hair for the last time.

When Lincoln boarded the train for Washington the "only person from his home that he selected to accompany him" was black-skinned William Johnson. On Lincoln's arrival at the nation's capital he was flanked by this Negro bodyguard and the Pinkerton men. Lincoln had planned to employ Johnson at the White House, but the opposition of the incumbent Negro domestics was too great. Thereupon, the President wrote several letters of recommendation for Johnson, finally succeeding in having him placed as a "Laborer in the Treasury Department, at a compensation of Six hundred Dollars, per annum."

Lincoln did not permit himself to get excited over such matters as social equality and intermarriage, which he regarded as emo-

tionally toned "false issues." Wrote he to David R. Locke on
September 16, 1859:

> I shall never marry a Negress, but I have no objection to
> anyone else doing so. If a White man wants to marry a
> Negro woman, let him if the Negro can stand it.

In the first of the famous Lincoln-Douglas debates in 1858,
at Ottawa, Illinois, on August 21, the "Little Giant" charged that
Lincoln was "worthy of a medal from Father Giddings and Fred
Douglass for his Abolitionism." This statement, made in an attempt to discredit a political rival, was far from factual. For
although Lincoln's deep humanity was touched by the sight of
manacled slaves, he tended "to bite my lips and keep quiet."
Lincoln was essentially a man with reservations. He believed
slavery wrong, but he deplored agitation on the subject. As a
Congressman he read a proposal for abolishing slavery in the
District of Columbia, but he attached a string of "ifs." His concern for the oppressed was strong, but he was ready to crucify
his feelings, as he informed Speed in 1855, in order to maintain
loyalty to the Constitution and to the Union. In the Douglas debates, Lincoln repeated that "the Union could not endure per-
manently half slave and half free," yet he was of the opinion
that Congress had no power to interfere with slavery in the
states.

After he became President, his natural conservatism and inclination to "bide his time" was strengthened by his grave
responsibilities. Lincoln took as something sacred his oath to support the Constitution and the laws. In his first inaugural address
he asserted that he had neither the purpose nor the right to interfere with slavery. Lincoln held that the Presidency did not confer on him the right to act upon his own feelings and beliefs —
that he was privileged to execute only the laws that he liked, "and
inexecute those he disliked." As a genuine believer in democracy,
Lincoln was guided by public opinion, and hence he tended to

delay action until the voice of the people had become clearly intelligible to him.

However, the shaping of public opinion was in some measure a Presidential responsibility, and Lincoln was not a man to dodge a public duty. He was not without a plan for the slave problem and for the free Negro problem. His plan for the slaves was gradual compensation — freeing them gradually over a period extending to some thirty years and paying their masters out of the national treasury.

Lincoln felt that if he could get one Border State to take this step the others would quickly follow. To this end he decided to sound out Delaware which had less than 2000 slaves (1798 in 1860). The cost of war for half a day, as Lincoln figured it out, would pay for all the slaves in Delaware at $400 apiece. In November 1861 he wrote out drafts of two separate bills for state action and placed them in the hands of his friend George Taylor, who represented Delaware in the House.

At a special session of the state legislature the proposal for gradual, compensated emancipation met with a stormy reception. Its opponents scoffed at it as "an abolition bribe" which would encourage the foes of slavery. If Delaware decided to emancipate her bondmen, said they, she would do so in her own good time. So vigorous was the criticism that the proponents of the bill withdrew it before it had been formally introduced.

Lincoln was not deterred by the puncture of this trial balloon. Early on the morning of March 6, 1862, he sent a request to Charles Sumner to come to the White House as soon after breakfast as was convenient. Sumner came at once. Lincoln picked up a manuscript and read the draft of a special message to Congress proposing compensated emancipation. When he had finished, Lincoln awaited the Senator's reactions. Sumner's feelings were mixed. He informed the President that he was cool about emancipation measures that were gradual and compensated, but that he welcomed even a half step in the right direction. Thus assured that the Massachusetts Senator would not raise his powerful voice against the proposal, Lincoln at once sent a message to Congress recommending a program of gradual emancipation, and proposing that the Federal government assist any state that would initiate such a plan.

Lincoln's proposal was widely discussed and the comment in the press was generally favorable. Wendell Phillips said "Yes," and Horace Greeley thanked God that America had "so wise a ruler." On April 10, therefore, Congress by joint resolution passed Lincoln's proposal exactly as he had worded it in his message:

> Resolved, That the United States ought to co-operate with any State which may adopt gradual abolishment of slavery, giving to such State pecuniary aid, to be used by such State in its discretion, to compensate for the inconveniences, public and private, produced by such change of system.

On the day following its sanction of the President's recommendation, Congress gave concrete evidence of its good faith by passing the District of Columbia Emancipation Act. This measure abolished slavery in the national capital and voted compensation to masters, not to exceed $300 for each bondman, to be paid out of the Federal treasury.

There was a final hurdle: would the President sign the bill? It was common knowledge that Lincoln was "a little uneasy" about having compensated emancipation receive its baptism in the District, for it had been his ardent desire to have the Border States make the first move. Moreover, if the first step had to come in Washington, the Chief Magistrate would have preferred that the recommendation originate with the qualified voters, rather than with Congress.

Fearful that the President would withhold his "A. Lincoln," the apprehensive Charles Sumner hurried to the Executive Mansion. Lincoln listened — there was a deep, mutual respect between the two—while the Massachusetts Senator spoke his mind:

"Do you know who at this moment is the largest slaveholder

in this country? It is Abraham Lincoln; for he holds all of the 3,000 slaves of the District, which is more than any other person in the country holds."

Another apprehensive visitor was Bishop Daniel A. Payne of the African Methodist Episcopal Church. On April 14, three days after Congress sent the bill to the President, the colored clergyman called at the White House and sent in his card. A Charleston-born Negro turning fifty, with graying chin whiskers, Payne was thin and emaciated, with the appearance of chronic invalidism. But he bore himself like a prelate, with an air of high seriousness.

When he entered the room the President instinctively exhibited that great skill in greeting people that had helped win for him the highest political office in the land; he repeated the bishop's name, gave him his sonorous title, and took him by the hand as though the two were cronies of long standing. He led Payne to the fireplace and introduced him to Congressman Elihu B. Washburne, a close friend who had been the sole person to greet him on his secret arrival in Washington for the inauguration of 1861. After Washburne and Payne had exchanged greetings, Lincoln pointed to an armchair. As the bishop sank into his seat, Carl Schurz unobtrusively entered. United States minister to Spain, Schurz had journeyed from Madrid to urge Lincoln to free the slaves as a means of gaining support abroad for the Union cause.

"I am here," began Payne, in his sharp, shrill tones, "to learn whether or not you intend to sign the bill of emancipation?" Too big to take offense at such blunt questioning, the President parried; he had been visited earlier in the day, said he, by a group that asked him not to sign it. German-born Carl Schurz injected a word, "All Europe is looking to see that you fail not."

"Mr. President," resumed Payne — his deep-set eyes piercing through thick lenses — "you will remember on the eve of your departure from Springfield, Illinois, you begged the citizens of the republic to pray for you?"

"Yes."

"From that moment, we the colored citizens of the republic have been praying:

O Lord, just as thou didst cause the throne of David to wax stronger and stronger, while that of Saul should wax weaker and weaker, so we beseech Thee cause the power at Washington to grow stronger and stronger, while that at Richmond shall grow weaker and weaker."

No scoffer in matters religious, Lincoln was quick to acknowledge the role of Higher Powers in shaping the course of the war, but in matters more temporal, such as his impending decision, Lincoln, as Payne discovered, could not be induced to answer "Yes" or "No" to a direct question. When forty-five minutes had ticked off, the bishop felt it his duty to withdraw. As he took his leave, he handed the President an armful of religious literature, including copies of the *Christian Recorder*, and asked him to look over the contents in a moment of leisure "so that he could see what the African Methodist Church was doing to improve the character and condition of our people in the republic."

Payne left with his question unanswered, but so graciously had he been received that he almost forgot his failure. He contrasted Lincoln with John Tyler who had been stiff and formal when Payne had come to a private parlor in the Presidential mansion to preach a funeral service over the coffin of a Tyler servant, who had been killed by the explosion of a gun on a warship.

The good bishop did not have long to wait in uncertainty. Two days after his visit, the President signed the bill. With a largeness of spirit that concealed his disappointment that the Border States had not taken the lead in compensated emancipation, Lincoln remarked that he had "ever desired to see the national capital freed from the institution in some satisfactory way."

When the news was flashed over the country, the Negroes lifted their voices in joy and thanksgiving. "It is the first step," intoned Frederick Douglass, "toward a redeemed and regenerated nation." In San Francisco, the Negro poet-plasterer, J. Madison

Bell, many of whose "brilliant gems of thought were born on the scaffold," laid down his trowel and tuned up his harp:

> Thank God! from our old ensign
> Is erased one mark of shame,
> Which leaves one less to rapine
> One less to blight our fame.

The Negroes in the District made no effort to conceal their exuberance. The handsome young Negro, Christian A. Fleetwood, received word from a friend on the spot: "Sights have I witnessed that I never anticipated." One slave chambermaid, upon hearing the news, took off her apron and dashed into the street, shouting, "Let me go tell my husband that Jesus has done all things well."

On the Sunday after the bill was passed every one of Washington's seventeen Negro churches had a day of prayerful celebration. At Union Bethel church, near the Capitol, the pastor attempted to sermonize on the general subject, so often heard from Negro pulpits, of Moses going down to Egypt's land and telling old Pharaoh to "let my people go." But for once Bethel's pastor could not make himself heard; his congregation was not in a listening mood. Some kept rubbing their hands in glee and some kept laughing outright. A few twisted themselves into grotesque positions, as if their joy was too great "to be entertained at a staid perpendicular." An elderly woman in a corner shouted and wept in turn, and a man who bore a deep scar across his nose kept hopping up and down, as if his soul were so happy that he couldn't sit still.

The pastor gave up trying to preach, and shouted, "Glory to God!" A voice to the right which belonged to a muscular mulatto yelled, "Glory to Lovejoy." "No," rebuked the pastor, finally coming into his own, "I tell you glory *to God*."

In one Washington household the servant had to prepare a late breakfast and could not get to church. Suddenly the Sabbath stillness was shattered by shouts from the kitchen. In great alarm, the master and mistress hastened below and found the servant on her knees, shouting, "Glory to God, the jubilee has come at last." Glancing up and noting the looks of mingled astonishment and annoyance on the faces of the whites, the servant explained, "I could not go to church but I thought I would do my part in giving thanks for the jubilee."

Negroes outside of Washington expressed an almost equal sense of gratification. At New Haven's Temple Hall a meeting of celebration was presided over by Amos G. Beman, a light-skinned, full-whiskered, dignified Congregational pastor who had been a tireless worker in all movements for Negro advancement and whose character was above reproach, but whose fortunes had declined after 1857 when he took a white woman as his second wife. The speeches at Temple Hall were received with great bursts of applause, and the group expressed thanks "to those philanthropic Christian statesmen, Messrs. Hale, Sumner, Wilson and Wade of the Senate, and Messrs. Lovejoy and Stevens of the House." At Boston, wrote Nell, "there gushed forth from the grateful hearts of colored men and women their expressions of joy and thanksgiving for this inauguration of emancipation by President Lincoln, destined, as they humbly trust, to spread out, and insure the healing of the nation."

At Rochester the colored people met at Zion church with Lewis Douglass as secretary of the meeting. His distinguished father helped shape the resolutions. At a Buffalo celebration, the Reverend George Weir took as his text, "Righteousness exalteth a nation, but sin is a reproach to any people." One of the resolutions passed by the Buffalo group showed that Negroes were no strangers to boastful grandiloquence about race:

> Resolved, That as we find from history that in East Africa and Asia the arts and sciences flourished in their greatest grandeur and perfection of any period known to man, we therefore recognize in the African race, untrammeled and free, a capacity for improvement and progress equal, if not surpassing, any other race now inhabiting this globe.

Negroes in the city of New York were not to be outdone in observing emancipation in the District. They set aside an entire day, Monday, May 5, for celebration. At five o'clock in the morning a public prayer meeting was held at Shiloh church. At three in the afternoon a flag-raising ceremony took place with Henry Highland Garnet as speaker; flanking him on the platform were thirteen Virginia contrabands. To Cooper Union, the scene of the evening meeting, came groups of Negroes from Brooklyn, Harlem, Astoria, Jamaica, Flushing, Tarrytown, Sing Sing, Troy, Newark, Paterson and Jersey City. An impressive panel of speakers included the printer John J. Zuille, William J. Wilson, George T. Downing, J. McCune Smith and Garnet.

Wilson, a Brooklyn schoolteacher whose witty, well-written essays, under the pseudonym, "Ethiope," enlivened the columns of the Negro journals, took the floor and characterized the men who came to these shores in the *Mayflower* as men of principle and purpose, while depicting those who landed in Virginia as men whose principle was acquisition and power. George T. Downing then reviewed the dark days of the past; Smith asserted that one prop after another was being knocked from under slavery; and Garnet proclaimed that the stars had now assumed a new beauty. Dr. George B. Cheever, an enthusiastic spectator, congratulated the Negroes on the activities of the evening.

Now that the District had initiated compensated emancipation, Lincoln hoped that the Border States would take their cues. In the middle of May he had reminded those states of Congress's resolution to authorize payment for the freeing of their slaves, and advised them that the "change it contemplates would come gently as the dews of heaven, not rending or wrecking anything." Lincoln expressed the hope that he could argue the case "persuasively" rather than "menacingly," but he could not refrain from warning the Border States that slavery was being worn out by the frictions of war.

The President's position was supported by the recommendations of a special House committee which had been appointed on April 7 to inquire into the feasibility of gradually liberating the African slaves, and colonizing them. In its report on July 16, this "Select Committee on Emancipation and Colonization" recommended that the President be empowered to deliver United States bonds, at the rate of $300 for each slave, to the states of Delaware, Maryland, Virginia, Kentucky, Tennessee and Missouri, when they "shall have emancipated their slaves." Still the Border States showed no signs of nibbling.

Lincoln was not a man to hurry things, but his patience would not endure forever. In the middle of July he invited the Congressmen from the Border States to come to the Executive Mansion. He informed his guests that the Confederacy was taking heart because of the continued existence of slavery in their states. Lincoln reiterated his warning that if the war continued, slavery would be abolished without a penny of compensation to slaveholders. The President then served a notice the significance of which the assembled Congressmen either ignored or missed completely: if the Border States took no steps toward compensated emancipation, he might feel called upon, in behalf of liberty and Union, to strike harder blows than theretofore.

The unconvinced legislators promised a written reply and filed glumly out. Within a few days two communications reached Lincoln's desk. A minority report, signed by seven, promised to lay the matter before their constituents and urge them to consider the President's recommendations "calmly, deliberately and fairly."

The majority report was, in essence, a rejection. The Border State citizens, said these twenty-one spokesmen, had a right to hold their slaves; why should they be asked to make sacrifices beyond those of other Americans? The majority report toyed with some figures: to pay $300 per head for 1,196,112 slaves (the report included the 1860 census figures for Virginia and Tennessee and ignored the thousands of Virginia slaves who had fled within the Union lines), plus $100 apiece for deporting them, would run to more than $478,000,000. If Lincoln raised that sum beforehand, said they, then the voters of their states might consider the proposition although, added the Congressmen, they knew that their constituents would not accept it even then. The attitude of most of the Border State spokesmen toward compensated emancipation was summed up by Kentucky Senator Lazarus Powell Whitehead: "I regard the whole thing, so far as the slave states are concerned, as full of arsenic, sugar-coated."

This sharp setback to compensated emancipation had a bogging-down effect on the second of Lincoln's plans for the Negro — free as well as slave — that of shipping him out of the country. Lincoln believed that deportation would simultaneously achieve two ends: to get rid of slavery and get rid of the Negro. The idea of removing the Negro was by no means original with Lincoln; it was as ancient as the question, "What should be done with the colored man?"

It had been natural for Lincoln to turn to deportation as a solution for the Negro problem. He was an admirer of colonizationalist Henry Clay, a Kentucky senator who had been a conspicuous figure in national politics for a third of a century. Moreover, Lincoln's own early political associations had been with Border State and Southern liberals who favored colonization, since it permitted them to show a coolness toward slavery without showing an enthusiasm for abolitionism. Hence, Lincoln's belief that Negroes should be deported antedated his election to the Presidency. Long before 1860 he had come to the conclusion that color prejudice is implanted in human nature and that the physical differences between whites and blacks would probably forever prevent a harmonious living together. "My first impulse," said Lincoln, in a speech at Peoria on October 16, 1854, "would be to free all the slaves, and send them back to Liberia, to their own native land." Three years later, noting that the progress of the movement had been at a snail's pace over the decades, Lincoln placed the blame on a general luke-warmness: "What colonization needs most is a hearty will."

In his first annual message to Congress, the President proposed colonizing the Negroes who were being freed during the course of the fighting on the battle front, and any free Negroes who were desirous of leaving the country. To the Chief Executive's plea for relieving the country of the colored population, Congress responded with three assists. By the District of Columbia Act of April 16, 1862, Congress set aside $100,000 to aid in colonizing and settling "such free persons of African descent now residing in said District, including those liberated by this act, as may desire to emigrate." Two months later Congress appropriated half a million dollars to colonize slaves whose masters were disloyal to the Union. On the same day (July 16) the House Committee on Emancipation and Colonization recommended an appropriation of twenty millions for settling the confiscated slaves beyond the limits of the United States. The Committee's action was based on its opinion that "the retention of the Negro among us with half privileges is but a bitter mockery to him, and that our duty is to find for him a congenial home and country."

Lincoln was quite pleased with this tangible support from the legislature. However, two formidable hurdles to removing the Negro still remained: getting him to agree to go, and finding some place to send him.

To handle the first of these problems Lincoln hit upon a clever scheme. He would get his recommendations before the colored people of the country by having an "interview" with a group of Negroes. In itself this would be a step calculated to win their approval since it would be the first time a delegation of blacks ever had an audience with a President to discuss a public issue. The details of the interview apparently were left in the hands of the Reverend James Mitchell, whom Lincoln had recently appointed as Commissioner of Emigration. An old-line drumbeater for Negro emigration, Mitchell had been an agent for the Indiana State Board of Colonization.

On August 14 Mitchell shepherded five hand-picked Negroes to the White House. Not one of them was prominent in Negro circles — four of them were contrabands. Lincoln, of course, wanted no firebrands like John Rock or Henry Highland Garnet; he wanted a sounding board, not an anvil chorus. Mitchell presented the five Negroes to the President. The colored delegation sat down in a tentative way, as if they were participants in a game of musical chairs and they might soon have to start moving again. Lincoln launched into the interview which, as the minutes wore on, turned out to be a monologue. Lincoln was a President who generally did more listening than talking, but this was a controlled situation, and he had not thought of having the colored visitors get in even an edgewise word. The Negroes, as one of them put it, "were here by invitation to hear what the President has to say."

Lincoln began by explaining that money had been made available for the colonizing of Negroes and that it had become his duty, as it already was his inclination, to favor such a move. Whites and blacks were different races, continued the President, and Negroes might go where they were treated the best in the United States and even there "the ban is still upon you." Moreover, American Negroes should sacrifice something of their present comfort and go to other countries and work to help those less fortunate than they. Liberia was all right, said Lincoln, but he had in mind a place only one fourth as far away as the African west coast, and unlike Liberia, this place was on a much-traveled highway. Moreover, it gave evidence of having rich coal mines which would give to migrants their daily bread as soon as they got there. A Negro colonization venture could be successful, ran the President's concluding remarks, even with a small nucleus: "If I could find twenty-five able-bodied men, with a mixture of women and children, good things in the family relation, I think I could make a successful commencement."

The chairman of the Negro delegation, Edward M. Thomas, said that the group would talk over the proposal and send an answer. "Take your time," replied Lincoln, "no hurry at all." Lincoln was in no hurry for an answer because his purpose was accomplished. James Mitchell would see to it that full reports of the interview would reach the newspapers.

As Lincoln expected, the interview was given wide circulation, and it at once became the leading topic of conversation among Negroes. "The President's address to the colored people of the District is being discussed in political Anglo-African circles," wrote Jacob C. White in Philadelphia to his cousin, Joseph C. Bustill, "and a diversity of opinion, of course, exists."

It was to be expected that on almost any public issue a diversity of opinion would exist among Negroes. Having no culture peculiar to a black skin, Negroes in the United States reflected an individualism typical of their native land. Negro Americans, like their compatriots, did not think in lock step.

However, a preponderant majority of Negroes opposed colonization, an issue which they had debated, pro and con, for more than half a century. One of their main objections to the deporting of Negroes was that such a policy assumed that there was no cure for color prejudice. For this reason Negro groups had assailed the American Colonization Society, asserting that there was a sympathetic relationship between the doctrines of slavery and the doctrines of colonization. The majority of colored people believed that the Colonization Society wished to expatriate the free Negro in order to make slavery secure. In 1834 William Hamilton, in an "Address to the Fourth Annual Convention of the Free People of Color in the United States," expressed an opinion commonly held among Negroes:

> However pure the motives of some of the members of that society may be, yet the master spirits thereof are evil minded toward us. They have put on the garb of angels of

light. Fold back their covering and you have in full array those of darkness.

Four months before Lincoln's interview with the colored delegation, the Negroes in Boston, at a meeting addressed by William C. Nell, J. Sella Martin, Robert Morris and William Wells Brown, drew up four blunt resolutions:

> Resolved, That when we wish to leave the United States we can find and pay for that territory which shall suit us best.
> Resolved, That when we are ready to leave, we shall be able to pay our own expenses of travel.
> Resolved, That we don't want to go now.
> Resolved, That if anybody else wants us to go, they must compel us.

A few days after their interview with the President the Negro delegates sent a reply. In the present condition of affairs, ran their resolution, they deemed it "inexpedient, inauspicious and impolitic to agitate the subject of the immigration of the colored people of this country anywhere, believing that time, the great arbiter of events and movements, will adjust the matter of so infinitely vital an interest to the colored people of the United States."

Other Negroes who opposed colonization held protest meetings. At a meeting held at Union Bethel church in Washington, the indignation ran so high that the presence of a white reporter was resented. Philadelphia Negroes formulated "An Appeal from the Colored Men of Philadelphia to the President of the United States," which opened on a moral note:

> We can find nothing in the religion of our Lord and Master teaching us that color is the standard by which He judges his creatures, either in this life or in the life to come.

Moreover, continued the "Appeal," many Pennsylvania Negroes owned their own houses and other property. Should they sacrifice this wealth, they asked, forsake their birthplace and journey to a strange land in order to placate traitors now in arms against the Union and their friends?

The Negroes at Newtown, Long Island denied that they were a different race. They then proceeded to make the eagle scream:

> This is our native country; we have as strong an attachment to our native hills, valleys, plains, luxuriant forests, flowing streams, mighty rivers, and lofty mountains, as any other people.

Hence, wrote they, "we conclude that the policy of the President toward the colored people of this country *is a mistaken policy*."

A number of Negroes wrote open letters. George B. Vashon, an Oberlin College graduate who had passed the bar, taught at Central College in McGrawville, New York, and sojourned in Haiti for thirty months, informed Lincoln that Negroes did not stay in American out of a feeling of selfishness and a dread of sacrifice; on the contrary, Negroes had "schooled themselves to labor and to wait." One letter, rare in its tone of sharpness to the Chief Executive, came from A. P. Smith of Saddle River, New Jersey: "Pray tell us is our right to a home in this country less than your own?" Smith would have Lincoln know that Negroes were with Warren at Bunker Hill, with Washington at Morristown and Valley Forge, with Lafayette at Yorktown, and with Perry and Decatur in their cruisings; "and when the history of this present atrocious insurrection is written, the historian will record that whoever was false, the blacks were true."

Correspondent Smith had a few cutting phrases concerning Lincoln's mention of coal mines at the interview with the colored men:

> "Coal land," you say, "is the best thing I know of to begin an enterprise." Astounding discovery! Worthy to be recorded in golden letters like the Lunar Cycle in the Temple

of Minerva. "Coal land," sir! If you please, give McClellan some, give Halleck some, and by all means, save a little strip for yourself. Twenty-five Negroes digging coal land in Central America! Mighty plan! Equal to about twenty-five Negroes splitting rails in Sangamon.

Despite such Negro denunciations of Lincoln's proposals, there was a minority wing which favored leaving the country. During the 'fifties the most prominent of these Negro emigrationists was Martin R. Delany, a dark-skinned Negro whose great abilities were spread over a variety of reform interests. The most race-conscious of Negroes, Delany admired heroes of "Hamitic extraction"; hence his five sons bore the baptismal names of Alexander Dumas, Toussaint L'Ouverture, St. Cyprian, Soulouque and Faustin, and his daughter was christened Ethiopia. In August 1854 Delany was the leading spirit at a National Emigration Convention of Colored People held at Cleveland. The convention proceedings, written by Delany and including an address by him, became the Bible of the Negro colonizationalists; indeed, so persuasively did it state the case for Negro emigration that the House Committee on Emancipation and Colonization, in its official published report, reprinted Delany's lengthy address *in toto*. In the late 'fifties Delany had conducted an exploring safari in the Niger Valley, but the tangible results of the expedition were meager.

Negro colonizationalists could point in 1860 to the successful efforts of the nearly 60,000 colored people in Canada. Fugitives from Southern plantations had flocked to the provinces, aware that in 1826 the Canadian government had notified the United States that it was "utterly impossible for them to agree to a stipulation for the surrender of fugitive slaves." These refugees from America had been made welcome; they were "building and painting houses, working in mills and engaged in every handicraft employment . . . shopkeepers and clerks . . . and busy upon their farms and gardens," as Benjamin Drew described their activities in *A North-Side View of Slavery*, after visiting Upper Canada in 1855.

Lincoln's proposal was favored by Negroes who supported emigration to Haiti. Since 1859 the Haitian government had officially encouraged such a movement, whose guiding spirit was James Redpath, General Agent of Emigration. So great was Redpath's admiration for the island republic that he requested the Haitian government to bestow upon him "the honor of being the first white adopted citizen of the republic." As general agent the zealous Redpath never took a holiday; he set up headquarters in Boston where he displayed certified copies of government guarantee, Haitian journals, books of reference and maps, and specimens of the island ores and staples. Redpath screened the recruiting agents, hiring John Brown, Jr., and Negroes of such prominence as William Wells Brown, William J. Watkins and H. Ford Douglass.

Redpath's appeal was threefold. He urged Negroes to leave a country which discriminated against them and he dwelt on such instances as that of "a distinguished colored lecturer, who refused a seat in a first-class car, payed his passage as freight, and was charged by his weight." Redpath urged Negroes to go to Haiti so that they would supply the competition of free labor to the slave-produced commodities of the South:

> Would you fight Virginia with a weapon that she will fear as much as she dreaded the rifles of John Brown? Grow tobacco in Haiti then, and fight her with it on the Liverpool exchanges. Would you retaliate on the Carolinas? . . . The way is open. Tar and cotton them in England. Hayti could produce enough sugar to drive Louisiana out of every market in the world, could raise cotton enough to corrupt the morals of a hundred generations of American politicians, could raise rice enough to bury Wilmington, Charleston and Savannah out of sight . . .

And finally Redpath urged Negroes to come to Haiti to help demonstrate the capacity of the colored race for self-government. Haiti, ran his prideful words, "invites you, common children of her ancient Motherland, to become a part of her household."

Lincoln's proposal also heartened the exponents of Liberian migration. The legislature of Liberia lent assistance by passing an act during its 1861–1862 session authorizing the appointment of commissioners "to itinerate among and lecture to the people of color of the United States of North-America, to present to them the claims of Liberia, and its superior advantages as a desirable home for persons of African descent." The legislature also set aside a large tract of land for colored emigrants, and the American Colonization Society promised to transport them and contribute to their support for six months for $100 per capita.

In the summer of 1862 Edward Wilmot Blyden, one of the Liberian "Commissioners to the Descendants of Africa in the United States and the West-Indies," arrived in America and spent several weeks. Born at St. Thomas in the Danish West Indies, Blyden as a young man of eighteen had come to the United States in 1850 to pursue his higher education. Unable to gain admission to any college and somewhat embittered by the several letters of rejection, Blyden went to Liberia in 1851. In the following ten years, he had become a Presbyterian minister and a professor of classical languages at Liberia College.

As Liberia's representative, Blyden spoke to Negro groups in New York, Philadelphia, Baltimore and Harrisburg. His appeal was much the same as Redpath's. In his prepared lecture, "Liberia's Offering," he urged American Negroes to leave the land of prejudice and oppression: "The moment a colored man from America lands in Liberia, he finds the galling chains of caste falling from his soul, and he can stand erect, and feel and realize that he is indeed a man." With outstretched arms, said Blyden, Liberia earnestly invited every black American to throw his lot with hers. "Come help us," pleaded he, "build up a Nationality in Africa."

Lincoln knew of the efforts of the Haitian and Liberian governments to secure immigrants — President Joseph Jenkins Roberts of the African republic had paid his respects at the White House early in August 1862 — but Lincoln was thinking of a different site. He had become enamored of the Chiriqui province located in present-day Panama. Four years earlier a Chiriqui Improvement Company, under Ambrose W. Thompson, had secured control of a substantial land grant of 2,000,000 acres. In August 1861 Thompson made a proposal to deliver coal to the navy for half the price then paid. Lincoln immediately grasped the possibilities: send the Negroes to Chiriqui and put them to work mining coal for the navy. Four months after Thompson's proposal, Lincoln ordered Henry T. Blow, United States minister to Brazil, to go on a secret mission and make a report concerning the lands and harbors of Chiriqui and its fitness as a place for colonizing the Negro.

During the spring and summer of 1862, Lincoln's interest in Chiriqui continued at fever-pitch. When he spoke to the colored delegation about having Negroes go to a spot in Central America, he was thinking of Chiriqui. On the day following the interview, Commissioner of Emigration James Mitchell began to compile a list of colored men who wished to settle abroad. Negroes who were interested were requested to send him their names and addresses and the numbers and ages of their families. Negroes read in the papers that an expedition, to be provisioned by the government, was scheduled to sail on October 1.

However, before the Chiriqui project could gain momentum, three discouraging factors became evident. There was the question of the legality of Thompson's title — his holdings had been secured from a number of private individuals, many of whose claims had undoubtedly lapsed. Thompson's business methods did not inspire confidence, and some of Lincoln's advisors, such as Secretary Welles, regarded the Chiriqui Improvement Company as "a swindling speculation." As if this were not enough, the scientist Joseph Henry of the Smithsonian Institute delivered a hard blow; early in September he reported that Chiriqui coal was "as nearly worthless as any fuel can be." There was still another disillusionment. Secretary of State Seward informed the President that a conflict existed between Costa Rica and New Granada over the title and jurisdiction of Chiriqui. It would be advisable, warned Seward, to call a halt lest the United States incur the ill-will of the Latin Americas.

This setback did not deter Lincoln. Sobered, however, by experience, he submitted to his cabinet the question of "the propriety of seeking to make treaties with Latin America or European countries or tropics" for the purpose of providing "a refuge for the colored people." On the last day of September, Seward addressed a circular letter to the governments of England, France, Holland and Denmark, informing them of Lincoln's colonization plans and asking their co-operation. Seward clearly stated the policy of the United States: every American Negro who went would go of his own free will; the vessels transporting emigrants must be seaworthy; there must be comfortable dwellings awaiting them when they debarked, and they were to remain forever free, enjoying liberty of conscience, property rights, and all the privileges commonly held by the country's inhabitants.

Seward received a few favorable replies to this appeal to the nations. The government secretary of British Guiana came to the United States expressly to lay plans for promoting Negro emigration to the colony. Before returning he appointed an agent of emigration with offices in New York. The Danish minister offered free transportation to St. Croix for all those who would contract to labor on the sugar plantations, with pay, for at least three years. The Dutch minister, Roest van Lamburg, reported that American Negroes would be cordially received in Surinam and that "the government of the King would desire them to engage for a certain number of years (five, for example) their labor to a planter, under the protection of the Netherlands laws."

On the whole, however, the response to Seward's letter would have discouraged a less sanguine temperament than Lincoln's. The proud and sensitive Hispanic nations were solidly arrayed against the plan. As Lincoln informed Congress in his annual message on December 1, 1862, "Several of the Spanish-American republics have protested against the sending of such colonists to their respective territories." Guatemala, Salvador, Costa Rica and Nicaragua sent word of their objection to Negro emigration. With a blindness rare in him, Lincoln did not perceive that the countries below the Rio Grande could scarcely be expected to welcome a class of people of whom the United States was attempting to rid itself. The Latin American countries, proud of their heritage, did not care to be considered a dumping ground for some other country's undesirables.

Within Lincoln's own borders there was far less enthusiasm for colonization than he cared to recognize. During the entire year of 1862 not more than a few hundred Negroes left the country. Despite James Redpath's heroic efforts, the Haitian Bureau of Emigration could report in May 1862 only 1573 recruits during the preceding eighteen months. The numbers fell off sharply during the summer and fall, as dozens of disillusioned former emigrants returned from Haiti and brought back word of poor living conditions and delays in distributing the promised lands. As for Liberia — far fewer went there than to Haiti. The distance from the United States to the west coast of Africa and the popular beliefs concerning Liberia's extreme heat continued to be deterring factors.

Lincoln in his annual report on December 1, 1862, asserted that colored Americans did not seem as willing to migrate to Liberia and Haiti as to some other countries. But the President was something less than candid. He specified no other countries for which United States Negroes expressed a preference, and he completely ignored the flood of public expressions such as the open letter which Robert Purvis sent to the government emigration agent on August 28, 1862:

> The children of the black man have enriched the soil by their tears, and sweat, and blood. Sir we were born here, and here we choose to remain.

❖

During the summer of 1862 one of Lincoln's chief reasons for pushing Negro migration was his momentous decision to issue a proclamation freeing the slaves. It would, reasoned Lincoln, be easier to defend such a step if there were a place to ship the freed slaves. But Lincoln was prepared to go through with the issuing of a proclamation, emigration or not. He made up his mind almost immediately after the Border States turned down his proposal for compensated emancipation. Lincoln realized the futility of any further attempt to free the slaves by paying their masters — it was then that he reached his conclusion about "laying a strong hand on the colored element," to use his expression.

Lincoln meant that he was thinking of using the Negro as a soldier. The need had become apparent. The war was going slowly; ill fortune and uninspired military tactics dogged the Virginia campaigns, and the general public was impatiently awaiting the day "when Johnny comes marching home." Northern governors were having trouble raising their quotas of troops and hoped to enlist Negroes in place of their white constituents. On the war front the soldiers were about-facing on the use of the Negro. "Everybody here is coming over to the notion of enlisting the darkeys," wrote John W. DeForest from Camp Parapet, Louisiana, on August 27. "Even old Democrats, even the Hibernian rank and file of the North Connecticut are in favor of it." At Washington a similar metamorphosis was taking place.

Wrote Senator John Sherman to his older brother, William Tecumseh, on August 24:

> You can form no conception at the change of opinion here on the Negro question. Men of all parties who now appreciate the magnitude of the contest and who are determined to preserve the unity of the government at all hazards, agree that we must seek and make it the interests of the Negroes to help us.

With such considerations in mind, Lincoln came to the conclusion that freeing the slaves of disloyal masters was an expedient step. Early in July he began to compose the first draft of this historic proclamation. He did the job at the office of his friend, Thomas T. Eckert, Superintendent of Military Telegraph of the Department of the Potomac. At the telegraph office Lincoln could concentrate in an atmosphere of quiet; at the White House he would be constantly interrupted. "Nearly every day for several weeks," wrote Eckert, Lincoln's routine never varied. He would arrive at Eckert's office and ask him for the carefully locked-up papers. Then he would read over the lines he had previously written and revise them, "studying carefully each sentence." This done, he would add a few lines. It was only after Lincoln had completed the document that Eckert, who had become understandably curious, learned that the President had been drafting the preliminary emancipation proclamation.

On July 13 Lincoln divulged his intentions to two of his cabinet members, Seward and Welles, as they rode in a carriage at the funeral of a baby of Stanton's. Lincoln informed them that he had given the matter much thought, wrote Welles in his diary, and dwelt "earnestly on the gravity, importance and delicacy of the movement." Lincoln asked their frank opinions. Seward, who was not a Secretary of State for nothing, replied that "the subject involved consequences so vast and momentous that he should wish to bestow on it mature reflection before giving a decisive answer." Welles murmured his concurrence.

Eight days later Lincoln took the next step. He summoned the cabinet and informed them of his intention to proclaim the emancipation of the slaves in those states which remained in rebellion on January 1, 1863. Lincoln made it clear to the secretaries that his mind was made up, but invited them to make comments.

The secretaries made various suggestions, most of which Lincoln had anticipated. However, Seward raised a question which gave pause to the President — a question of timing. In view of the recent military reverses, the public might view a proclamation issued at that time as an act of desperation — "a cry for help; the government stretching forth its hands to Ethiopia instead of Ethiopia stretching forth her hands to the government." It would be better, advised Seward, to wait for a military success before issuing the document. Lincoln was impressed by this line of reasoning; reluctantly he put the draft proclamation back in his desk and waited for his generals to produce a victory in the field.

Until September 22 when the proclamation was issued, Lincoln had sixty-two days to mark time — days in which he was criticized and taunted by the abolitionists, who little suspected that the tortoise President had finally got a move on. One of these critics was the explosive Horace Greeley, whose New York *Tribune* reached a readership in excess of a million. On August 19 Greeley wrote an editorial which he titled a "Prayer of Twenty Millions." Addressed to Lincoln, the editorial commented on the "seeming subserviency of your policy to the slave-holding, slavery-upholding interest." A great majority of the loyal population, said Greeley, wanted the President to enforce the confiscation acts, abolish slavery and use Negro troops.

The "Prayer" was a forceful challenge and it was widely circulated throughout the Union and in western Europe. Lincoln read it thoughtfully. Lying in his desk was the proclamation that would effectively answer the bumptious editor, but the military victory still lagged. In the meantime, the "Prayer" could not be

ignored, and Lincoln did not propose to ignore it. Indeed, he perhaps welcomed the opportunity of making his views explicit. He
wrote out a reply, held it up for two days, then released it to the
press.

A document of four paragraphs, it was one of Lincoln's most
memorable efforts. Shrewdly conceived and superbly executed;
it did not address itself directly to Greeley's question. The
"Prayer" had asked for enforcement of an existing law; Lincoln's answer addressed itself only to the question of the abolition of slavery. Its opening sentences were calm and measured;
if, wrote the President, Greeley's letter revealed an impatient
and dictatorial tone, he waived it in deference to an old friend.
Lincoln then proceeded to explain that to him the abolition of
slavery might become an incident of the war, but was not its
object:

> My paramount object in this struggle is to save the
> Union, and is not either to save or to destroy slavery. . . .
> What I do about slavery and the colored race, I do because
> I believe it helps to save the Union; and what I forbear, I
> forbear because I do not believe it would help to save the
> Union. . . .
> I have here stated my purpose according to my view
> of official duty; and I intend no modification of my oft-
> expressed personal wish that all men everywhere could be
> free.

This answer, clear as it was, did not quiet the clamor for a
Presidential proclamation. On September 13, a delegation representing the religious denominations of Chicago called upon Lincoln and asked him to proclaim emancipation. Although his decision had already been made, the President argued the subject
aloud, pro and con, for the benefit of the Christian leaders. He
asked them what good would such a proclamation do: would
it not seem ridiculous, "like the Pope's bull against the comet?"
He conceded that slavery was the cause of the rebellion and that

emancipation would help the Union cause in England. But he raised questions about arming the slaves, and he pointed out that in the Union armies there were 50,000 bayonets from the Border States whose bearers might object to a proclamation freeing slaves.

A week after the visit of the Chicago delegation, Lincoln summoned his cabinet to a special meeting. The battle of Antietam on September 17, although not a clear-cut Northern victory, gave him the military excuse for which he had been waiting. At noon on Monday, September 22, the cabinet assembled at the White House. There were no absences. The secretaries sensed that the occasion was important, although the meeting opened with "some general talk," after which Lincoln read a short passage from the humorist, Artemus Ward. Then assuming a graver tone, the President informed his attentive listeners that he had made a promise to himself and His Maker to issue a "Proclamation of Emancipation" as soon as the Rebel army was driven out of Maryland. Now the hour had come to fulfill that promise.

Just before going over the document, Lincoln invited comments on any of the expressions he used, "or in any other minor matter." He then proceeded to read the proclamation, "making remarks," wrote Secretary Chase in his diary, "on several points as he went on." He finished reading and paused. Seward suggested two slight modifications, both of which Lincoln accepted, and a few minutes later the secretaries were dismissed.

The heart of this preliminary emancipation proclamation was the passage declaring forever free the slaves in those states, or parts of states, which had not laid down their arms by January 1, 1863 — exactly a hundred days away. The Confederate states were thus given some fourteen weeks of grace; if by the end of that period they were still in rebellion, Lincoln would issue a definitive proclamation freeing their slaves.

To the Negroes and to the abolitionists this edict was a mighty step forward in making the war a crusade for freedom. Of course, the proclamation was by no means everything they could have wished. It actually did not go much further than declaring that the President would thenceforth carry out the antislavery measures of Congress, particularly the Confiscation Act of July 17, 1862, which declared free the slaves who escaped from masters who were Rebels. Moreover, the proclamation again stated Lincoln's primary concern for the restoration of the Union. It was evident, too, that to Lincoln the proclamation was primarily a military measure (in it he referred three times to his authority as commander in chief) to weaken the enemy. And in the proclamation he had again referred to the deportation of the Negro — his favorite blueprint for blacks.

Despite these limitations in the edict, the abolitionists acclaimed it joyfully. They would of course have to wait until January 1 before it would be proclaimed, but no abolitionist (or anyone else) expected the Southern states to lay down their arms by then. Hence, it was simply a matter of clocks ticking and days passing. Ralph Waldo Emerson regarded this one-hundred-day period of advent as of such historical significance as to justify nature suspending its laws. He asked that until January 1, 1863, death give up its legacies, that no chariot swing low:

> Do not let the dying die; hold them back to this world until you have charged their ear and heart with this message to other spiritual societies, announcing the melioration of our planet.

CHAPTER VIII

Sixty-three Is the Jubilee

WHEN YOU FEELS de Sperrit," said old Sister Bemaugh, "you mustn't squench him." Sister Bemaugh's thoughts were much like those of Henry Highland Garnet, who, however, would have used more elegant language. The Reverend Mr. Garnet, as soon as he read the preliminary proclamation, was moved by the spirit to call a mass meeting in celebration. Many of his friends advised against such a step. There was a danger, ran their words of warning, that hoodlums and other mischief-makers would disrupt the proceedings. Moreover, cautioned they, such a meeting might be inopportune since Lincoln's preliminary proclamation was nothing more than a declaration of an intention which might or might not be kept.

But Garnet went ahead. On September 29, a week after Lincoln's announcement, Garnet presided over a meeting at Shiloh church, at the corner of Hammond and Prince streets, in New York. Garnet held his audience as he told them of his early boyhood days on a Maryland plantation. Here, as he related it, he had often heard his father and his grandfather "sing a ditty that had in view the present period, although they were a little in advance of the times." The ditty "was somewhat to this effect":

— in 1833
They say the people shall be free,
There's a better day a-coming
Oh, sound the jubilee.

Garnet was followed on the platform by a galaxy of some-what lesser lights. George Levere, pastor of a Brooklyn flock, proclaimed that it was high time for colored men "to stand up against the outrages heaped upon them by the brutal portion of society." Another clergyman, R. H. Cane of Bethel church, de-scribed the war "as the ultimation of the contending principles planted on this continent at Plymouth Rock and the James River." Robert Hamilton, editor of the *Anglo-African*, then sang a song whose verses he had composed just for that occa-sion. The tune was taken from "Wait for the Wagon," and the audience joined in the singing after Hamilton read out the words. The last speaker, Jeremiah Powers, confessed that he was puz-zled as to whether to pray for the submission of the Rebels before January 1, emancipation being dependent upon their not laying down their arms. He had compromised, said Powers, "by hoping that General McClellan might find new swamps to dig until that time." When the laughter and applause had subsided, Garnet arose to pronounce the benediction and to bring the meeting to its close.

The meeting at Shiloh church was one of the few celebrations following the preliminary emancipation proclamation. Most Ne-groes did not care to risk jumping the gun; they preferred to wait until January 1, when the definitive edict was promised.

In the meantime the colored people noted with great satis-faction some of the results of the preliminary proclamation. "It has thrown a moral bombshell in the Confederacy," exulted Frederick Douglass. Negroes had heard of it and were "flock-ing in thousands to the lines of our army." Although it was com-monly asserted that the proclamation wouldn't reach the slaves, it soon became evident, as pointed out in the New York *Times*, September 29, 1862, "that there is a far more rapid and secret diffusing of intelligence and news throughout the plantations than was ever dreamed of in the North."

Unquestionably thousands of slaves got wind of Lincoln's edict.

The news of the preliminary proclamation seeped so widely among Kentucky slaves held to service that one of the state's leading dailies sought to counter the general impression among them that they would be free. The Louisville *Journal* urged colored clergymen in the state "to set themselves earnestly, zealously, and energetically to explain" to the slaves of Kentucky that the proclamation had no application to them since Kentucky was not one of the states in rebellion. Similarly in Louisiana, the uneasiness over the proclamation among the planters in the Union-held sections of the state, prompted the commander of the Department of the Gulf, N. P. Banks, to issue an order advising slaves in loyal portions of the state to remain on the plantations.

Negroes and abolitionists were pleased upon reading reports that the preliminary proclamation had so disturbed many slave-holders as to cause them to abandon their landholdings, gather up their able-bodied chattels, and hurry southward. In middle Tennessee, according to a contemporary account, as a result of the preliminary edict, "whole plantations which once counted their scores of bondsmen — coal black, chestnut-brown, saddle-colored, olive-tinted and Saxon-hued — are now depopulated. Their former inhabitants have

> Laid down the shovel and the hoe,
> And hung up the fiddle and the bow . . ."

To the satisfaction of the Northern Negroes and their abolitionist allies, the preliminary emancipation proclamation caused considerable alarm in the Confederacy. Many white Southerners interpreted the measure as an invitation to the Negroes to murder their masters. The ever-present fear of slave insurrections again became a sectional obsession as rumors of servile uprisings became common. There were demands for a more rigid enforcement of the patrol regulations, and the state governors of South Carolina and Georgia urged their constituents not to delay in taking precautionary steps. Within a week after it had been issued, the preliminary proclamation was brought up for discussion in the Confederate upper house. "Some of the gravest of our senators favor the raising of the black flag," wrote war clerk J. B. Jones on September 30, "asking and giving no quarter thereafter."

Although the preliminary proclamation accomplished much that was pleasing to the abolitionists, the measure was bitterly assailed in the Border States and in the big-city strongholds of the Democratic party. The most common of the objections was that it was impotent and would be laughed to scorn in the South. "You must first catch your hare," warned these critics. Another charge centered around the alleged abuse of Presidential authority. Lincoln was usurping his powers, so ran the accusation, for legally he had no right to issue a proclamation that was more sweeping in its pretensions than a ukase decreed by the Czar of All the Russias or an imperial edict issued by the Roman Caesars.

A contention that carried great weight in urban centers was that the proclamation would flood the North with blacks fresh from the cotton fields and rice swamps. Politicians and newspaper editors played upon the natural resentments which the Northern workingmen felt toward any great influx of labor competitors. Loudest in voicing this not wholly phantom fear of a Negro influx was James Gordon Bennett's New York *Herald*, which had no peer in stirring up Negro-white antagonism. "The Irish and German immigrants, to say nothing of native laborers of the white race," wrote Bennett on October 20, 1862, "must feel enraptured at the prospect of hordes of darkeys overrunning the Northern States and working for half wages, and thus ousting them from employment."

Negroes and their friends were quite aware of the strong hostility aroused by the preliminary edict, and they hoped Lincoln would not weaken in his promise to issue the definitive decree. However, there could be no confident answer to the question, "Will he go through with it?" Indeed, there were some disquieting straws in the wind. The Congressional elections of November 1862 went heavily against the administration. This could not be ascribed to any single cause, but foes of the proclamation trumpeted that the verdict of the public was a resounding "No."

In his second annual message to Congress, delivered on December 1, 1862, the President did not mention the proclamation. Lincoln pitched his concluding passage on a high moral level:

> Fellow-citizens, we cannot escape history. . . . The fiery trial through which we pass will light us down, in honor or dishonor, to the latest generation. . . . In giving freedom to the slave we assure freedom to the free, honorable alike in what we give and what we preserve. We shall nobly save, or meanly lose, the last, best hope of earth.

This was memorable prose, and it did not ignore the slave. Nevertheless, it was ominously silent on the proclamation.

Lincoln was bombarded by antiproclamation appeals from the Border States. As the capital city correspondent of the Cincinnati *Gazette* wired from Washington on December 22, 1862, "The border state pressure on the President to withdraw the emancipation proclamation grows intense as the day for its taking effect approaches." There was a feeling in Washington, continued the reporter, that Lincoln might "undertake by some sort of plastering generality to keep on both sides, as usual."

Noting these signs, the abolitionists were uneasy. Among the reformers impatiently perched on anxious seats was Mrs. Harriet Beecher Stowe. Finding the position intolerable, Mrs. Stowe decided to go to Washington and have a tête-à-tête with Lincoln. Late in November, Mrs. Stowe was escorted into the presence of the Chief Executive by Henry Wilson. The Senator introduced his world-renowed constituent, and Lincoln seized her hand, saying, "So this is the little lady who made this big war." During the unrecorded conversation, Mrs. Stowe asked Lincoln whether he intended to issue the edict of freedom. It is unlikely that the cagey Mr. Lincoln said either "Yes," or "No." Mrs. Stowe came away from the White House with a slight twinge of misgiving, although she was convinced, she let it be known, of the President's good faith.

Negroes took some encouragement from Mrs. Stowe's hopefulness. Another omen which they interpreted as favorable was an opinion handed down by Attorney General Edward W. Bates to the effect that the Negro was a citizen of the United States. Bates rendered this opinion as a result of a request from Secretary of the Treasury Chase. The latter had written to Bates informing him that a schooner, the *Elizabeth and Margaret* of New Brunswick, was being detained by a revenue cutter at Perth Amboy because the vessel was commanded by a Negro, and therefore by a person not technically meeting the requirement of United States citizenship. "As colored masters are numerous in our coasting trade," continued Chase, "I submit, for your opinion the question: 'Are colored men citizens of the United States, and therefore competent to command American vessels?'"

Bates got busy with his books. Since the Constitution did not define the word "citizen," Bates examined history and the civil law from the days of the great Roman jurists. After a lengthy written analysis, the attorney general tersely summarized his researches:

> And now, upon the whole matter, I give it my opinion that the free man of color mentioned in your letter, if born in the United States, is a citizen of the United States.

The knowledge that the attorney general's office had declared that the boon of citizenship was theirs was inspiring to Negroes, and seemed to them to foretell the doom of slavery.

Perhaps Lincoln too foresaw the end of the South's "peculiar institution." He had admonished in his message to Congress on December 1, 1862: "The dogmas of the quiet past are inadequate to the stormy present." At any rate, he had made up his mind on the proclamation. The Radicals in Congress — those explosive advocates of drastic measures against the South — had threatened to hold up all army appropriations if the President reneged on the edict and Congressman James M. Ashley, of Ohio, warned Lincoln that if he receded one step from his antislavery position, there would be a counterrevolution in the North. But these threats were unnecessary: this decision was Lincoln's own.

Not that advice was lacking — recommendations were thrust upon the President until the very last hour. On the evening of December 31, three abolitionists, George B. Cheever, William Goodell and Nathan Brown, were admitted to the Executive Mansion. They instructed the patient Mr. Lincoln that he had missed the heart of the slavery question, and that since human bondage was an intolerable wrong, it should be abolished as a matter of simple justice rather than on the grounds of political expediency.

Mr. Lincoln slept on such last-minute advice. The next day — the fateful first of January — dawned chilly and depressing. A driving snow and rain had racked the Atlantic coast during the night, and the morning sun struggled to pierce the veil of murky vapors. Despite the overcast morning, Negroes and their friends hopefully went forward with their meetings, which had been arranged, as announced by the sponsors of a Brooklyn meeting scheduled at the Bridge Street African Methodist church, "in anticipation that the President of the United States will be faithful to his Proclamation, whereby millions may be redeemed from the yoke of Human Bondage, and our beloved country, we trust, saved from being much longer under the misrule of Rebel Power."

Lincoln had a busy day. In the morning he had rewritten the proclamation, slowly and with good penmanship, and sent it to the State Department to be engrossed. He spent the afternoon hours shaking hands with the inevitable procession of New Year's well-wishers who came to pay their respects at this annual Presidential reception. Late in the afternoon, the last caller having pumped the Presidential hand and been borne off by carriage, Secretary of State Seward brought to the President's office the broad sheet on which the proclamation was written. Lincoln affixed his signature to the historic document. His *Abraham Lincoln* — this time he did not abbreviate his first name — appeared somewhat uneven and shaky: "Not because of any uncertainty or hesitation on my part," remarked he to Schuyler Colfax that evening, "but it was just after the public reception, and three hours of hand shaking is not calculated to improve a man's chirography."

The proclamation was phrased in a dry, matter-of-fact style, as befitted "a necessary war measure for suppressing said rebellion." In it Lincoln called attention to his earlier edict of September 22. Then he specifically named those states and parts of states whose inhabitants had not laid down their arms. In those places, and this was the heart of the proclamation, all persons held as slaves "are and henceforward shall be free," and their freedom would be maintained by the full powers of "the Executive government of the United States."

At the numerous celebration meetings held that evening, audiences did not wait to learn the specific content of the proclamation. Indeed in many instances, the celebrations had begun many hours before Lincoln dipped his pen into the inkstand. In Boston, where the preparations were especially noteworthy, "proclamation meetings" had begun on New Year's eve when at the colored churches, prayer meetings were held by "ye watchers and ye holy ones."

On the afternoon of January 1, a grand jubilee concert was held at the Music Hall in Boston. The roster of those present read like a *Who's Who* of literary New England — Henry Wadsworth Longfellow, Oliver Wendell Holmes, Charles Eliot Norton, John Greenleaf Whittier, Edward Everett Hale, Francis Parkman and Ralph Waldo Emerson. The meeting opened with the reading of "a string of verses, a sort of Boston Hymn," according to the description by composer Emerson. The stanzas had been completed that very day, and the responsive audience quickly caught the poem's mood of elation:

> Up! and the dusky race
> That sat in darkness long.
> Be swift their feet as antelopes,
> And as behemoth strong.

As Emerson sat down, Carl Zerrahn's Philharmonic Orchestra, "greatly augmented," tuned up for Beethoven's impressive *Fifth Symphony*. The orchestra was followed by a chorus which sang Mendelssohn's "Hymn of Praise," and then "Mr. Dresel performed at the Chickering grand." The large gathering was uplifted by the poetry and the music, but the uncertainty as to whether Lincoln would issue the edict had somewhat restrained the enthusiasm. Toward the close of the lengthy program, a man in formal attire came out of the wings and announced that the message was coming over the wires. Above the terrific din that followed, there was heard a rhythmic call for Harriet Beecher Stowe, sitting in the balcony. The "crusader in crinoline," deeply affected, moved down to the rail and looked into the hundreds of upturned faces: "She could only bow and dab her eyes with her handkerchief."

Music Hall was not the only scene of celebration in the Hub. At Tremont Temple the Union Progressive Association, under Negro leadership, had arranged a series of three monster meetings — morning, afternoon and evening. At the morning session the preliminary proclamation was read, whereupon William C. Nell, the presiding officer, contrasted New Year's Day, then and now. Cried he:

> New Year's day — proverbially known throughout the South as "Heart-Break Day," from the trials and horrors peculiar to sales and separations of parents and children, wives and husbands — by this proclamation is henceforth invested with new significance and imperishable glory in the calendar of time.

Nell was followed by William Wells Brown, and the remarks of both were duly recorded by secretary Edwin M. Bannister, a thirty-two-year-old painter already known for his landscapes and portraits and destined for a wider fame.

At the afternoon session, following speeches by Dr. J. B. Smith and the Reverend James Freeman Clarke, a collection was lifted for the benefit of the freedmen. The closing speaker was Frederick Douglass, who declared that he was thankful to be living at that hour. The dark yesterdays were now to be followed by days made luminous "by the rosy dawning of the new truth of freedom." He praised his Maker that "we are here to rejoice in it." Douglass's closing sentences were punctuated by cries of "Amen," and "Bless the Lord."

The morning and afternoon gatherings had been enthusiastic, but everyone looked forward to the evening session, for by then Lincoln was expected to have signed the proclamation. A meeting-goer nearing Tremont Temple at seven o'clock might have been struck by the singular beauty of the evening as contrasted with the storminess of the early morning. The fresh snow glistened as the night took on an unusual brightness from the lanterns and giant candles. Entering the Temple, one laid down his ten cents to help defray expenses and picked up his ticket of admission. The charge was modest in view of the number of speakers engaged by the "Committee of Arrangements."

During the ninety minutes of waiting for the President's edict of freedom, the audience listened to a variety of personages: Attorney John S. Rock, Clergyman J. Sella Martin, Charles E. Slack, who in the Massachusetts legislature had led the movement against separate schools for Negroes, and the young and good-looking woman's righter, Anna E. Dickinson, who in 1861 had been discharged from the United States mint as a consequence of her ultraabolitionist sentiments. Edward Atkinson held up a sample of Sea Island cotton cultivated by free black labor, and

Army Chaplain C. W. Dennison spoke in high praise of the former slave's willingness and capacity to work.

These presentations took well over an hour, and still no news from Washington. A general restlessness pervaded the hall. William Wells Brown and then Frederick Douglass spoke in hopeful terms. But the customary talisman of their words seemed powerless to stay the rising mood of doubt. Just as Douglass himself was about to succumb to a morose state, a messenger, bursting with the good news, hastened into the hall, exclaiming, "It is coming! It is on the wires." A tumultuous chorus sounded to the Boston Common.

The excited audience could not restrain itself during the reading of the proclamation. Overcharged emotions demanded release. Cheers and shouts finally gave way to more formal group expression. All voices joined in as Douglass's rich baritone swelled the song, "Blow ye the trumpet, blow." A Negro minister led in another stirring anthem:

> Sound the loud timbrel o'er Egypt's dark sea,
> Jehovah hath triumphed, his people are free.

For two hours the celebration continued. The Tremont Temple had been hired until twelve o'clock, but enthusiasm was still at a high pitch when the hour of midnight struck. Few of the celebrators were in a mood to go to bed. A proposal that the meeting continue elsewhere was adopted by acclamation.

In less than an hour the transplanted audience was crammed into the Twelfth Baptist Church on Phillips Street, known to the abolitionist faithful as "the Fugitive Slave's Church." Its pastor, Leonard A. Grimes, a truly Christian man, stood in the vestibule in his neat suit of rusty black and beamed a welcome. Perhaps as he greeted the throng of merrymakers, thoughts may have run through his mind of three turbulent episodes of the 'fifties — of the day when twenty colored men from "Nigger Hill" had stormed the Boston courthouse and seized runaway slave Shadrach, spiriting him off to Canada; of the morning of April 23, 1852, when he (Grimes) stood sorrowfully with the Death Watch at a 4 A.M. vigil, as the marshal's guard led fugitive Thomas Sims to the Long Wharf, where the Savannah-bound *Acorn* was steamed up for sailing; and of that tense June morning of 1854 when he and Richard Henry Dana accompanied heavily guarded Anthony Burns, the last fugitive to be returned from Boston, through the surging streets to the dock, the air heavy with dirges from the tolling church bells.

When the two-storied church was packed, Grimes wormed his way to the pulpit, and led in public prayer. Spontaneous singing followed, echoing from the rafters. Everyone wished to raise an exultant voice. "At Grimes' church," said Douglass, "we got into such a state of enthusiasm that almost everything seemed to be witty and appropriate to the occasion." Speaking and singing were interrupted only for the enjoyment of refreshments, as the rejoicing continued into the small hours.

Throughout the North — New Bedford, Orange, Ypsilanti, to name a representative sampling — the Negro proclamation meetings were scenes of joy. "Well, did you ever expect to see this day?" queried Frances Ellen Watkins Harper, in rising tones of incredulity, to a Columbus, Ohio, audience. The most popular of war songs among Negroes, "Sixty-three is the Jubilee," seemed prophetic. Now the American Negro would have a day of his own to celebrate — he would no longer have to borrow August 1 — the anniversary of emancipation in the British West Indies — he had a more glorious date.

At Washington, as in many other places, watch meetings preceded the proclamation celebrations. As midnight approached at the Union Bethel church, the pastor told the congregation that "he wanted no one to pray standing up with bowed head; nobody sitting down, with bended neck praying; and no brother kneeling on one knee, because his pants were too tight for him, but to get down on *both knees* to thank Almighty God for his freedom and President Lincoln too."

On the last night of the old year, nearly six hundred Negroes — men, women and children — from the two long rows of temporary barracks in Washington, known as the "Contraband Camp." assembled at the headquarters of Superintendent D. B. Nichols. They spent the "forepart of the night" in praying and singing. Periodically the singers came back to the chantlike, "Go Down, Moses," obviously identifying themselves with the Israelites. One sister supplied her own version:

> Go down, Abraham, away down in Dixie's land,
> Tell Jeff Davis to let my people go.

Between vocal numbers, those who wished to speak waited for no formal introduction. One of those who held forth was a patriarch known as "John de Baptis' " because he invariably took his text from the "regulations ob de 3d chapter of Matthew, 'And in those days came John de Baptis'." One woman shouted in a high-pitched voice:

> If de Debble do not ketch
> Jeff Davis, dat infernal wretch,
> An' roast and frigazee dat rebble,
> What is de use of any Debble?

Superintendent Nichols called for volunteers to give their experiences in slavery. An old man, Thornton by name, got up and testified, "I cried all night. What de matter, Thornton? Tomorrow my child is to be sold, neber more see it till judgment — no more dat; no more dat! no more dat! With my hands on my breast, going to work, I feel bad, overseer behind me. No more dat! No more dat! No more dat!"

Two minutes before midnight the whole group dropped to its knees in silent prayer. After the hour of twelve had struck, the singing and shouting commenced anew, to which dancing was soon added. About one o'clock a procession formed and its participants paraded around the campgrounds. They serenaded the superintendent, "in whose honor a sable improvisatore carolled forth an original ode." This spontaneous song, "I's a free man," had an arresting chorus: "Forever free! Forever free!" Then the contrabands sang the "Negro Boatman's Song," with a volume "heard miles off." Never was Whittier's stirring composition so rapturously voiced. They sang until dawn.

Further to the South a similarly fervent celebration was observed in the Port Royal region. The Sea Islanders, however, had a preliminary demonstration, due largely to the efforts of Charlotte S. Forten, an attractive young woman with soft, dark eyes and raven-colored hair. Miss Forten had come to the islands as a teacher. The granddaughter of James Forten, she had been sent to Salem, Massachusetts for her education, since her father, Robert Bridges Forten, refused to enroll her in the segregated Philadelphia colored schools. A serious young woman who lived, as she confided to her diary, "for the good I can do my oppressed and suffering fellow creatures," Charlotte had applied herself diligently to her studies at the State Normal School. She was, as a local newspaper phrased it, "graduated with decided éclat." An ardent abolitionist, she soon came to know Garrison, Phillips and Whittier personally, and before she was twenty-one she was corresponding with Charles Sumner and Harriet Martineau. In late October 1862 Miss Forten sailed from New York, bound for the Sea Islands to assist with the freedmen. She was sent to St. Helena's where she was assigned to teach under the efficient guidance of Laura M. Towne.

As Christmas approached, Miss Forten laid plans for a celebration. Toward the close of November she sent word of her plans to Whittier: "I wish someone would write a little Christmas hymn for our children to sing," she added; "the little creatures love to sing."

Four days before Christmas, a package came from the poet.

Whittier enclosed "a little song for your Christmas festival," explaining that although he was ill, he could not resist the temptation "to comply with thy request." The package also contained a volume of Alexander Crummell's, *The Greatness of Christ, and Other Sermons*. "Its author," wrote Whittier, "is a churchman and a conservative, but his writings are a noble refutation of the charge of the black man's inferiority. They are model discourses, clear, classic and chaste."

Miss Forten did not open *The Greatness of Christ* until some four weeks later, but she got busy on the hymn at once. The children learned it without effort and enjoyed rehearsing it. That it had been written for them made them take to it all the more.

Christmas was a full day for Charlotte Forten. In the morning she went out among the islanders and distributed presents — for each baby a bright red dress, and for each of the other children an apron and an orange. Then she went to the church and decorated the interior with hanging moss, holly, pine and mistletoe, taking note how prettily the evergreen glistened in the bright morning light. When the 150 expectant children arrived she gave them presents sent down by the Philadelphia ladies — dresses for the girls, shirt and trousers materials for the boys, and picture books for all. It was the most wonderful Christmas the young colored children had ever known. After examining their gifts, they delivered their repertoire of songs, including the John Brown number, "Sing, Oh Graveyard," and "Roll, Jordan, Roll." They poured their voices into Whittier's seven-stanza'd, "Christmas Hymn":

> O, none in all the world before
> Were ever so glad as we!
> We're free on Carolina's shore
> We're all at home and free.

When night fell the children were too excited to keep quiet. "O Miss," exclaimed Armaretta, "all I want to do is to sing and shout." Armaretta was not alone in her wish. All the children, as Miss Forten observed, "had the shouting spirit tonight." The young teacher from Salem was particularly moved by their rendition of "Look Upon the Lord," which she considered the most moving of all their shouting hymns: "There is something in it that goes to the depths of one's soul."

A week later, on January 1, came the grand celebration at the Smith plantation on Port Royal, where the regiment of First South Carolina Volunteers was encamped. By ten o'clock the people had begun to gather, many of them arriving on steamers sent out by Brigadier General Rufus Saxton. Some came by rowboat, and white passengers heard anew the deep-throated and rhythmic rowing songs which were such an important addition to the work of the oarsmen. Near the landing, soldiers from the regiment stood drawn up in line to receive the visitors. Incoming celebrators became aware that Port Royal wore a holiday air — wrapped around the heads of the colored women were the gayest of handkerchiefs, and from their waistlines hung the whitest of aprons. The faces of the men bore "that peculiarly respectable look which these people always have on Sundays and holidays." The spectators — white and colored — assembled at a beautiful grove of live oaks adjoining the camp. Through the great oak branches and the trailing moss, a patch of the blue river was visible.

The exercises began with the reading of the preliminary proclamation by Dr. W. H. Brisbane, a South Carolinian who twenty years previously had been driven from the state for freeing his thirty slaves. Next came the presentation of two flags to the regiment. Colonel Thomas W. Higginson stepped forward to accept them, and as he was on the point of replying, a woman's voice was heard:

> My country, 'tis of thee,
> Sweet land of liberty.
> Of thee I sing . . .

Other Negroes quickly took up the refrain. The whites started to join in, but Higginson, deeply touched, motioned them to silence.

When the song was ended, the well-loved "Cunnel" Higginson made his short speech, pointing out that the spontaneous singing was a far more moving reply than anything he might say. Thereupon he delivered the flags to the "jet-black" guards, Prince Rivers and Robert Sutton, each of whom spoke to loud applause. The entire regiment responded with a full-throated singing of "Marching Along." Then came a "few earnest words," from Mrs. Frances D. Gage, Sea Islands correspondent for the *Independent*, and a reformer of long standing. The formal portion of the program closed with the John Brown song.

The dress parade which followed was colorful — the men in their blue coats and scarlet pantaloons all spick and span — and it put everyone in good appetite for the grand barbecue. Laid out on the wooden table, and flanked by plates of bread and jugs of molasses, were twelve roasted oxen which had been cooked the night before, a detail of soldiers sitting up all night watching the great fires smoldering in the pit. Many of the colored celebrators helped themselves without inhibition: "The way some of the Negroes put into the beef was astonishing," wrote a reporter. They paused in the eating long enough to drink a toast to the health of President Lincoln in molasses and water.

Those who lived on other islands, like Miss Forten, were a little unhappy when the sun went down and they had to board the waiting transports. They would have given much to stay and listen to the grand "shout" which the soldiers had planned.

In the soft and lovely Sea Island moonlight the uniformed men sang until taps sounded. "The day was perfect," summarized Colonel Higginson.

Below the Mason-Dixon line the Emancipation Proclamation was greeted with scorn and ridicule, and compared in futility with the Chinese Army's practice of waving flags and beating drums in the face of an enemy charge. In his message to the Confederate Congress on January 12, 1862, President Davis expressed the official attitude of the South: "Our own detestation of those who have attempted the most execrable measure recorded in the history of guilty man is tempered by profound contempt for the impotent rage it discloses." In Border-State Kentucky a widely circulated weekly pointed out that Davis could declare the Negroes in the North to be slaves and his proclamation would have as much effect as that of Lincoln in declaring slaves in the Confederacy free.

Davis himself toyed with something of that idea. In a broadside dated January 5, 1863, and published at Richmond, "An Address To the People of the Free States by the President of the Southern Confederacy," Davis notified the North that since it had "degraded" itself by inviting the co-operation of the black race, he thereby declared that on and after February 22, 1863, "all free Negroes in the Southern Confederacy shall be placed on the slave status, and deemed to be chattels, they and their issue forever." Moreover, continued Davis, all Negroes who were captured in states where slavery did not exist were to be adjudged to occupy the status of slaves, "so that the respective normal condition of the white and black races may be ultimately placed on a permanent basis."

Davis's "Address" was preposterous, and he knew it. And yet it was not any more powerless, in the opinion of many Northerners, than Lincoln's edict. Lincoln, said these critics, had issued "a proclamation that did not emancipate," since his measure proposed to free only the slaves of persons in rebellion, and such persons would do everything in their power to retain their chattels. But those critics who called attention to the fine-print specifications of the proclamation, and those who charged that it made the war "a nigger crusade," soon found themselves drowned out. For the proclamation, although not couched in the moving quality of prose Lincoln could summon, was psychologically effective.

The Negroes and the abolitionists were in approval. They did not pay close attention to every line — they preferred to interpret the edict in the light of their wishes and aspirations. Like Frederick Douglass, they "saw in its spirit a life and power beyond its letter." To them it was a notable gain to have the Union committed to the extinction of slavery, even though military necessity was set forth as the reason. Wrote Douglass: "I approved the one-spur-wisdom of Paddy, who thought that if he could get one side of his horse to go, he could trust the speed of the other side."

The favorable reaction of the reformers was matched by those newspapers which closely followed Republican party lines. "God Bless Abraham Lincoln," editorialized Horace Greeley's daily. Its namesake on the banks of Lake Michigan, the Chicago *Tribune*, was also most fulsome in its praise: "The President has affixed the great seal to the grandest proclamation ever issued by man. So splendid a vision has hardly shone upon the world since the days of the Messiah."

The Emancipation Proclamation won an approval that was not confined to the ranks of the abolitionists and the editors of the party press. Soon the North as a whole also gave its approval. For the proclamation, almost in spite of itself, was a challenge to one of man's loftiest aspirations — the quest for freedom. More of a rallying cry and a slogan rather than an enforceable edict, it pinned the fight to a high-sounding cause. A war to re-establish the Union was not enough to move men's hearts deeply. But a holy war for freedom — a new birth of freedom — was a goal which could hardly fail to stir the most sluggish soul. "The Emancipation Proclamation was uttered in the first gun fired at Fort Sumner," remarked Secretary of State Seward to Donn Piatt. But to Americans the significant thing was not the unchaining of nearly four million bondsmen, as important as that was. The freedom that caught the imagination of the American people, and the freedom which they identified with the Emancipation Proclamation, was a generalized freedom – a broad charter of human rights whose espousal came naturally to the citizens of a country which envisioned itself as the haven of human liberty and the asylum of the oppressed for freedom's sake.

In February 1865, as Lincoln reflected on the effect of the Emancipation Proclamation – how it had broken the backbone of the Confederacy, and how it had been so favorably received by public opinion in Europe – he informed portrait painter Frank B. Carpenter that as affairs had turned out, the edict of freedom was "the central act of my administration, and the greatest event of the nineteenth century." In this appraisal Lincoln had been anticipated by Frances Ellen Watkins Harper, the Negro woman of letters:

> It shall flash through all the ages;
>   It shall light the distant years;
> And eyes now dim with sorrow
>   Shall be brighter through their tears.

❖

The definitive proclamation, unlike the preliminary edict of September 22, 1862, contained a declaration that freed slaves "of suitable condition" would be "received into the armed service of the United States, to garrison forts, positions, stations, and other places, and to man vessels of all sorts in said service." This was the signal that Negroes had been waiting for. North and South, they prepared to join up.

Anoder ting is, suppose you had kept your freedom without enlisting in dis army; your chillen might have grown up free and been well cultivated so as to be equal to any business, but it would have been always flung in dere faces — "Your fader never fought for he own freedom."

PRIVATE THOMAS LONG
FIRST SOUTH CAROLINA VOLUNTEERS

CHAPTER IX

Do You Think I'll Make a Soldier?

IRISH WOMEN are incensed when they think they are to be deprived of the companionship of their husbands," wrote Jacob C. White to Joseph C. Bustill on August 19, 1862, "while no such sad catastrophe is likely to befall the *nagur* women." The attitude of the Irish women is symptomatic of the change of heart in the North concerning the use of Negro soldiers. "We needed that the vast tide of death should roll by our own doors," wrote Chaplain George H. Hepworth of the Forty-seventh Massachusetts, in November 1863, "and sweep away our fathers and sons, before we could come to our senses and give the black man the one boon he has been asking for so long — permission to fight for our common country."

In the South, as has been noted, the movement for Negro troops had gotten underway before the Emancipation Proclamation — Hunter had made a beginning at Hilton Head, and Butler had issued a call at New Orleans. In the North with the coming of 1863, many state governors took the initiative in enlisting Negro regiments. These governors were finding it hard to raise their quotas of troops and hoped to use Negroes in place of whites.

By 1863 the national government was in a co-operative mood.

The Federal government had authority to determine who might join the militia, and in 1792 Congress had decreed that only white male citizens should be enrolled. But in July 1862 the racial tag was left out, and Congress said simply that the enrollment of militia should include all able-bodied male citizens between the ages of eighteen and forty-five. The Emancipation Proclamation favored arming the freed slaves, and less than four weeks after it was issued, Secretary of War Stanton authorized the governor of Massachusetts to enlist Negro volunteers.

Governor John A. Andrew, in addition to wishing to fill the Massachusetts quota, was moved to use Negro troops by a zeal for the welfare of the colored man. It was Andrew who had spear-headed the movement to raise the Massachusetts Fifty-fourth, the first Negro regiment recruited in the North. Andrew had appointed George L. Stearns as supervisor of enlistments, and Stearns in turn had chosen as recruiting agents a roster of well-known Negro leaders.

Each of these agents was assigned a specific region, and by exhortation at public meetings, by visiting homes, barbershops and cracker-barrel crossroads stores, they prevailed upon young Negroes to sign up. Their chief argument was forcefully stated by Frederick Douglass, who shrewdly divined in the Negro as soldier a foundation for the Negro as citizen and the Negro as voter:

> Once let the black man get upon his person the brass letters, *U.S.*; let him get an eagle on his button, and a musket on his shoulder and bullets in his pocket, and there is no power on earth which can deny that he has earned the right to citizenship in the United States.

The recruiting agents sent to the Readville barracks more than enough men to fill the quota of the Fifty-fourth. "I can fill up another regiment for you in less than six weeks," wired Stearns to Andrew late in April. This newly enlisted complement of volunteers, the Massachusetts Fifty-fifth, like most of the regiments to be raised under state auspices, came from every walk of Negro life. Of the total of 980 recruits, 287 had been slaves. Five hundred and fifty were listed as "pure blacks," and 430 were of "mixed blood." Nearly 500 could read and over 300 could both read and write. Forty-six trades and occupations were represented, although farming, with 596, comprised more than all the others combined. The birthplaces of the men covered twenty-five states, the District of Columbia, Canada and Africa. From the last named came Nicolas Said, a native of Bornu, Eastern Sudan, Central Africa. As a member of the ruling class of his tribe, Said was tattooed on the forehead. During the period of his service, Private Said, according to the commanding officer of the regiment, "spoke and wrote English, French, German and Italian, while there is no doubt that he is master of Kanouri [his vernacular], Mandra, Arabic, Turkish and Russian."

Rhode Island had the distinction of raising the first colored artillery regiment in the North. As early as August 4, 1862, the governor of the state had issued a call for a regiment to consist "entirely of colored citizens." Four days later at a meeting held in the Colored Baptist Church, the Negroes had responded enthusiastically. "I would rather lose my life than have the Southern Confederacy rule over us," was the sentiment of the meeting as expressed by one speaker. But the then-hesitant policy of the national government had prevented any successful recruiting effort. On June 17, 1863, the War Office gave Rhode Island permission to organize a colored company of heavy artillery. A few weeks later this permission was extended to include a battalion, and still later, to include a full regiment of twelve companies. Within two weeks after the authorization from Washington, Negroes were drilling at the Dexter Training Ground at Providence. Within eight weeks after the call, the first two companies held a street parade. A reporter for the Providence *Journal* (August 28, 1863) commented on the many fine physical specimens:

Look, for instance, at the two Freeman boys. Peter the file leader is a splendidly formed man, huge, muscular, and powerfully built. Charles Freeman is his equal. Though they are of the same name and fashioned after the same mould, they are in no other way relatives. Peter is from the border and hails from slavery. Charles is of Rhode Island stock and hails from Bristol. Jeremiah Noka, who stands near the right, is also a noteworthy specimen of a Rhode Islander. He is one of the finest examples which a modern intermingling of African blood has left to us of the once all powerful tribe of Narragansetts.

Four weeks after the parade, the regiment, headed by Colonel Nelson Viall, established headquarters on Dutch Island in the harbor where their brawn could be used in constructing defensive works for the city of Providence. On November 19 the governor and the state legislature, in a body, visited the island to review the Fourteenth Rhode Island Heavy Artillery and present to them a stand of colors. One of the speakers, Senator Henry B. Anthony, reminded the soldiers that it was "nigh upon a hundred years since a Rhode Island colored regiment under Colonel Christopher Greene, as brave a man as ever drew a sword, received the praises of George Washington."

Late in November Major General Halleck ordered the Fourteenth to proceed to New Orleans. Shortly before they sailed, the colored people of Providence held a celebration in their honor. The colored women of the city presented the regiment with a handsome silk flag. The speakers included the governor, the lieutenant governor and the mayor. "See to it," exhorted Negro John T. Waugh, "that history writes that you nobly sustained the honor of the flag." On December 19 the regiment left Providence, bound for the distant Crescent City.

The success in recruiting the Massachusetts and Rhode Island regiments had its influence on Pennsylvania. For a Northern state, Pennsylvania had lagged behind on matters Negro. In 1862 its legislature had considered a bill to punish by fine and imprisonment any colored person coming into the state. In Philadelphia, Negroes were still excluded from riding the city passenger cars, despite repeated petitions to the Board of Passenger Railway Presidents sent by Quaker City Negroes like William Still, Isaiah C. Wares and Samuel S. Smith, and Negro civic organizations such as the "Social and Statistical Association." On February 6, 1863, when Frederick Douglass asked Governor Andrew G. Curtin if he would accept colored troops the governor said No. During the same month, when Robert E. Corson was in Philadelphia recruiting for the Massachusetts Fifty-fourth, he bought tickets for the men and got them into cars one at a time, in order to avoid any scenes. But Confederate General Robert E. Lee's invasion of southeastern Pennsylvania in the early summer of 1863, and the subsequent battle of Gettysburg early in July, had alarmed the state and made many of its citizens less hostile to the idea of blacks in blue.

In the early summer of 1863 a committee of prominent civic leaders in Philadelphia secured authorization to recruit Negro soldiers. Headed by Thomas Webster as chairman and Cadwalader Biddle as secretary, this "Supervisory Committee for Colored Enlistments" had to expand its membership from twenty-five to fifty, and finally up to seventy-five, so great was the desire of public-spirited merchants, bankers and professional men to serve on it. These men quickly raised $33,388 to promote the work of recruitment — for agents' expenses, and for travel and subsistence allowances to volunteers while en route to Camp William Penn, near Philadelphia. On June 23, 1863, the camp received its first recruits, pitching tent for eighty men.

The Negroes in Philadelphia were pleased with this development. At a public meeting they passed a resolution which declared that colored Philadelphians, "throwing aside the unpleasant memories of the past, looking only to the future, and asking merely the same guarantees, the same open field and fair play that are given to our white fellow-countrymen, desire here and now to express our willingness and readiness to come forward to the defence of our imperilled country."

Recruitment for the Pennsylvania regiments proceeded rapidly. In less than ten months after the first call for volunteers, Webster's committee was able to report the organizing of ten full regiments, one of which, the Third United States Regiment, "was in front of Fort Wagner when it surrendered." Social register Philadelphians, particularly the members of the Union League Club, were proud of the black troops: "Camp William Penn became a fashionable resort," wrote a contemporary, "and fine equipages filled the road thither every afternoon."

In New York state the enlistment of Negro troops was delayed by the attitude of Democratic Governor Horatio Seymour. When he showed a reluctance to take any action whatsoever, a committee of thirteen prominent New Yorkers, among whom were Horace Greeley, Peter Cooper, William Cullen Bryant, Parke Godwin and Horace Bushnell, sent a delegation on May 3, 1863, to Lincoln to find out what the national government would do to assist in raising troops in the state. Successful in obtaining an audience with the President, the delegates told him of the pledges of enlistment they had received from 3000 Negroes, and pointed out that 7000 additional colored men could be signed up.

The delegation recommended John C. Frémont as commander of the 10,000 Negro soldiers who would constitute a "Grand Army of Liberation."

Lincoln listened "with earnestness and indeed solemnity," but in essence he threw the matter back into the lap of New York's own chief executive. Governor Seymour was the titular head of a loyal state, replied Lincoln, and hence the national government would not act concerning colored enlistments unless Seymour specifically refused to do so. Returning to New York, the delegation made its report at a public meeting held at the Church of the Puritans. Thereupon the sponsoring committee, the Association for Promoting Colored Volunteering, submitted a formal application to the governor on July 9.

While the committee was waiting for an answer, the colored citizens were not idle. A convention was held at Poughkeepsie on July 15 and 16 "for the Purpose of Facilitating the Introduction of Colored Troops into the Service of the United States." In the name of the colored citizens of the state, the delegates drew up a manifesto declaring that the Negro was loyal to the national government and that he was ready to bear arms. One of the resolutions urged that a more effective remedy for the rebellion ought to be tried, "in the shape of warm lead and cold steel, duly administered by two hundred thousand black doctors, more or less, under the direction of Surgeon John Charles Frémont, or such other person." The convention appointed a State Central Committee, under the chairmanship of P. B. Randolph, to canvass for recruits and to enroll and organize colored troops.

In the meantime Governor Seymour had not replied to the letter from the Association for Promoting Colored Volunteering. The committee sent another letter. Seven weeks later, with still no word from Albany, the committee called on the governor. If Seymour's reply was long in coming, it was short and to the point, "I do not deem it advisable to give such authorization, and I have therefore declined to give it."

A mass meeting was called for November 16 to map out the next steps. Henry Highland Garnet, one of the speakers, proclaimed that the colored men "were most anxious to do their utmost to put down the rebellion." A General Committee of Twenty-five was appointed, including Henry J. Raymond, David Dudley Field and Peter Cooper, and from this committee a smaller group was selected to wait upon President Lincoln. Cooper dispatched a long letter to the White House. Simultaneously the subcommittee sent a letter to Stanton on November 21 informing him of the refusal of "certain State functionaries to recognize colored men in the call for volunteers."

Stanton sent an immediate reply. Upon application by suitable persons, wrote he, the War Department would grant authorization to raise colored troops whose membership would be credited to the state. These recruits would be paid $10 a month, and would receive no bounty. Thus, finally, Washington had flashed the go-ahead signal.

On December 5 the Association for Promoting Colored Volunteering was joined by the Union League Club. The latter had raised considerable monies to promote enlistments in white regiments and was well financed. These two groups united to form a Joint Committee on Volunteers, and with combined funds, amounting to nearly $20,000, they proceeded to recruit Negroes to help fill New York's draft quota.

The Joint Committee established a camp at Rikers Island, to which the recruits were sent as soon as they were mustered in. Within two weeks the quota was filled; on January 4, 1864, Colonel George Bliss, Jr. informed Stanton that the regiment had reached its maximum strength of 1000 men. Bliss recommended that the regiment be allowed to remain in camp for another month so that the men might become more proficient as soldiers.

When the troops got ready to break camp, a committee of citizens arranged for a public reception in the city. The committee sent word to the regimental commander, Colonel Nelson B. Bartram, asking if he thought his soldiers would be prepared to cope with any hostile demonstrations. Bartram's answer was brief: "Give me room to land my regiment, and if it cannot march through New York it is not fit to go into the field."

On March 5, 1864, the Twentieth United States Colored Troops left Rikers Island in the morning and were transported to the foot of Thirty-sixth Street, East River, where they disembarked, formed in regimental line, and with loaded muskets and fixed bayonets marched to Union Square. At one o'clock they arrived in front of the Union League clubhouse where flag presentation ceremonies had been arranged. A newspaper reporter described the scene: "A vast crowd of citizens of every shade of color, every phase of social and political life, filled the square and streets, and every door, window, veranda, tree and house-top that commanded a view of the scene, was peopled with spectators."

Two large platforms, one over the entrance to the League clubroom and the other in the middle of the street, had been erected, and were "ornamented with flags and filled with ladies." From the platform in the street President Charles King, of Columbia College, presented two flags; one was from the mothers, wives and sisters of the New York Union League Club, and the other, a regimental banner showing a conquering eagle, a broken yoke and the armed figure of liberty, was presented by a group of loyal women. "When you put on the uniform and swear allegiance to the standard of the Union," said President King, "you stand emancipated, regenerated and disenthralled — the peer of the proudest soldier in the land."

After the flag-presentation ceremonies were over, the regiment stacked arms, and moved with good appetite to the refreshment tables where coffee and sandwiches had been prepared. The line of march was then re-formed. It was led by the superintendent of police and one hundred of his force, followed in order by Union League Club, "the Colored Friends of the Recruits, marching with hands joined," the Governor's Island Band and the regiment. Down Broadway to the Canal, the civilians and the soldiers marched to the strains of martial music and the applause of the crowd. At North River the black soldiers embarked on board the *Ericsson*, bound for New Orleans.

Like Pennsylvania's Governor Curtin, the chief executive of Ohio, David Tod, experienced a change of heart concerning colored troops. Negroes had offered their services in 1861 and 1862, and Tod had turned them down. He had been following precedent; in Ohio the Negro had never been called on to perform military service. The companies of state militia had been somewhat of a semisocial organization and the presence of Negroes would have destroyed their "companionable character."

By the summer of 1863 things had changed. Cincinnati Negroes had proved their willingness to be of service when, in September 1862, the mayor of the city, in alarm lest the Confederate Army sweep into their streets, closed all the business houses, had all the cash removed from the bank vaults, and called upon all voters to report for assignments in erecting fortifications. General Lew Wallace requested Colonel William M. Dickson to raise a voluntary brigade of Negroes for the work of throwing up defenses. For three weeks the black brigade worked night and day. "You have labored faithfully," said Colonel Dickson, at a celebration in which the six hundred colored men presented him with a sword for his kindness. "You have made miles of military roads, miles of rifle pits, fallen hundreds of acres of the largest and loftiest trees, and built magazines and forts." Early in October the Confederates marched out of Kentucky, thus removing the military threat to the Queen City. But Cincinnati citizens had been given an object lesson in Negro co-operation in a common cause.

By the summer of 1863, leading Ohio newspapers such as the Toledo *Blade* and the Cincinnati *Gazette* were urging Tod to use Negro troops in order to meet the state's draft quota. Ohio was proving to be a recruiting ground for Massachusetts, and Ohioans wanted to arrest the exodus. "Let their own state," said the *Gazette* in a front-page editorial on July 17, 1863, "have credit for their services."

It was a request from a Negro recruiting agent that prompted Governor Tod to wire Stanton and thus to obtain official permission to raise colored regiments. O. S. B. Wall, a prosperous Negro merchant who ran a boot and shoe store at Oberlin, had raised a squad of forty-eight recruits for the Massachusetts Fifty-fifth. Just as Wall was ready to forward the men to the camp at Readville, Massachusetts, he received a wire from George Stearns stating that the regiment was full. Housing the volunteers with hospitable Negro families in Columbus, Wall hastened to the state house and explained the situation to the governor. Tod promised to get in touch with Stanton at once. The next morning, June 16, brought a telegram from the war office granting permission.

With Wall's nucleus, Tod began the recruiting of Negro troops in Ohio. He issued an appeal to raise funds for colored families whose breadwinners might wish to join up. One of his chief agents was John Mercer Langston, now finished with his effort in the enlisting of the Massachusetts regiments. Recruited almost exclusively from Ohio, the Fifth United States Colored Troops, with Colonel G. W. Shurtliff commanding, filled its regimental quota in November 1863. At the flag presentation ceremonies at Camp Delaware, the two chief speakers were Tod and his predecessor in the governor's chair, William Dennison. During the second week in November the regiment entrained for Portsmouth to join the Army of the James, its men little dreaming that they would see action in ten battles in Virginia.

Other commonwealths in the North — Connecticut, Michigan, Illinois, Indiana, Iowa, Kansas — raised one or more regiments of black troops, but state efforts were soon slowed down by sheer lack of numbers — there were simply not enough Negroes above the Mason-Dixon line. Congress thereupon obligingly passed a conscription act (July 4, 1864) which authorized Northern governors to send agents into the Confederate states to recruit Negroes, who would be credited to the state's quota. During the eight months this act was on the books, a total of 1405 agents were sent into the South by Northern state governors. The number of recruits enlisted by the combined efforts of these state agents was an unimpressive 5052.

One reason for the limited success of the agents was the attitude of the field commanders. Many of the Union generals, fearing that the enlisting of Negroes might rob them of their military laborers, were cool in their reception to the state agents. William

T. Sherman obeyed the law halfheartedly, and then only after Lincoln had sent him a tactful letter urging compliance.

Fortunately for the Union cause, the national government supplemented state recruiting by efforts of its own. In the spring of 1863 Washington launched a vigorous program to recruit an army of blacks. Wrote ranking general H. W. Halleck to Ulysses S. Grant on the last day of March 1863, "And it is the opinion of many who have examined the question without passion or prejudice, that they can also be used as a military force. It certainly is good policy to use them to the very best advantage we can."

A week earlier, on March 25, Adjutant General Lorenzo Thomas had been dispatched to the Mississippi Valley with orders to recruit and officer as many Negro regiments as possible. The choice of Thomas was a good one. With a strong belief in the ability of the Negro to make a first-rate soldier, Thomas took up his new duties with zeal and efficiency. He visited centers where Negroes were congregated, addressing them and urging them to rally to the flag. "They eagerly seek to enter military organization," wrote he in optimistic vein to Stanton on April 22, 1863, from Milliken's Bend.

Thomas also made trips to military camps, speaking before white brigades and informing them of the changed policy of the government concerning Negro troops. On April 6 after addressing 7000 white troops at Helena, Thomas sent word to the Secretary of War that the policy of arming the blacks was "most enthusiastically received," and "infused new spirit into the troops." Two days later, at Lake Providence, Thomas announced the new policy to 11,000 enlisted men. The troops received the information with cheers, and many of the officers including General John A. Logan, praised the step. "I asked each of these division officers to raise two Negro regiments," wrote Thomas to the war office, "but the difficulty will be to restrict them to that number."

So successful were Thomas's efforts in enlisting Negroes that a special bureau, under the adjutant general's office, was set up in order to systematize the work. On May 22, 1863, the War Department announced the establishing of a Bureau of Colored Troops whose functions embraced all matters pertaining to the recruitment, organization and service of black regiments and the officers thereof. Provision was made for the appointment of field inspectors, and for the examining of candidates for officers' commissions. By this order the use of the Negro as a soldier became a fixed and permanent policy of the national government.

Thomas, the head of the bureau, raised black troops through the use of special officers of recruiting and regular field officers. Among the former was George L. Stearns, a Massachusetts abolitionist who had been a confidant of John Brown. In June 1863 Stearns had completed his work of organizing the two Massachusetts regiments, and Stanton prevailed upon him to become a recruiting commissioner for Negro troops, with the rank of major. Sent to Nashville in September, Stearns soon came under the technical authority of Thomas, whose jurisdiction was extended on October 13, 1863, to include Maryland, Missouri and Tennessee. A true friend of the black man, Stearns quickly won the confidence of Nashville Negroes, signing up three hundred in one day. He also sought to persuade the War Office to use Negro recruiting agents, but to no avail.

Perhaps the most successful of Adjutant General Thomas's special officers of recruiting was Augustus L. Chetlain, Brigadier General of Volunteers. With headquarters at Memphis, Chetlain was authorized to enlist and organize colored troops in Tennessee and western Kentucky, reporting monthly to Thomas. The energetic Chetlain soon had a chain of enlisting stations — Knoxville, Chattanooga, Nashville, Corinth, and Columbus, Kentucky. In June 1864 his scope of operations was enlarged to include central and eastern Kentucky, with headquarters at Louisville.

Eastern Kentucky tested Chetlain's recruiting mettle. At Louisville so great was the opposition to Negro troops that when the black soldiers got ready to attend a Fourth of July picnic given in their honor by local Negroes, Chetlain took the precaution of ordering each soldier to carry ten rounds of armament. The black regiment marched by fours through the heart of the city, impressive in their new uniforms, new arms and white cotton gloves. The streets were thronged, but there were no demonstrations; there was no applause, nothing but thunders of silence.

Chetlain did not have the last laugh. Four weeks later the order to recruit in central and eastern Kentucky was revoked. Tobacco growers had complained that the crop would go to ruin for want of labor if the recruiting of blacks continued. The administration lent an ear — national elections were approaching, and Chetlain was ordered back to Memphis.

Here he resumed his vigorous efforts, inspecting Negro troops at such points as Paducah, Nashville, Knoxville, Johnsonville and Athens, Alabama. At the end of 1864 as a result of his nine months' work Chetlain reported the organizing of eighteen regiments of infantry, three regiments of heavy artillery of 1700 each, and one battery of light artillery.

In addition to making effective use of special commissioners of recruiting, Adjutant General Thomas utilized a ready-at-hand instrument — the field officer. Thomas sent orders to division commanders to busy themselves in recruiting black regiments. In May 1863, for example, he ordered Stephen A. Hurlburt, commanding the District of West Tennessee, to raise six regiments of colored troops. Hurlburt in turn ordered each of his six brigade commanders to organize a regiment. Thomas, in his Special Orders No. 17, issued on February 19, 1864, ordered that regiments of infantry be raised from Negroes "who may hereafter come within our lines."

Brigade commanders quickly found two convenient ways to enlist the required black regiment. One was to select its prospective officers and detail them to go out and do the recruiting. Indeed, commissions were often awarded on the basis of the ability to secure enlistments. As soon as the prospective officer had collected the required number of volunteers and had them mustered in, he would be discharged from his former regiment and take his commissioned rank in the newly organized colored body of soldiers.

The prospect of securing a commission in a Negro regiment was one of the powerful factors in overriding Billy Yank's opposition to Negro troops. Since all commissioned officers, according to Thomas's orders, were to be white, this presented a splendid opportunity to an ambitious enlisted man who might have little chance to rise from the ranks in his own outfit. White soldiers did not object to serving in the same unit with Negroes if there was a sufficient difference in their respective rank. Horace Greeley stated this point in a piquant way:

> There are few, if any, instances of a White sergeant or corporal whose dignity or whose nose revolted at the proximity of Blacks as private soldiers, if he might secure a lieutenancy by deeming them not unsavory, or not quite intolerably so; while there is no case on record where a soldier deemed fit for a captaincy in a colored regiment rejected it and clung to the ranks, in deference to his invincible antipathy to "niggers."

Another troop-raising technique employed by brigade commanders was to order that a group of men be detailed on recruiting service. The methods used by these soldier-recruiters were much like those of the state agents, except that they offered no bounty and they were not averse to using strong-arm methods if sweet reasonableness failed.

In the towns their usual method was to nail up attractive posters announcing a mass meeting. When the Negroes had gathered, the recruiters would inform them that they should sign up in order to strike a blow against slavery. Prospective volunteers were assured that in their absence their families would be protected by the Union Army. They were promised a salary of $7.00 a month, plus free issues of rations and clothing. Sometimes the allotment would be read off: one coat, one trousers, one blanket, one cap, one pair of shoes, one knapsack, one canteen, one haversack, one pair of overalls, two shirts and two pairs of socks.

In the rurals the recruiters split up, each party covering all the plantations within a radius of twenty miles. Each party rode from plantation to plantation, buttonholing all able-bodied Negroes and giving them the sales talk. If the Negro was receptive and a single man, he simply joined the recruiting party on the spot, since usually he had no real estate matters to settle, or personal possessions to assign.

The recruiters did not have to contend with state authority since they were operating in conquered territory, but the opposition of the resident whites was strong. Local citizens condemned the intruders as troublemakers and incendiaries. In his diary on May 4, 1864, at Huntsville, Alabama, one of these scorned recruiters, James M. Ayres, an elderly ex-clergyman of salty temper who was on detached service from the Illinois One Hundred Twenty-ninth Infantry, described the woes encountered in "geathering up Sambo":

> Sometimes it had been attended with great danger and Risk. And many unpleasant things has occurred. I have stood allmost as A lone tree where A forest once was, forsaken by all the South, and while my Brother soaldiers and officers would occasionally meet a smile from Southern faces, in Shape of Southern Women, My Lot was Sneers and Curses. "Ther goes that oald nigger Recreuter, thats that oald man was at our House the other day and took pops or dads Niggers Away." And Oh such Eyes and Daggers I got.

As a result of the efforts of his Bureau of Colored Troops, Adjutant General Thomas reported that from April 1, 1863, to December 24, 1863, a total of 20,830 Negro volunteers had been raised in the Valley of the Mississippi — 825 in the cavalry, 4517 in the artillery and 15,448 in the infantry. This nearly 21,000 troops did not include the 15,000 which had been recruited lower down the Mississippi, in the Department of the Gulf, through the pioneer work of General Benjamin F. Butler and the later efforts of Generals N. P. Banks and Daniel Ullman.

The number raised in the Valley would have been much larger, wrote Thomas to Stanton, but for two factors: "several thousand" of the Negro volunteers had to be rejected before muster, on account of disease or disability; and the Rebels ran their slaves off to Texas and other points beyond reach of the Union lines. "It is to be presumed that as our armies advance, the number of our Colored organizations will be largely increased." Thomas's presumption was a safe one. When, within four weeks after Lee's surrender, Provost Marshal James B. Fry, in an order dated April 29, 1865, terminated the recruitment of Negroes, the number of Negro regiments had climbed to 166 — of which 145 were infantry, 7 cavalry, 12 heavy artillery, 1 light artillery and 1 engineers — and the number of enlisted men had soared to 178,975, approximately one eighth of the entire Union army.

✤

"Do you think I'll make a soldier?" is the opening line of a popular Negro spiritual. The singer who voices the inquiry has no doubt that he'll make a soldier; he only raises the question as to whether his listener thinks so too. The nearly 180,000 blacks who donned the Union blue had no misgivings about their ability to make efficient soldiers. "What are you, anyhow?" was the question asked in an insulting tone to one of Colonel Thomas W. Higginson's men. The soldier drew himself erect, "When God made me, I wasn't much, but I's a man now."

The Negro who joined the army was not likely to "crack up," even though he faced problems not met by the white soldier. The Negro recruit had steeled himself from the beginning to meet these difficulties, even though many of them were not in-inconsiderable. Perhaps it did not matter much if his regiment was listed under "United States Colored Troops" by an order from the Adjutant General's office dated March 11, 1864, which stated that thenceforth all black regiments be designated by numbers and include the word "colored." Perhaps it did not matter much if the War Department, with Lincoln's approval, issued on March 9, 1863, a "United States Infantry Tactics for the Use of Colored Troops."

A much sorer spot, however, was the matter of pay. Negroes in the army received $10 a month, of which $3 was paid in clothing; white soldiers received $13, plus clothing — a difference of $6 a month. The pay of the Negro was based on a decision of the solicitor of the War Department, William Whiting, who on June 4, 1863, ruled that Negro soldiers were to be paid under the pro-visions of the Militia Act of July 17, 1862, which stipulated that persons of African descent could be used for military service, for which they would be entitled to $10 a month, $3 of which might be in clothing. This act did not have in mind Negroes actually bearing arms, and it referred only to those Negroes who had recently been freed from bondage. Nonetheless until Congress acted, Negro soldiers were to be paid, said Whiting, as military laborers, under the act of July 17, 1862.

John A. Andrew, governor of Massachusetts, was greatly troubled over the solicitor's ruling since he had promised the men of the Fifty-fourth and Fifty-fifth equality in every respect with the other state regiments. Andrew hastened to Washington and talked to Lincoln, Stanton, Secretary of the Treasury Chase and Secretary of State Seward. He urged the President to get an opinion from the attorney general. Lincoln did so. Supporting Andrew, Bates's reply stated that the $10 a month pay was meant solely for those Negroes who had been slaves.

Lincoln did nothing — elections were approaching. Stanton moved slowly too, doubtless because he feared that equal pay might interfere with the recruitment of white soldiers. When asked by John Mercer Langston what was the duty of colored men in view of the lower wage, Stanton took refuge in the clouds:

> The duty of the colored man is to defend his country, whenever, wherever and in whatever form, is the same with that of the white men. It does not depend on, nor is it affected by, what the country pays. The true way to secure her rewards and win her confidence is not to stipulate for them, but to deserve them.

Disappointed over his failure at Washington, Andrew returned to the state house and sent a recommendation to the legislature that corrective action be taken. In quick response the Massachusetts lawmakers passed an act on November 16 to make up the deficiencies in the monthly pay of the Fifty-fourth and Fifty-fifth. Andrew then mailed to the two regiments duplicates of his address to the legislature and copies of the legislative enactment equalizing pay.

A week later the governor received an answer from the Fifty-fourth declining to accept any money from Massachusetts. Notwithstanding the generous action of the legislature, wrote Colonel Hallowell, the men of the Fifty-fourth wanted it known that they had enlisted as other soldiers from the state, and that they would rather continue to serve without pay until their enlistments ran out, rather than accept from the national government less than the amount paid to other soldiers.

This stand did not come as a complete surprise. Three times previously had the Fifty-fourth been mustered in for pay; three times had they declined, refusing the money until they could get justice with it. And while they were appreciative of the deficiency enactment of the state legislature, they were not willing, as Theodore Tilton put it, "that the Federal Government should throw mud upon them, even though Massachusetts stands ready to wipe it off."

The action of the Fifty-fourth in refusing to accept less than a soldier's pay stirred the country. In the halls of Congress the hot debates flared up anew after February 2, 1864, when Senator Wilson of Massachusetts introduced a joint resolution to equalize pay. After endless argument, Congress passed an act on June 15, 1864, which provided retroactively that as of January 1, 1864, colored soldiers were to receive the same uniform, clothing, arms, equipments, camp equipage, rations, medical and hospital attendance, pay, and emoluments, other than bounty, as other soldiers . . ." The law further provided that if the Negro soldier had been free on April 19, 1861, he would be paid the difference, from the time of his enlistment to January 1, 1864, between what he had received and the full pay allowed by law during the same period to white soldiers.

Most Negro soldiers who had enlisted prior to January 1, 1864, found it easy to qualify for this back pay since "the fact of freedom is to be determined by the statement of the soldier, under oath," as ordered by the War Department in a communication on August 1, 1864, to all officers commanding Negro troops. Officers were not required to go behind the oaths, and few ex-slave soldiers would have any compunctions in swearing that they "owed no man unrequited labor on or before the 19th day of April, 1861."

The Massachusetts regiments had a red-letter day when Paymaster Lockwood arrived at Folly Island in late September. It required $170,000 to pay the Fifty-fourth for its eighteen months of unsalaried service. The pay average was about $200 per volunteer. The men were overjoyed. "Songs burst out everywhere," wrote Captain Emilio. "The fiddle and other music long neglected enlivens the tents night and day."

The Fifty-fifth likewise had a gala celebration upon receiving the arrears in pay. "The boys are in great glee," wrote bronzed and bearded Sergeant James Ruffin of Company F to his sister-in-law, Josephine Ruffin. "We had a glorious celebration, there was a procession, then a mass meeting when speeches of various gentlemen were made, and readings of resolutions to be published in the papers. In the evening we had a Grand Supper. All passed off very creditable." The soldiers paid off all their loans to the officers and their indebtedness to the sutlers, wrote Burt G. Wilder, an officer in the Fifty-fifth, and sent home over $60,000 by Adams Express.

A grievance of the Negro soldier, which the Army Appropriation Act of June 15, 1864, proposed to remedy was that of "medical and hospital attendance." In colored units there was a serious shortage of surgeons: "The subject of obtaining suitable Medical Officers," wrote Adjutant General Thomas to his assistant, Colonel E. D. Townsend, on December 8, 1863, "has given me much uneasiness." Six months later, on June 14, 1864, the adjutant general tersely notified the Secretary of War: "Colonel Wood, Assistant Surgeon General, informs me that he cannot find any Assistant Surgeons for Colored Regiments."

It was not easy to induce medical officers to accept commissions in Negro regiments. Hence, "in very many cases," wrote N. P. Banks, commanding in the Department of the Gulf, "Hospital Stewards of low order of qualification were appointed to the office of Assistant Surgeon and Surgeon. Well-grounded objections were made from every quarter against the inhumanity of subjecting the colored soldiers to medical treatment and surgical operations from such men."

The available Negro physicians faced hardships if they attempted to serve, as illustrated by the experience of Alexander T. Augusta, one of the eight Negro physicians to be commissioned during the war. A native of Virginia, Augusta had received his medical education at Trinity College and had remained in Toronto, where he became a leading physician with a large practice, mostly white. On April 14, 1863, Augusta was given a surgeon's commission, "having been examined and found qualified." A month later as he boarded a northbound train at Baltimore and took his seat in the car, the railroad guard and "8 or 10 toughs" tore off one of the oak leaf straps from his major's uniform. Augusta got off the train, left the station, and went to the provost guard to report the incident. The black officer was escorted back to the depot by a military squad and a detachment of detectives. Despite such a formidable bodyguard, Augusta, as he entered the station, was dealt a powerful blow in the face. The guards displayed their arms, and the Negro officer was conducted to the cars with drawn revolvers.

Augusta had two discouraging experiences of an official nature. Early in February 1864, at Camp Stanton, Maryland, where he was senior surgeon, the white assistant surgeons wrote to Lincoln informing him of their surprise upon reporting to the regiment to find that the senior surgeon was a Negro. They requested "most respectfully, yet earnestly," that a termination be put to "this unexpected, unusual, and most unpleasant relationship in which we have been placed." Augusta was soon removed from Camp Stanton and placed on detached service. Dr. Augusta had a final difficulty — that of collecting a surgeon's salary. The paymaster at Baltimore insisted that his pay should be $7.00 a month. Following a letter from Senator Wilson to Secretary Stanton and an order from the latter to the paymaster general, Major Augusta was finally compensated according to his rank, after a delay of fifty-three weeks.

Another hazard run by the Negro volunteer was that of inferior arms and equipment. The ordnance department often sent materials that were either obsolete or faultily constructed — bayonets, for example, that did not fit muskets. Brigadier General Ullman expressed his distress, in a letter to Henry Wilson early in December 1863, at having to send his Negro soldiers into battle with "arms almost entirely unserviceable." Lorenzo Thomas, after an inspection of the eight companies of a colored regiment stationed on Ship Island, Mississippi, advised Stanton on April 7, 1864, that the men be furnished with Springfield muskets:

This Regiment, like most of this class of soldiers, have the old flintlock muskets, altered to percussion, which have been in use for a long time. The muskets of this Regiment were condemned once, and have been condemned by an Inspector a second time.

Negro regiments also faced the performing of an excessive amount of fatigue duty. Aside from the seven colored regiments which were specifically organized for assignment on labor details, Negro troops were usually given garrison duty rather than field service. The garrisoning of forts and arsenals, month in and month out, became dull, monotonous and demoralizing. A Negro soldier might become dispirited, feeling that he was being singled out as a common laborer to perform such tasks as building bridges, draining marshes, filling sandbags, unloading vessels, throwing up entrenchments and drawing cannon to the front and mounting them. The War Department, perhaps unwittingly, strengthened this attitude that fatigue duty was the natural lot of the black enlisted man by issuing in April 1863 Special Order No. 13, addressed to the commanders of Negro troops in the Valley of the Mississippi:

> One of the duties to be required of Regiments of African descent, will be to secure abandoned Cotton, and have it conveyed to the Levee for shipment to the Quartermaster at Memphis, Tennessee.

Greatest of the grievances of the black volunteer was the dread of the fate that might be his if he fell into the hands of the enemy. A Negro in martial regalia "offended the Southern view of 'the eternal fitness of things.'" Hence Confederate military and civilian officials never referred to blacks in blue as soldiers — they were designated "slaves in arms," or "slaves in armed rebellion." This was a natural attitude for a slaveholding society. As a Virginia daily explained: "The very foundation of slavery would be fatally wounded if we were insane enough to treat black men as the equal of white, and insurgent slaves as equivalent to our brave white soldiers."

On the last day in April 1863, the Confederate Congress, in line with a proclamation made by President Davis four months previously and in accordance with his subsequent recommendations, passed a law decreeing that Negroes who were "taken in arms against the Confederate States," or who gave aid and comfort to its enemies, should if captured in the South be dealt with according to the laws of the state in which they were seized. This punishment was the equivalent of a death sentence since the law in every one of the seceded states would have branded such Negroes as incendiaries and insurrectionists.

Disliking an-eye-for-an-eye policy, Lincoln at first had thought of limiting the employment of Negro military laborers to places sufficiently removed from the war fronts as to prevent their being captured. In early January he discussed such a course with Secretaries Stanton and Welles.

But increasingly public opinion in the North cried out for repayment in kind. "They have proposed in Richmond to sell our cooks &c into slavery," wired Assistant Secretary of the Navy G. V. Fox to Admiral S. F. Du Pont. "If they do, I think we can retaliate." Bowing to the storm, Lincoln issued an order on July 30, 1863, that for every Union soldier killed in violation of the laws of war, a Rebel soldier would be put to death, and that for every Union soldier enslaved or sold into slavery, a Rebel soldier would be placed at hard labor on the public works.

As the war progressed and the number of Negro regiments multiplied, the South modified its stated policy as to captured blacks. Not many were sold into slavery — that practice was rare. In a few instances Negroes were killed rather than captured, notably at Fort Pillow, on the east bank of the Mississippi, some forty miles above Memphis, where on April 12, 1864, a Rebel force swept into the garrison, and of the 262 Negro soldiers stationed there, 229 were killed, wounded in escape or buried alive.

Major General Nathan Bedford Forrest, the able and ruthless Confederate commander, was not squeamish about bloodletting: "War means fighting, and fighting means killing," was a favorite maxim of his. Doubtless, too, there were instances in which Negro troops were slain after they were captured. "I hope I may never see a Negro Soldier," wrote a Mississippi boy to his mother, "or I cannot be a Christian Soldier."

The South consistently contended that slaves captured in arms should be returned to their masters, but in actual practice, Negro soldiers, ex-slave and freeborn, although not formally regarded as prisoners of war, were treated about as humanely as white prisoners. Perhaps Negro captives were discriminated against as to daily rations, shelter and prison duties, but there was no such officially stated policy. If captured Negroes were sometimes put to work building Rebel fortifications, this circumstance was not wholly disadvantageous. Such prisoner-laborers would be reasonably sure of getting enough to eat, and would not be penned up in such a notorious prison slaughterhouse as Andersonville where the death rate of Union soldiers averaged eight and one half per hour.

There was little likelihood that captured Negro soldiers would be exchanged. The Confederate agent of exchange, Robert Ould, declared that the South "would die in the last ditch" rather than to return an ex-slave to the Union Armies. The Confederacy's firmness on this point had led in the summer of 1863 to a suspension of the general exchange of prisoners. But by the spring of 1864, the Richmond government, feeling the pinch of a growing manpower shortage, instructed Commissioner Ould to agree that freeborn Negroes might be considered as prisoners of war and hence subject to exchange. The Confederacy hoped that this concession would lead to the drafting of a general cartel of exchange. Ould sent word of the new ruling on free Negroes to the Union Commissioner of Exchange, Major General Benjamin Butler.

But Ulysses S. Grant, now promoted to ranking general, was averse to effecting any exchange of prisoners, relying on the North's great superiority in numbers. Grant did not need the Union prisoners held by Rebels nearly as much as Lee needed the Confederate prisoners held by the North. Moreover, the realistic Grant was reluctant to exchange the relatively hearty and well-fed Rebel prisoners held by the Union forces in order to get the half-starved, sick and emaciated Yankees from such notorious prisons as Andersonville and Libby. Grant therefore forbade Butler to come to any agreement with Ould. It would have provoked much criticism in the North had Grant's orders not to exchange prisoners been known. But Butler pretended, in his long-drawn-out correspondence with Ould, that the exchange of prisoners was being held up because the South refused to consider captured ex-slaves as exchangeables.

The colored volunteer was aware of the hardships that he faced by virtue of having a black skin, but these discouragements did not prevent him from striving to become a good soldier. Fortunately the caliber of officers in Negro regiments was on the whole conducive to making a soldier. A regiment that was well trained and disciplined and whose morale was good was one in which the officers had gained the confidence of the men in the ranks and won their devotion.

The commissioned officers in Negro units were almost always white men — fewer than one hundred Negroes were commissioned during the war — and this scarcity of black officers was vigorously condemned by colored spokesmen, especially since those who led troops into battle did well under fire. But the whites who commanded Negro regiments were, as a group, officers of above average character and efficiency. True, there were white officers like the coarse and brutal Lieutenant Colonel Augustus Benedict who had to be reduced from an officer after horsewhipping two members of a regimental band, the Fourth Regiment Corps d'Afrique, at Fort Jackson, Louisiana, on December 8, 1863, and thereby precipitating a camp mutiny in which 125 soldiers fired their guns off. But although Negro troops had to suffer their share of officers with a sadistic love of cruelty, an Augustus Benedict was the exception rather than the rule.

Commissions in colored regiments raised in the seceded states were issued by the War Department. In the Valley of the Mississippi it was the practice to give commissions to men who were successful in recruiting Negro volunteers, but, according to the head of the Bureau of Colored Troops, "None but intelligent officers and enlisted men have been detached from their Regiments for the purpose of raising Colored Troops." In nearly every instance, wrote General Thomas to Secretary Stanton on December 24, 1863, those officers in Negro regiments were filling their positions with credit, and "when found unfitted, their appointments have been revoked."

In order to screen the officer candidates, the Bureau established in May 1863 a Board of Examiners for the Command of Colored Troops. With Brigadier General Silas Casey as permanent president, the Board of Examiners was made up of two colonels, one lieutenant colonel, one surgeon and one lieutenant, the last-named being a recorder or secretary. Before giving the candidate a written examination, the board first assured itself that he was loyal to the Union, had a good moral character and was physically sound. If a candidate met these tests he was given an examination in infantry tactics, army regulations and "capacity to command." A successful applicant was recommended to the War Department for a commission according to his merits. In the two years of its existence the board examined approximately 3000 candidates, 1700 of whom they recommended for commissions from colonel down to second lieutenant.

The board did a conscientious job. Its president, General Casey, believed that whoever placed an inefficient officer in command was guilty of manslaughter. Hence the board would recommend no candidate simply because he "had connections," no matter

how influential. One of the unsuccessful applicants for a commission was a friend of Lincoln's. On November 11, 1863, the
President sent a peremptory note to Stanton:

> DEAR SIR: I personally wish Jacob Freese, of New Jersey, to
> be appointed colonel for a colored regiment, and this re-
> gardless of whether he can tell the exact shade of Julius
> Caesar's hair.

Good officers helped in making good soldiers, but the greatest
asset of the Negro volunteer was his own spirit and outlook. He
was prepared to keep his chin up despite the enemy on the battle
front and a skeptical public opinion on the home front. His
morale was up because he had convincing reasons for enlisting.
He felt that he was striking a body blow at slavery: H. Ford
Douglass who prior to the organizing of colored regiments,
managed to join a white unit, the Ninety-fifth Regiment of
Illinois Volunteers, was anxious to serve so that, as he phrased it,
he might "be better prepared to play his part in the great drama
of the Negro's redemption." The black soldier felt that he had
a personal stake in the war: "I in dis army still, Cunnel," dog-
gedly said Abram Fuller of the First South Carolina Volunteers,
as he was handed his discharge papers for physical disability on
November 21, 1863. "To save the country from ruin," was the
announced reason that induced the enlistment of Christian A.
Fleetwood, Sergeant Major of the Fourth United States Colored
Troops, and one of the fourteen Negro recipients of the Congressional Medal for heroic conduct on the field of battle.

Many of the Negro volunteers were able to adjust easily to
army life because they had been military laborers. As teamsters,
cooks and servants, they had been in the front lines of the armies
of both the blue and the gray. Hence they were not raw recruits;
they knew what to expect. It was unlikely that they would ever
join the ranks of the deserters.

The army, moreover, had something to offer to many Negroes,
especially former slaves. The black volunteer was often better

fed and clothed than ever before in his life, and hence he spent little time in "griping" over camp inconveniences and discomforts; he did not say much if the shoddy clothing turned to rags, if the soles fell off his shoes, if the rations were delayed and if the gritty hardtack required soaking in boiling coffee until it became malleable enough to fry in pork grease.

The white soldier not engaged in combat tended to become restless and fidgety under the monotonous daily routine, doing the same thing over day after day from morning gun at sunrise until taps at ten-thirty. But the one-time slave had come from an even more simple and monotonous plantation round. Hence he was exhilarated by army life with its din and bustle — its marchings and countermarchings, its blowing of bugles, beating of drums and playing of fifes. Negro volunteers other than those in fatigue regiments had little incentive to count the number of days to the end of enlistment.

Because the Negro recruit was not bored by army life, his regiments were relatively free from camp vices. Drinking was rare. Thomas W. Higginson reported that in his regiment, even though whiskey was easily purchasable and the men had money, he "had never heard of a glass of liquor in camp." James Shaw, an officer in the Seventh U. S. Colored Troops, bore a similar testimony: "The regiment seldom, if ever, had a man drunk." Officers in Negro units in the Department of the Gulf were thankful that Negro volunteers showed self-control, since army commanders had soon discovered that "no stimulant was more demoralizing than Louisiana rum."

Scarcely more prevalent than drinking in Negro regiments was gambling. In the army as a whole gambling was a natural pastime "since a pack of cards occupies less space than a Testament, one sixth of the room which a Shakespeare requires, and is capable of indefinite combinations." Negro regiments were relatively free of cardsharps, the best paid men in the army. In one of the few reported instances of gambling in a colored unit, all of the players lost. Captain J. M. Addeman of the Fourteenth Rhode Island Heavy Artillery, coming upon a group bent over the pasteboards, scooped up both cards and stakes. One of the players ruefully remarked that "it was no use to play against the Captain, for he got high, low, jack and the game."

The Negro recruits were likely to have good morale because they took pride in being elevated to the rank of soldier. Hence, they kept their campgrounds neat and clean; spit-and-polish staff officers making inspection delighted in the orderly appearance of the barracks, and in the punctilious pains of the black recruits to do the militarily correct thing. For dress parade, Negro soldiers reported with arms burnished, belts polished, shoes blacked and clothes brushed.

Negroes showed a proficiency for military service, especially drill. Most officers in black regiments were struck by the aptitude with which the colored volunteer mastered the manual of arms. His ear for time was perfect. "They take to drill as a child takes to its mother's milk," reported folksy Jim Lane.

It was on dress parade that the ex-slave showed his greatest liking for army life. Somewhat of an exhibitionist, he loved to march. He could make out quite well with a few drummers, or to the martial music of his own singing. And a brass band would "send" him: "And when dat band wheel in before us and march on," exclaimed one of Higginson's sergeants, "My God! I quit dis world altogeder." A similar suffusion of feeling characterized a colored drummer observed by Theodore Lyman, a volunteer aide on the staff of George Gordon Meade, at the headquarters of the Army of the Potomac. This drummer "felt a *ruat-coelum-fiat-big-drum* sentiment in his deepest heart!" wrote Colonel Lyman on November 10, 1864, to his wife. "No man ever felt more that the success of great things lay in the whacking of that sheepskin with vigor and precision. Te-de-bung, de-de-bung, bung, bung! could be heard far and near." To the colored volunteer music had charms — heard melodies were sweet.

And, finally, because the Negro recruit believed in the Union cause and felt proud of his trust in wearing the blue, he was thoroughly loyal. He felt no inclination to be traitorous, to "go over" to the enemy, or even to listen to the defeatist talk of malcontents. On guard duty he never betrayed a countersign, if an exception could be made of that overzealous sentinel who challenged a party with the words: "Who comes dar? Halt, an' gib de countersign, *Charleston*."

By his motivation and by his aptitude for soldiering the Negro volunteer was ready for the trial by battle — ready, as he soon proved, to pay "the last full measure of devotion."

NURSE CLARA BARTON: "*Ah, Sam, that's bad for you.*"
PRIVATE SAM: "*Yes, miss, I knows it. I'm a gwine, but thank God my childers free.*"

CHAPTER X

Anselmas Reports to God

COLOR-GUARD, protect, defend, die for, but do not surrender these flags."

Flag Sergeant Anselmas Planciancois stepped forward and took a firm grip on the unfurled banners: "Colonel, I will bring these colors to you in honor or report to God the reason why."

Cheers broke out from Planciancois's regimental comrades, a stalwart, heavy-chested set of fellows who dressed into line magnificently. The men of the First Louisiana Native Guards were in high spirits, having just learned that they were soon to see action. They were an outfit suited for military service. "As far as the privates are concerned, a more decent, orderly, obedient and soldierly set I never saw," wrote the New Orleans correspondent of the New York *Times*, in February 1863, "while as regards the officers, had I come in contact with the same number of white men, taken at random, I could not have expected to find more general intelligence, education and refinement."

The First Louisiana had spent months camping in the mud, first at Algiers and then at Baton Rouge. Since the day of mustering in, all their assignments had been drudgery — building forts and repairing bridges — and the nearest they had come to military action was rubbing the barrels of their guns. This had been somewhat galling since many of the regiment's volunteers were New Orleans "f. m. c.'s" of wealth and culture. Now at last they had been

ordered to a scene of impending action, Port Hudson, a Confederate-held stronghold nearly thirty miles above Baton Rouge on
the left bank of a sudden bend in the river.

Port Hudson in the spring of 1863 was the last remaining Rebel
fortification on the Lower Mississippi. The river above and below
was controlled by Union gunboats, but unconquered Port Hudson
still stood to point a threatening, death-charged finger at any
Yankee vessel that ran by its batteries, day or night. If Port
Hudson fell, Vicksburg, two hundred miles up the river, would
fall, thus "redeeming" the Mississippi and cutting the Confederacy
in two. General N. P. Banks, commanding in the Department of
the Gulf, was ordered to reduce Port Hudson in co-operation
with General Grant's operations against Vicksburg.

Assaulting Port Hudson was no holiday task. Built by slave
labor, that formidable work presented a strong profile along its
entire length of line stretching over three miles. Its face to the
Mississippi River was an eighty foot bluff. Its semicircle of abatis
— felled trees with the branches sharpened and turned toward the
enemy — was buttressed by a series of rifle pits and outworks. Its
parapets averaged twenty feet in thickness, and below the parapets was a fifteen-foot ditch. The Port mounted twenty siege guns
and thirty pieces of field artillery, and its rear grounds afforded
first-rate facilities for the prompt shifting of troops from one
point to another. On May 25 the Confederates retired into this
stronghold, having been compelled to contract their outer lines.
The time had come.

On the early morning of May 27, the air already sultry and
the heat oppressive, the Union artillery opened up a brisk can-
nonade against Port Hudson, preparatory to the assault. "About
half an hour by the sun this morning," reported Rebel officer,
W. R. Miller, "the enemy opened up an infernal fire on our lines."
The Union strategy was to subject the stronghold to four hours
of bombardment and then to rush in simultaneously all along
the line.

On the extreme right facing two forts, Banks had placed the Native Guards. Numbering 1080,. they formed into four lines. At ten o'clock the bugle sounded, followed by the sharp command, "Charge!" The response of the troops was described by the well-known contemporary poet, George H. Boker:

> "Now," the flag-sergeant cried,
> "Though death and hell betide,
> Let the whole nation see
> If we are fit to be
> Free in this land; or bound
> Down, like the whining hound —
> Bound with red stripes of pain
> In our old chains again!"
> Oh! what a shout there went
> From the black regiment!

Unaffected by all the talk of the Negro's lack of soldierly qualities, which they had heard since the first hour of their enlistments, the two black regiments moved forward in quick time and with spirit and dash, entering the woods in their immediate front. The terrain over the half mile from their camp to the works of the enemy was pockmarked with gullies and ravines, strewn with felled trees, and interlaced with entangled brushwood like an obstacle race.

The Rebels were ready for the stormers. "We are laying in our rifle-pits, awaiting the hated foe," wrote John A. Kennedy of Company H, First Alabama, in his diary. "If they come in sight they will catch it, shure as two and two makes four."

As the assaulting soldiers emerged from the wooded area and started their charge up to the works in full face of the batteries, the Rebels opened up with everything — grape, canister, shell and musketry. Sheets of flame flashed along the forts as the Negro soldiers reeled from the direct fire upon them from the front and an enfilading, raking cross fire along their length, spewn from a six-gun battery on the left and a redoubt of six pieces of artillery on the right.

Men spun and fell before the deadly hail, their last cries hushed and unheard in the roaring thunder of the enemy artillery. Their comrades, many of whom had never smelled powder before, charged into the storm of bullets, moving with fixed purpose toward the string of Rebel batteries lined up against the high bluff.

"Steady men, steady," said Captain André Cailloux of Company E, First Native Guards, his dark skin actually a bit ashen from the sulphurous smoke. A prominent Catholic layman of wealth and attainment who liked to boast that he was "the blackest man in America," Cailloux had received his civil and military education in Paris. The idol of his men, he moved along the line speaking words of encouragement, now in French and now in English. His company, the color company, was an especial target for Rebel sharpshooters. Cailloux's left arm was shattered, but he refused to leave the field. Just as he reached the flooded ditch, he shouted, "Follow me," his last words. A second later a shell hit him and he fell with his body facing forwards to the foe.

His followers were halted by the ditch, eight feet deep and twenty feet wide. Their losses already severe, there was no alternative except to retire. They had expected to engage the Rebels but had met the backflow of the river. As they withdrew, they were severely cut up.

The shattered columns wheeled to the rear and re-formed. A second time on the double quick they rushed square up to the edge of the ditch, some fifty yards from the enemy guns. Easy targets, they could scarcely hope to cross or ford the gully. "Yet," wrote eyewitness John A. Foster, colonel of the One Hundred Seventy-fifth New York Volunteers, "they made several efforts to swim and cross it, preparatory to an assault on the enemy's works, and this, too, in fair view of the enemy, and at short musket range." A score of volunteers from Companies E and G, Third Native Guards, recklessly plunged into the water, holding their rifles and cartridge boxes above their heads. They would never answer roll call again.

At the field hospital many of the black soldiers whose wounds were slight, asked that their cuts and bruises be dressed as soon as possible, so that they might rejoin their comrades. One soldier returning to the front limping painfully was halted and asked where he was going. His explanation was revealing: "I am shot bad in de leg, and dey want me to go to the hospital, but I guess I can give 'em a little more yet." The surgeon in charge over the two regiments, J. T. Paine, a busy man on that day of carnage, wrote that he had "seen all kinds of soldiers, yet I have never seen any who, for courage and unflinching bravery, surpass our colored."

Yet the second assault, like the first, was repulsed. Almost incredibly, during these two operations the center and the left wings of the Union forces had failed to mount their offensives. Their four-hour delay in attacking meant that from ten in the morning until two in the afternoon, the right had borne the complete burden of the battle and thus had received the undivided attention of the Rebel guns. However, even under the combined attack of the three wings, it would not have been easy to take an elaborate and skillfully planned work like Port Hudson. Hurling against it masses of men, no matter how gallant, was not a good answer. Indeed, the combined land assaults probably did less damage to the Confederates than did the Union fleet of six vessels — the sloop of war *Hartford* and the gunboat *Albatross* above the stronghold, and the sloops of war *Monongahela* and *Richmond*, the gunboat *Genesee* and the ironclad *Essex* below — whose total of eighty-six guns rained shot and shell into the Rebel fortification.

But Brigadier General William F. Dwight needed one final illustration before he would learn the lesson. He sent word by an aide: "Tell Colonel Nelson that I shall consider that he has accomplished nothing unless he takes those guns."

For the third time the Negro regiments dressed into line, their ranks now thinned. Again they charged and again they were greeted with volleys of musketry. Falling treetops, severed by Rebel shells, crashed down on the advancing blacks. On they went, vainly attempting to ignore the tempest of rifle bullets and the iron shower of grape and round shot.

Anselmas Planciancois was bearing the flag in front of the enemy's works when the top of his head was lifted off by a six-pounder. As he fell, still clutching the banner, a struggle ensued between the two color-corporals, each wishing to have the honor of bearing the blood-bespattered flag. The issue was settled only after one had been seriously injured in the set-to. The victorious bearer did not enjoy his triumph long — he was soon picked off. Indeed, the honor of that flag cost the lives of six men.

With a final desperate charge the black soldiers rushed forward and again reached a point only fifty yards from the Rebel batteries. So vigorous was their forward thrust, that a newspaper reporter covering the battle, expressed a belief that "if only ordinarily supported by artillery and reserve, no one can convince us that they would not have opened a passage through the enemy's works." But the Rebel defenders emptied their rifles, cannon and mortars upon the heads of their colored adversaries. Severe fighting continued on the right part of the line until four o'clock in the afternoon, but Port Hudson was not to be taken that day. Finally came the inevitable order to retreat, and the Negro troops "marched off as if on parade."

As a military operation the assault was entirely unsuccessful. Yet the behavior of the black regiments was one bright spot. Their conduct had been under especial scrutiny since Port Hudson was the first real battle in which Negro soldiers were engaged. Had they flinched under fire, the future of the Negro soldier would have been jeopardized. But they had not flinched. "No body of troops — Western, Eastern or rebel — have fought better in the war," editorialized the New York *Times* on June 13, 1863.

General Banks in his report to H. W. Halleck reflected the attitude of all officers who commanded on the right:

> The position occupied by these troops was one of importance, and called for the utmost steadiness and bravery . . . It gives me pleasure to report that they answered every expectation. No troops could be more determined or more daring . . . The history of this day proves conclusively that the Government will find in this class of troops effective supporters and defenders.

The casualties sustained by the colored regiments gave evidence of their role. They suffered 37 killed, 155 wounded and 116 missing. Comprising one twelfth of the Union troops engaged, they bore one-eighth of the loss in numbers killed, one tenth in wounded and three fourths in missing.

❧

Ten days after the assault on Port Hudson, another engagement, further up the river, took place which became famous for the conduct of Negro troops. The scene of this encounter was a small Louisiana town, Milliken's Bend, about twenty miles upstream from Vicksburg. The latter, a Confederate stronghold crowning a great bluff, lay under a siege conducted by Ulysses S. Grant. Needing to summon his total strength in order to invest the well-defended Mississippi city, Grant had stripped to the bone the forts higher up the river. One of these was Milliken's Bend.

Lying immediately below the town of that name, Milliken's Bend was a Union camp fifteen feet above the right bank of the Mississippi. The camp, 150 yards wide, was sheltered by two levees, one on its river face and the other on its land side. In front of the forward levee the fort was protected by a thick Osage orange hedge averaging fifteen feet in height. To the right and to the left were open fields, trailing off in each direction into densely wooded areas. On its rear flanks the fort could be protected by supporting gunboats.

In the late spring of 1863, Milliken's Bend had been left with a detachment of 1410 men, of whom 160 were whites, the Twenty-third Iowa, and the remainder were ex-slaves from Louisiana and Mississippi, organized into three incomplete regiments, the Ninth Louisiana, the Eleventh Louisiana and the First Mississippi. These 1250 contrabands had been mustered in at Milliken's Bend on May 22, 1863, according to Lieutenant Colonel Cyrus Sears, one of their officers. The black volunteers were destined to go into battle exactly sixteen days later.

Early in June the Confederates decided to launch an assault on Milliken's Bend, an attack destined to be their most serious threat from the west during the siege of Vicksburg. The Rebels knew that the fort's defenses had been thinned. With Milliken's Bend taken, weakly guarded Young's Point, eleven miles below, would certainly fall, and thus Confederate General J. C. Pemberton's forces at Vicksburg would be covered if he found it necessary to move them out of the city and across the river.

On the night of June 6, four Rebel regiments of Texans — three infantry and one cavalry — left Richmond, Louisiana, for Milliken's Bend, ten miles to the northeast. Marching at night to escape the sun's strong rays, Brigadier General Henry E. McCulloch planned an attack before dawn in order to lessen the amount of assistance the fort's defenders could receive from the gunboats. The Confederates hoped to have driven the Union soldiers into the river by 8 A.M.

On Sunday morning at 2:30 A.M., when they were within a mile and a half of the fort, the Texas regiments encountered the Union pickets. The Rebel skirmishers pressed forward, driving the enemy pickets in front of them. Half an hour after the pickets were driven in, the Confederates appeared in force, marching on the left in close column. Their advance was slowed up by black skirmishers, whom they drove back, hedge by hedge, over ground made rough by running briars and tie-vines.

Finally the Confederates reached the open spaces between the two levees. Within twenty-five paces of the river levee, they charged with a shout on their lips, "No quarter."

The Union troops had been deployed along the rifle pits: on the extreme left the Ninth Louisiana had been stationed; in the center the First Mississippi, and on the right the Eleventh Louisiana. They had been ordered to withhold their fire until the enemy was within musket-shot range. As the Rebels ran forward along the open ground, the air was suddenly pierced with volleys of shot from the fort. The Confederate line wavered and recoiled.

But the Texans rallied and came on, charging the breastworks in close-order ranks. The Negro soldiers had trouble reloading their faultily constructed guns. One black regiment was inexperienced in handling the guns, having just received them the previous day. Nevertheless, as Confederate General McCulloch observed, "This charge was resisted by the Negro portion of the enemy's force with considerable obstinacy."

Rushing upon and over the entrenchments and flanking the fort, the Rebels closed in on the defenders of Milliken's Bend. Thereupon ensued a bloody hand-to-hand fight which ranked as one of the most bitter knock-down-and-drag-out struggles during the course of a war famous for its hard-fought actions. It was a contest between enraged men fighting with bayonets and musket butts. Both sides freely used the bayonet — a rare occurrence in warfare, as General Lorenzo Thomas observed in commenting on the battle, since usually "one of the party gives up before coming in contact with steel." In one instance two men lay side by side, each having the other's bayonet in his body. A new recruit to whom young Captain Matthew M. Miller of Company I, Ninth Louisiana, had issued a gun the day before was "found dead with a firm grasp on his gun, the bayonet of which was broken in three places." A teen-age cook, who had begged for a gun when the enemy was seen approaching, was badly wounded with one gunshot and two bayonet wounds. In one Negro company there were six broken bayonets.

The scathing ordeal continued all during the morning, each man on his own hook. Until the hour of high noon the rival infantrymen contested the field, in the longest bayonet-charge engagement of the war. Broken limbs and mangled bodies were strewn in profusion along the breastworks. Confederate General McCulloch reported that of the wounds received by his men, "More are severe and fewer slight than I have ever witnessed among the same number in my former military experience."

At twelve o'clock the tide turned with the arrival of the Federal warship *Choctaw*, rushed down from Helena by Acting Rear Admiral David D. Porter. Saving the day for the men in blue, the *Choctaw* immediately opened on the enemy, dropping shells in their midst. Undoubtedly, the warship's guns killed a few Union soldiers, but a half dozen well-placed shells on the Rebels' right hastened their decision to withdraw. Moreover the Confederate soldiers had now become exhausted by the 95 degree in the shade temperature and the serious lack of drinking water.

As the Texas regiments retreated, the Union soldiers, encouraged by the turn of events, followed after them across the open field. The pursuit ceased as the Rebels crossed the outer confines of the fort. Before the retreat had been completed, one Negro took his former master a prisoner "and brought him into camp with great gusto."

That afternoon Admiral Porter arrived in his flagship, *Black Hawk*, having pulled up anchor the moment he heard of the assault. What he saw at Milliken's Bend he described in a letter to U. S. Grant:

> The dead Negroes lined the ditch inside of the parapet or levee and were mostly shot on the top of the head. In front of them, close to the levee, lay an equal number of rebels, stinking in the sun.

A day later another correspondent of Grant's, Captain A. E. Strickle, sent word from Milliken's Bend: "The capacity of the Negro to defend his liberty, and his susceptibility to appreciate

the power of motives . . . have been put to such a test under
our observation as to be beyond further doubt." Brigadier General Elias S. Dennis, commanding the District of Northeast Louisiana, voiced a similar opinion: "It is impossible for men to show
greater bravery than the Negro troops in that fight." Colonel
Herman Lieb, who commanded the Ninth Louisiana, and whose
military experience extended to Continental battlefields, bore cor-
roborative testimony: "There is no better material for soldiers
than they."

If the record of casualties is the best gauge of severe and gallant
action, the black soldiers truly distinguished themselves on that
sweltering June morning. Thirty-nine per cent of them were killed
or wounded. Out of a regimental total of 285, the Ninth Louisiana
sustained 66 killed and 62 mortally wounded. This was 45 per cent
of its strength, the highest per cent in killed and wounded suffered
by any unit in a single engagement during the course of the war.

Milliken's Bend was thus one of the hardest fought encounters
in the annals of American military history. Its lesson was not lost
on the Union high brass: "The bravery of the blacks at Milliken's
Bend," observed Assistant Secretary of War Charles A. Dana,
"completely revolutionized the sentiment of the army with regard
to the employment of Negro troops."

This change in army sentiment produced by Port Hudson,
Milliken's Bend and Battery Wagner did not escape the watchful
eye of Abraham Lincoln. Late in August 1863 he sent a message
to James C. Conkling for the latter to present at a mass meeting
of "unconditional Union men" scheduled for Springfield, Illinois.
"Read it very slowly," cautioned Lincoln:

> I know as fully as one can know the opinions of others,
> that some of the commanders of our armies in the field,
> who have given us our most important successes, believe that
> the emancipation policy and the use of colored troops con-
> stitute the heaviest blow yet dealt to the rebellion, and
> that at least one of these important successes could not have

been achieved when it was but for the aid of black soldiers. Among the commanders holding these views are some who never had any affinity with what is called Abolitionism, or with Republican party politics, but who hold them purely as military opinions.

✦

Not every Negro who smelled smoke on the battlefield and who served within the lines was a male. From the headquarters of Lieutenant Colonel George S. Hollister, commanding the Sixteenth New York Cavalry encamped at Vienna, Virginia, came an authorization, dated February 27, 1864, to his adjutant to issue to a contraband woman a written permission to go and come:

Guards and Patrols
    Will you pass Lucy Carter, Colored, through the lines of the 16th Regiment New York Cavalry at pleasure until further Orders.

Of the Negro women receiving passes to go within the lines, by far the most notable was Harriet Tubman, the fabulous underground railroad operator of the antebellum years. The permits issued to this ex-slave bore the signatures of top military officials. "Pass the bearer, Harriet Tubman . . . wherever she wishes to go; and give her free passage, at all times, on all government transports," ordered Major General David Hunter, commanding in the Department of the South, in a written statement issued from Hilton Head on February 19, 1863. Three weeks after relieving Hunter, Brigadier General Quincy A. Gillmore affixed his signature to the same pass, adding, "Continued in force, July 1, 1863." On March 20, 1865, Secretary Stanton ordered Brevet Brigadier General S. Van Vliet, stationed in New York, to "pass Mrs. Harriet Tubman (colored) to Hilton Head and Charleston, S. C., with free transportation on a Government transport."

Harriet's work as a nurse and as a scout merited this attention.

For nearly two years she gave her services in the badly under-staffed hospitals in the Sea Islands. Orthodox medical men did not fully share her enthusiasm for roots and herbs remedies, although they were much less skeptical about her prescriptions in liquid form, judging by an order from Acting Assistant Surgeon Henry K. Durrant: "Will Captain Warfield please let 'Moses' have a little Bourbon whiskey for medicinal purposes."

In caring for the sick and wounded, Mrs. Tubman's influence was unique. Coming with a reputation as "the Moses of her people," and as one whom John Brown had dubbed "General," she was believed to possess great powers of healing. Many a soldier tossing with fever in a stifling hospital tent felt better when he saw her coming through the opening. Durrant, who had observed her over a two-year period as she moved among the bedridden, white and colored, wrote a "To-Whom-It-May-Concern," dated May 3, 1864, commending her for "kindness and attention to the sick and suffering."

As a scout, Mrs. Tubman's deceptive appearance was a great asset. Who would have thought that this short, gnarled black woman with a bandanna wrapped around her head was engaged in such a bold venture as entering Rebel-held territory for the purposes of urging slaves to take to their heels, appraising military and naval defenses, and taking in with a knowing eye the location and quantity of supplies, provisions and livestock? Rufus Saxton, Brigadier General of Volunteers, recorded that she "made many a raid inside the enemy's lines, displaying remarkable courage, zeal and fidelity."

Many of Mrs. Tubman's excursions into enemy territory were made in company with soldier details from Colonel James Mont-gomery's Negro brigade, the Second South Carolina Volunteers. A former Kansas associate of John Brown, Montgomery was one of the war's ablest guerrillas and foragers. Of unparalleled au-dacity, he reveled in upcountry raids — the St. John's and the Combahee especially — appearing unexpectedly before a small settlement, seizing its foodstuffs and supplies, freeing its slaves, and sometimes burning its buildings.

Montgomery used the former underground railroad operator both as a scout and as a liaison between the military officers and the slaves in the raided regions. The elderly, inoffensive-looking Negro woman could quickly win the confidence of frightened slaves, quieting the fears of any who remembered the stories their masters had spread concerning the deviltry of the Yankees. "I wish," wrote Montgomery to General Gillmore, on July 6, 1863, after one of these raids, "to commend to your attention Mrs. Harriet Tubman, a most remarkable woman, and invaluable as a scout."

Another colored woman who served the Union cause in the Sea Islands was Susie King Taylor, young wife of a noncommissioned officer in Company E of the First South Carolina Volunteers, later the Thirty-third United States Colored Infantry. Slender, dark-skinned, with a friendly countenance and sympathetic eyes, Mrs. Taylor was enrolled as company laundress, but of her own volition she also acted as teacher and nurse.

Her ability to handle the written word proved a great asset in serving the soldiers. As a girl in Savannah, she had learned to read and write by going to the house of a friend with her "books wrapped in paper to prevent the police or white persons from seeing them." Mrs. Taylor took charge of the Company E mail pouch, reading letters to illiterate recipients and writing and dispatching their replies. She conducted informal instruction for those who wished to learn the mysteries of the alphabet.

As a volunteer nurse, Mrs. Taylor's efforts were welcomed by medical officers. A resourceful woman, when she was unable, on one occasion, to get soup for the convalescent, she materialized as from a void some turtle eggs and a few cans of condensed milk and made a custard. Her patients were grateful at being spared the unvarying hospital menu of dip toast, meat cooked dry and tea without milk.

At Beaufort during the summer of 1863 young Susie met Clara Barton, foremost of the war's "angels of mercy," and later the moving spirit in the founding of the American Red Cross. Oftentimes as Miss Barton made the rounds in the hospital during her eight months in the Sea Islands, she was accompanied by the colored volunteer nurse, whom she treated with cordiality. As Miss Barton moved from bed to bed, her companion took note of her solicitude for the Negro soldiers: "I honored her," wrote Mrs. Taylor, "for her devotion and care of these men."

As described in the pages of her *Reminiscences of My Life in Camp*, Mrs. Taylor's varied experiences included contact with enemy sentinels. When Company E was on picket duty at the Barnwell Plantation on Port Royal, the young laundress would frequently stroll along the picket line, where she could detect the boys in gray on the opposite side of the river: "Sometimes as they were changing pickets they would call over to our men and ask for something to eat, or for tobacco, and our men would tell them to come over."

Another Negro woman who knew her way around an army camp was Sojourner Truth. This legendary character confined her visits to camps in the North, particularly those in Michigan — she was perhaps a bit too old to go to camps located in the South (she admitted to being over seventy, although she indignantly denied the widespread rumor that she had nursed George Washington). As a rule whenever she showed up in camp, the regiment would be ordered into line, and she would display the boxes of gifts she had solicited. Then she would distribute the contents, interspersing bits of motherly advice.

She raised money for these gifts by lecturing and singing. One of the numbers in her fund-raising repertoire was of her own composition. Written to the John Brown tune and entitled, "The Valiant Soldier," its flavor may be sampled by one of its six stanzas:

We are done with hoeing cotton, we are done with hoeing
    corn;
We are colored Yankee soldiers, as sure as you are born.
When Massa hears us shouting, he will think 'tis Gabriel's
    horn,
    As we go marching on.

For her services in the Union cause, one of Sojourner's admirers in Wisconsin hymned her praises:

> The world grows just at last, for who like thou
> E'er wore an aureole on a living brow?

❖

While the Negro soldier was proving his mettle, the Negro
sailor was going unobtrusively ahead in his service to the country.
Throughout its history, the navy had never barred free Negroes
from enlisting, and in September 1861 it had adopted the policy
of signing up former slaves. Suffering during the entire course
of the war from a shortage of men, the navy encouraged the
blacks to join the service. "Fill up the crews with contrabands
obtained from Major-General Dix, as there is not an available
sailor North," was the advice sent by Secretary Welles on August
5, 1862, to Commodore Charles Wilkes, commanding the James
River Flotilla. "Don't be astonished at the lists of niggers I send
you," wrote Admiral Porter to Rear Admiral A. H. Foote, on
January 3, 1863, "I could get no men. They do first-rate." Five
months later Rear Admiral S. F. Du Pont informed Welles that
the contrabands on board the vessels in the South Atlantic Blockading Squadron were "very useful, particularly as there is difficulty in obtaining men in the North ports."

Anxious to attract black recruits and to have them re-enlist
when their terms expired, the navy tended to treat them fairly
well. Segregation and discrimination were at a minimum. Negroes
were messed and quartered with other crew members; it might

have been impractical, of course, to have adopted a Jim Crow policy within the close confines of the crew quarters of the average warship. In prisoner exchange the Negro sailor was spared the uncertainty experienced by his black brother in the army: "No question of color has ever come up in regard to naval exchange," wrote Secretary Welles in his diary on October 5, 1864.

The Negroes responded in goodly numbers to the navy's beckoning, eventually comprising one quarter of the men sailing the Union fleet. Although precise figures on colored naval personnel are lacking, Secretary of the Navy John D. Long, in a letter written on April 2, 1902, quotes the Superintendent of the Naval War Records Office as reporting that of the 118,044 enlistments in the navy during the Civil War, one fourth, or 29,511, was Negro. This estimate was found to be remarkably accurate in a spot check made by Herbert Aptheker, a contemporary student of the Negro in the Union Navy, who examined the muster rolls of three Federal vessels, *New Hampshire*, *Argosy* and *Avenger*, and found that of their total crews of 1150, the Negro sailors numbered 296, or 26 per cent. A check by the same scholar on the rolls of additional Union warships revealed not a single one without Negro crewmen.

A few Union vessels were manned by a predominantly colored personnel. The gunboat *Glide*, accidentally burned at Cairo, Illinois, in February 1863, had a crew of eight whites and thirty contrabands. When *Stepping Stones*, a paddle wheeler of light draft attached to the Potomac Flotilla, conducted operations in Mattox Creek, Virginia, in March 1865, only two of her crew of thirty were white, the ensign and the master's mate.

Below the officer level, Negroes could be found in all ranks. On board a typical ship the gamut of positions discharged by blacks was wide. Herbert Aptheker's tabulation of the colored crewmen of eight Union vessels showed that, of a total of 364, there were 279 landsmen, 44 boys, 18 coal heavers, 7 seamen, 5 stewards, 5 ordinary seamen, 4 cooks, 1 first-class fireman and

1 second-class fireman. This was a cross section of the general proportion of these ratings in the navy as a whole. When the daring Confederate raider *Alabama* steamed out of the Cherbourg harbor on a Sunday morning to meet its doom in an engagement with the *Kearsarge*, there were fifteen Negro enlisted men of various ratings serving on the Union gunboat. They included 8 landsmen, 2 coal heavers, 1 seaman, 1 ordinary seaman, 1 officers' cook, 1 captain's cook and 1 captain's steward.

In this historic duel in which the famed *Alabama* went down in forty fathoms of water, Joachim Pease, a colored crewman of the Union gunboat, won a navy Medal of Honor. For his services as "loader of the No. 1 gun" when the *Kearsarge* gave tongue, Pease was cited by his superior officer, Acting Master David H. Sumner, as possessing qualities even higher than courage or fortitude. Sumner did not name these qualities, but according to his official report, Pease's conduct during the combat "fully sustained his reputation as one of the best men on the ship."

For their outstanding gallantry three other Negroes won the coveted navy medal. Ex-slave Robert Blake distinguished himself while serving as a powder boy on board the U.S.S. *Marblehead* in an engagement with the Confederates in the Stono River, off Legaréville, South Carolina, on December 25, 1863. The commander of the *Marblehead*, Richard W. Meade, Jr., reported that Blake "excited my admiration by the cool and brave manner in which he served the rifle gun." The action of the Union warship on that Christmas day caused the Confederates to abandon their island position, leaving a caisson behind.

John Lawson, colored landsman of the gunboat *Hartford*, won the star-shaped medal of bronze for his bravery at the battle of Mobile Bay on August 5, 1864, during the successful triple-pronged attack against Fort Morgan, the ram *Tennessee* and the Rebel gunboats. Of the fleet of fourteen Union vessels that forced their way into the bay of Mobile on that midsummer day, the *Hartford* could expect her share of the enemy fire, for she was the flagship, and conspicuously stationed on her maintop was Rear Admiral David D. Farragut. Two days after the desperate encounter, Captain Percival Drayton officially informed Farragut of Lawson's conduct The captain reported that when an enemy shell exploded in the midst of the six-man crew at the shellwhip on the berth deck, Lawson had been severely wounded in the leg and thrown violently against the side of the ship. As soon as the Negro landsman had regained his composure, he had returned to his station, refusing to go below for treatment. He had remained at his post above deck until the badly crippled *Tennessee* had run up the white flag.

The last of the four Negroes to receive the navy Medal of Honor was Aaron Anderson, a landsman of the *Wyandank*. During a boat expedition on March 17, 1865, to clear the Mattox Creek, the colored crewman, according to the official citation, "carried out his duties courageously in face of a devastating fire which cut away half the oars, pierced the launch in many places and cut the barrel off a musket being fired at the enemy."

The navy had its roster of unsung blacks who discharged their duties effectively during battle action, but who did not do anything sufficiently spectacular to win official commendation. At least forty-nine Union vessels had Negro crewmen who were killed, captured or wounded in action. Colored naval casualties numbered an estimated 800, approximately one quarter of the navy total of 3220. To these battle casualties of 800 must be listed another estimated 2000 Negro seamen who died of disease.

While the Negro in uniform was reporting from battlefield and seacoast to a heroes' Valhalla, the Negro civilian was not neglectful of home-front responsibilities. He, too, was taking at the flood the tide in the affairs of his country.

*The efforts we are making to secure rights for the
colored men is also one to secure recognition of the
rights for the white men of this country.*

COLORED NATIONAL CONVENTION, SYRACUSE, 1864

CHAPTER XI

Home Front: Group Portrait in Sepia

THE FASHIONABLE Fifteenth Street Presbyterian Church was a
most appropriate setting for the "Grand Emancipation Celebration," held by Washington Negroes on April 16, 1863, one
year after Lincoln signed the bill freeing the slaves in the District
of Columbia. The beautiful interior of the church was conducive
to decorous worship: its seats were cushioned, its aisles carpeted,
its pews gold-lettered, its pulpit stand marble-topped and its
chandeliers ornate. Its well-trained choir heightened the mood of
exaltation. "Caucasians hurrying away from the jarring discords
of their own church-choirs," wrote a contemporary reporter,
"sometimes paused at the door to hear the rich swell and fine
harmonies of Grant's choir or the delicate grace of Boston's
voluntaries." The congregation was well dressed; no finer bonnets
could be seen in the city.

The celebration program had been arranged by a committee of
three, two of whom worked in the White House and hence
represented the cream of Washington colored society: the styl-
ishly beautiful Elizabeth Keckley, dressmaker to Mrs. Lincoln
and President of the Ladies' Contraband Relief Association, and
William Slade, White House butler and confidential messenger,
a man of medium height with straight chestnut-colored hair and

a little goatee. With John F. Cook presiding, the meeting began at ten in the morning.

The committee had engaged six speakers (the seats were cushioned, but colored audiences were inured to lengthy meetings — sometimes a presiding officer at a Negro gathering would unconsciously select as the closing number the popular spiritual, "I been a lis'nin' all de night, been a lis'nin' all de day"). All of the addresses were models in delivery and composition — during the entire evening few sentences were uttered which would have offended the ear of a purist. A white newspaperman reported that the only questionable English usage he found was "the scarcely defensible figure" pictured by one speaker, "of representing slavery as a 'dragon, scattering lava throughout the land.' "

One of the speakers, William E. Matthews, urged his fellow Negroes to celebrate the birthdays of their great men — "the birthday of Hannibal, who crossed the Alps, and compelled the Romans to cringe at his feet (applause), of Toussaint L'Ouverture, who worked successfully the greater than mathematical problem, that they who would be free must themselves strike the first blow, and Benjamin Banneker, the Negro astronomer, who first gave an almanac to Maryland, Virginia, and the District."

The poet, J. Willis Menard, delivered a talk prior to the reading of the verses he had composed for the occasion. Menard was a clerk in the department of immigration, the first Negro to hold a white-collar job in the national government, and was later to be prominent in reconstruction affairs in New Orleans. He remarked that he was happy to note the presence of the newly commissioned A. T. Augusta, sporting the glittering gold-leaf epaulettes of a major. The speaker added that he would cease to be an advocate of emigration if he could only see a major general's epaulettes on a black man. Menard then read his poem, "One Year Ago Today," dedicated to the emancipated slaves of the District. The burden of the five stanzas ran thus:

Almighty God! we praise thy name
For having heard us pray;
For having freed us from our chains,
One year ago today.

The celebration concluded with musical numbers, including "Viva l'America," and "John Brown's Body," sung by the audience.

The tone of the celebration was congratulatory and optimistic, and indeed the colored people had much for which to be thankful. But throughout the North during the middle of the war the position of the Negro was still hazardous. The full extent of his exposure was given its most dramatic expression in the famous New York riots of July 1863, the bloodiest race riots in the annals of American social pathology. Like many such explosive outbursts, the riots were a demonstration of the fear and resentment engendered by the upward climb of the Negro.

By the middle of 1863 the fear of the competition of the black laborer had grown into an obsession. White workingmen in the North were apprehensive about an influx of Negroes, or foreigners, "who would fill the shops, yards and other places of labor, and by that means compel us to compete with them for the support of our families." The belief was widespread that if the slaves were liberated they would overrun the North. "Free the slaves," screamed the Boston *Post*, "and your poor-houses will be filled with them."

There was actually little likelihood of such an overflowing immigration. The Southern Negro was predominantly rural agricultural rather than urban industrial. Moreover, he loved his native surroundings. When General Hunter was commanding the Department of the South he never refused a Negro a pass to go to the North, but "not more than a dozen applications have been made since our occupation began," wrote Charles Nordhoff in March 1863. "Once let liberty be established at the South," intoned Henry Ward Beecher from his Plymouth church pulpit, "and the North will be whiter than ever."

Although the white workingman's fear of a mass migration of plantation blacks was imaginary, there was no question about the dread prospect of the Northern Negro as a labor competitor. For despite manpower shortages, due to army enlistments and to the war-created industrial boom, wage increases tended to lag behind price rises. Therefore the white laborer felt compelled to use his most powerful weapon — the strike. But this technique would be far less potent if the owners of factories and ships had a reserve pool of black brawn to draw upon. And with strikes more frequent, the use of colored strikebreakers mounted.

Particularly was this the case along the waterfront. Stevedoring was a casual and oversupplied occupation and its Irish personnel, who virtually monopolized the work, were incensed by any competition from Negroes, no matter how small. When in March 1863 the longshoremen working on the North River piers of the Erie Railroad Company struck for $1.50 a day, and the longshoremen of the Hudson River Railroad struck for a like amount, both blamed the failure to win wage increases on their black replacements. Similar unsuccessful strikes in Boston, Brooklyn, Albany, Buffalo, Cleveland, Detroit and Chicago were attributed to Negro strikebreakers.

In vain might Negro spokesmen point out that before the influx of the sons of Erin in the late 'forties, colored men and women had furnished practically all of the unskilled and domestic service labor. These black workers had been driven out by the willingness of the freshly arrived immigrants to take jobs at whatever wage they could get. In vain might a Negro editor raise the questions: "Who has a better right to find work in this country than he who was born in this country? Who has a fairer claim to keep clear of the almshouse than he who from childhood has considered the almshouse a disgrace?" In their bitter struggle for jobs with the wearers of the green, Negroes took little comfort in remembering that the great Irish patriot Daniel O'Connell had summoned his matchless oratory in the service of the American slave, and that the sympathies of Irish nationalists like Robert Emmet and Henry Grattan had extended to the downtrodden blacks across the water.

In their efforts to reduce Negro competition the white workers resorted to all-white Unions. An everyday experience among Negroes was the story, as reported by the New York *Times*, of a Negro cooper who made the rounds of several barrel-making factories and at each employment window received the same answer: "Yes, I have work; I would like to employ you; but my journeymen would all leave me if I did, and I cannot."

Violence was an instrument often used to reduce Negro labor competition. In July 1862 when Cincinnati Negroes were hired as stevedores on boats plying the Ohio River waters, the Negro section of the city was invaded and homes set afire. After the Negroes retaliated and put the torch to several dwellings in the Irish quarter, Mayor George Hatch issued a public notice proclaiming that a posse of one hundred men stood ready to assist the police in keeping the peace.

In Brooklyn four weeks later a stone-throwing, brickbat-hurling mob smashed its way into Watson's tobacco factory, which employed some twenty-five Negroes. Hastening to an upper floor, the colored workers bolted the doors and barricaded themselves. The assaulting party then attempted to set the building on fire, but this attempt was thwarted by the arrival of the police, who caught the blaze within a few minutes after it had been started. The New York *Times* for August 5 urged editorially that the Catholic clergy encourage the members of their parishes to live in amity and good will, adding that "no class of persons were more quiet, orderly, peaceful, respectful, and even courteous, than the colored people."

The pattern of violence was displayed in other Northern centers — Chicago, Detroit, Cleveland, Albany and Boston. "In Harrisburg it is dangerous for colored people to walk the street after night" — ran a letter by Jacob C. White, addressed from Philadelphia on August 19, 1862, to his cousin, Joseph C. Bustill — "and I have concluded that it is wise policy for Jacob to move around cautiously and to go home early." A week before the New York riots, upstate Buffalo put on a dress rehearsal. When the shippers of the city put Negroes to work loading and unloading cargoes, the white longshoremen took direct action. Three Negroes were killed and twelve were severely beaten. "This, we fear, is but the beginning of the end," predicted *Fincher's Trades Review.*

The white workingman's mood to riot was strengthened by his opposition to the enforcement of the draft law. On March 3, 1863, Congress passed the first comprehensive conscription law in the country's history. Denounced as unconstitutional and despotic, the measure favored the rich since a drafted man could obtain release by paying $300. Many of the white workers who could not raise this sum were inflamed by "Copperhead" orators who, anxious to undermine the war effort, proclaimed that the white workingman was being made to shoulder a gun to free the slave who would soon become his rival for a job. On Sunday, July 12, the names of the drafted men for that city were printed in the New York papers. The fat was in the fire.

The next morning the enrollment office on Third Avenue and Forty-sixth Street, where the draft names had been drawn, was stormed by a mob. The police squad and the guard of invalided soldiers were powerless to prevent the wrecking of the lottery machine and the looting of the office. Another downtown draft headquarters was assaulted by a crowd armed with clubs and paving stones.

In the afternoon the mobs increased in numbers as the thousands of factory and shipyard workers joined in the looting of stores and the burning of warehouses. No saloon or dramshop escaped a raid on its bottled goods. Before long the rioters were grogged to the gills, their restraining inhibitions drowned in whiskey without a chaser. The furies now issued from the latent volcano which had lain dormant in the heart of the city.

Those policemen with whole skins abandoned the streets and the growing mobs pillaged and burned without hindrance. They smashed the windows of Horace Greeley's *Tribune* office and tore up the ground floor. Whoever got in their way was clubbed without mercy. A colored face was fair game: several Negroes were left dangling from lampposts and trees. "Small mobs are chasing isolated Negroes as hounds would chase a fox," wired Edward S. Sanford of the United States Military Telegraph Service to the Secretary of War.

The Reverend William Massie, in Gotham as the bearer of an antislavery petition signed by more than 4000 British clergymen to their American fellow pastors, learned something of the fear that gripped the Negro people. He had been scheduled for a speaking engagement that evening at Henry Highland Garnet's Shiloh church. When he reached the building, he found it in total darkness. After much knocking, he succeeded in getting the sexton. When Massie finally convinced the old man of his good intentions, he was conducted to Garnet's house, where earlier in the day Garnet's daughter had taken the precaution of removing the name plate from the door. Massie was ushered into the darkened parlor where Garnet and four friends, one of whom had barely escaped with his life, sat in tense and watchful silence, growing rigid every time a footfall seemed to approach the steps to the front door.

The evening was not far spent when the rioters began to light bonfires in the middle of the streets. "The city of New York is tonight at the mercy of a mob," wired Sanford to Stanton.

On the second day the ranks of the demonstrators were swelled by the criminal and gang element – the thieves, burglars, jailbirds, arsonists, hoodlums and thugs. The mobs' numbers were also increased by thousands of workingmen, their factory places of employment having been closed by order of the ringleaders of the rioters. Taking advantage of the absence of Federal troops, which had been sent to Pennsylvania to halt Lee's thrust at Gettysburg, the mobsters took up their unfinished business. The objection to the draft was no longer uppermost in their minds; they now seemed bent on sacking public buildings and private residences, plundering shops and stores and pursuing and punishing Negroes and their benefactors.

People who had employed Negroes could prepare for the worst. Houses where Negroes buttled or cooked were marked for a visit. Downtown restaurants and hotels that hired colored waiters, bellhops and maids could steel themselves for a calling upon, which would end only when the furniture was broken up and the linen and silverware carted off. One business firm, fearful that its property might be leveled to the ground by rioters who believed that it employed Negroes, sought to avert the wrath to come by hanging out a window-length sign: *No niggers in the rear.* The rioters remembered that the home of the Quaker abolitionists, James and Abby Hopper Gibbons, had been a station on the underground railroad; it was sacked and looted. A group of hoodlums seized Elizabeth Cady Stanton's young son Neil, who thereupon invited them to the nearest saloon for a drink. The tipsy group let Stanton go, unharmed. His mother was overjoyed, although she deplored her son's "departure from principle."

The outbreaks continued throughout the day, a pall of smoke settling on the city as the marauding bands danced and howled around the red flames of the burning buildings. The shouts of the crowds mingled with the bells ringing out the alarm of some new fire. The looting continued; Mayor George Opydyke's house suffered a common misfortune in being stripped of its furniture. Many plunderers, laden with spoils, hastened home to store their loot in cellar or attic.

The reign of terror continued during the next day. No street-cars were running, no peddler pushed his cart, no milkman came and no grocer's boy. There was no letup in the hunting down of Negroes. Many of them had gone down to the waterfront and crawled under the piers. The barns of farmers in Long Island and Morrisania were swarming with black refugees. Some fled to Blackwell's Island, hiding in the woods; others lost themselves in the swamps and groves bordering towns in nearby New Jersey.

Some Negroes stayed put, such as the eight athletic black women on Thompson Street. They had filled several boilers with a mixture of water, soap and ashes, a combination which when heated to the proper temperature they called "the King of Pain." As William Wells Brown entered the room he saw the huge, tin boilers which were steaming away on an old-fashioned cookstove, filling the room with a dense fog. Encircling the boilers was the octet of Amazons, armed with dippers.

"How will you manage if they attempt to come into this room?" asked Brown.

"We'll fling hot water on 'em, an' scall dar very harts out."

"Can you all throw water without injuring each other?"

"O yes, honey, we's been practicin' all day."

Two persons paid the penalty of their lives for being identified with Negroes — one was identified by virtue of his skin color and the other by virtue of her marriage. Peter Hueston, a Mohawk Indian who had served with the New York Volunteers in the Mexican War, was mistaken for a Negro by one of the marauding gangs. He was assaulted, beaten, and left senseless. Finally he was taken to Bellevue Hospital where he died of his injuries, leaving a parentless boy. The rioters made it a point to deal very severely with white women who had married across the color line. Anna Derickson, white wife of a Negro, was bruised and beaten with a cart rung while attempting to save the life of her son, whose clothes and hair had been saturated with camphene, preparatory to applying a match to him. Like Hueston, Mrs.

Derickson died from her injuries, leaving her son without father or mother.

No act of the rioters was more universally condemned than the sacking and burning of the home for colored orphans. This agency, the Colored Orphan Asylum and Association for the Benefit of Colored Children in the City of New York, had been founded by two young Quakers, Mary Murray and Anna H. Shotwell, who were shocked by the practice of placing destitute Negro children in the jails and poorhouses. In 1836 these two women, with Hetty King, went to the almshouse and brought away eleven youngsters. Three of them were tots unable to walk to the site of the new home. Ignoring the astonished gaping of pedestrians and street loafers, the three young women, their white skins in marked contrast with the brown babies in their arms, made their way along the sidewalk, trailed by eight straggling children of varied hues.

In 1843 the orphanage was able to expand its services by securing a fine site on Fifth Avenue, running the entire block between Forty-third and Forty-fourth streets. A large building of four stories, veiled in the summer with green foliage, it was directly on the line of travel, and the children could look out and see the fine carriages roll by. The school was supported mainly by public-spirited citizens, the colored women of New York raising $1464 in 1862 for its support. A small portion of the upkeep came from the fee of fifty cents a week which the surviving parent of a "half orphan" was asked to pay. The administrative staff served gratuitously, among them J. McCune Smith, the physician to the orphanage and the only Negro board member. The young inmates contributed something toward their own support, making their clothes and doing the "housework." Characteristic of the Quaker attitude toward life, the atmosphere of the school was informed by religious influences: after each evening meal the matron read from the Scriptures, and concluded with a "Lord, dismiss us with thy blessing."

On the first afternoon of the riots, as the 233 children were seated quietly in the schoolroom late in the afternoon, they heard a distant rumble. Like the poet Charles de Lay, listening at the University Towers, they may have speculated:

> Is it the wind, the many-tongued, the weird,
> That cries in sharp distress among the eaves?

But they were not long in doubt — it soon became evident that the rumble was the salutation of an oncoming mob. As the disorderly crowd drew nearer, the children could tell from the shouts and curses that the orphanage was in for it. The superintendent, William E. Davis, stepped outside; standing on the front steps he appealed to the howling throng, 2000 strong, to spare the building. But like many of the marauders, reason had taken a holiday. Hastening back into the building and bolting the door, the superintendent quickly rounded up the orphans and led them out of the building through a rear entrance rarely used.

The last child had just filed out when the mob, brushing aside the few policemen, stormed into the building, having employed the rather direct technique of laying an axe to the front door. They ransacked the building, carrying out into the street whatever they could lay their hands on — beds, bedding, carpets and kitchen utensils. Still unsatisfied, they decided to burn the building. Twice their efforts were thwarted by a squad of firemen headed by Chief John Decker, a powerfully built man. But with fires all over the city, the department's forces had been spread quite thin, and Decker had only a small detachment of ten firemen and two hoses. To quench the blazes from fires kindled at fifteen different parts of the building was an impossibility, and soon thick smoke and lurid tongues of flame were seen rising from the caved-in roof.

As the blazes roared and hissed, one little eight-year-old orphan broke out of line and dashed into the home. In a few moments she reappeared, bearing triumphantly, if a bit unsteadily, the heavy Bible from which the daily lesson had been read. This was the only article saved as the $80,000 building was laid level to the ground.

Some of the roofless children were taken to the Thirty-fourth Street police station, and others to the Seventh Avenue arsenal. Here they remained for three days, and were then taken to Blackwell's Island under an escort of twenty Zouaves with bayonets drawn and forty policemen.

By Thursday night, after four days of uproar, the mob spirit had subsided. From Washington word had come that the provost marshal general had ordered the draft suspended in New York. Moreover, four regiments of troops had arrived in the city, and Governor Seymour and Archbishop Hughes had made addresses appealing to the better nature of the populace. The businessmen had also met and organized "to take immediate action in the present crisis."

It was the businessmen who, three days after the rioting ended, organized the "Committee of Merchants for the Relief of Colored People Suffering from the Late Riots." At the first meeting on Monday, July 20, the committee raised $6500. "Those who know the colored people of this city," said Jonathan Sturges from the chair, "can testify to their being a peaceable, industrious people, having their own churches, Sunday schools and charitable societies, and that, as a class, they seldom depend upon charity; they not only labor to support themselves, but to aid those who need aid."

The merchants hired Vincent Colyer, who had worked with contrabands in North Carolina, as general agent, and ran advertisements in the papers, advising Negroes who were without food, or whose property had been lost, or whose breadwinner had disappeared, to report to the office established on Fourth Street to assist them. The committee asked employers not to discharge their colored workers. They also recruited a battery of lawyers who served two hours a day without fee. On behalf of their colored clients, these attorneys filed 1000 claims for damages against the city.

The hungry were furnished with small sums of cash. Those who claimed to need continuing relief were visited by a colored clergyman who determined the truth of their statements. Appointed by the committee, this panel of pastors — Henry Highland Garnet, Charles B. Ray, John Cary, Clinton Leonard, and John Peterson — made a total of 3090 visits over a period of four weeks.

The committee solicited gifts of clothing and donations of cash. Business firms were the largest subscribers to the relief fund, which eventually totaled $40,779.08, but many other groups and hundreds of individuals responded generously within their means. Group givers included Sunday school classes and church congregations: in New York City church groups of all denominations rallied to the support of the fund, and contributions came from out-of-state congregations, such as the First Congregational Church of Waterbury, Connecticut, which sent $47, and "the Colored Churches in Cincinnati, through Peter H. Clark," which raised $100. The waiters of the United States Hotel at Saratoga Springs made a $113 contribution, and the sum of $6.65 came from a group which described its modest offering as "Mites from Sundry Poor." Individual donors included "a one-armed soldier" ($1.00), "a sewing girl" ($3.00), and "A Lost Bet" ($5.00). In a spontaneous outburst of good will, hundreds of other Gothamites opened their purses.

On August 22, five weeks after the riots, the merchants' committee received an expression of appreciation from the colored people. A committee of Negro ministers and laymen presented to the white merchants a framed address which had been engraved on parchment by Patrick Reason. "We were hungry, and you fed us," ran one of the phrases in the statement. The businessmen were thanked for their exhibition of "generous moral courage" in rolling back the tide of violence. The "Address" closed on a note of respectful suggestion:

> If in the labors of Christian philanthropy, you ask what is the best that can be done for us, — this is our answer, "Give us a fair and open field and let us work out our own destiny, and we ask no more."

Generous giving also enabled the colored orphanage to reopen in October 1863 at a new site on Fiftieth Street. Among the contributors to the fund-raising campaign was a group of Negro women in New York who periodically had assisted the home. The role of relief giving was not new to colored women. During the war they expanded their charity in order to embrace the freedmen. Money was raised for the contrabands by Negro women from Boston where, according to the church's historian, George W. Williams, the "Ladies of the Twelfth Baptist church were busy with their needles," down to Washington, where the "Visiting Committee" of Mrs. Keckley's Contraband Relief Society distributed groceries and wearing apparel to the colored refugees. From London Mrs. Ellen Craft sent bundles of clothing made by her own hands.

Like others of their sex who were keeping the home fires burning, the colored women raised money to send boxes to the soldiers. The women of Washington, North Carolina, formed a sewing circle to assist the Second North Carolina. Another of these needle-plying groups was the Ladies' Aid Society, of Norwich, Connecticut, which held a week-long fair at Breed's Hall, placing on sale the articles, "fancy and useful," which they had fashioned at their weekly sewing circle meeting. The hall was decorated with flags and banners, and the display tables were attractively decorated. Many well-to-do white persons who were unable to attend sent in cash contributions.

A favorite project was the raising of money to purchase a flag or banner for a newly formed regiment. When Brigadier General E. A. Wild's brigade of 2154 men left New Bern on July 30, 1863, it flaunted a beautiful banner which had been presented by the Colored Ladies' Union Relief Association. The women of New Bern had collected the purchase price "from their own people in small sums." Two weeks later the ladies in the nation's capital presented a regimental flag to the First District Colored Volunteers. Designed by D. B. Bowser, a colored artist of Philadelphia, the flag portrayed the Goddess of Liberty, her foot on a serpent's head, handing a musket to a Negro soldier. The usefulness of Negro women was evidenced by a War Department order of January 16, 1864, authorizing all "United States General Hospitals" to employ them as cooks or nurses, for which they were to be paid $10 a month and one ration.

✣

The advance in the Negro's fortunes, to which the riots were a reaction, was heralded in December 1863 at the annual meeting of the American Anti-Slavery Society. The meeting was held in Philadelphia to commemorate the founding of the society in that city thirty years previously. On hand for the meeting were all of the old-line Garrisonians whose health permitted — William Lloyd himself, Wendell Phillips, Stephen and Abby Foster, Robert Purvis and Henry C. Wright, among others. At the opening session a squad of colored soldiers from Camp William Penn occupied platform seats. To add another dramatic touch, a slave auction block, placed on the rostrum, served as a stand for the speakers.

The rejoicing over the decline of slavery took on a tone of reminiscence as Samuel J. May, the greathearted clergyman from Syracuse, Lucretia Mott, one of the attractive spirits of the nineteenth-century reform movements, and J. Miller McKim, former underground railroad operator, spoke of the historic first convention held at Adelphi Hall in 1833. If the abolitionists were in a self-congratulatory mood, they had not yet forgotten how they had been stoned by the lawless, scandalized by the penny press, and treated as untouchables by the men "of property and standing."

Of all the addresses to which the reformers gave ear during the two days of the convention, the one receiving the loudest and most frequent applause was delivered by an old scene-stealer, Frederick Douglass. Not scheduled to speak, he took the platform in response to several calls from the floor. Never more brilliant, the Negro orator told his fellow abolitionists that even though "it had been a meeting of reminiscences," the work of the Society was not done. The freeing of the slaves was simply the first step; it now became the duty of the reformers to work for his elevation. The best way to advance the black man's interest, said Douglass, was to help him get the ballot. If the Negro knew enough to take up arms in defense of the Stars and Stripes, and bare his breast to the fire of Rebel artillery, he knew enough to vote. Emboldened by the storm of applause greeting this remark, Douglass proceeded to assert that Negroes should sit in the halls of Congress: "You may as well make up your minds that you have got to see something dark down that way."

Many present did not agree with Douglass as to the new obligation he believed the American Anti-Slavery Society should assume, but in abolitionist circles the issue did not come to a head until two years later. The most important work of the convention was the drafting of a resolution requesting Congress to submit to the states a constitutional amendment abolishing slavery forever in the United States.

But Douglass had accurately mirrored the sentiment of the Negroes. Their thinking had passed beyond the freeing of the chattels; their sights were now set on the franchise. A case in point was the action of the New Orleans Negroes. A month after the abolitionists held their third decade meeting, a group of 1000 Crescent City colored men asked the President and Congress to use their offices to obtain for all loyal Louisianians the right to vote. The signers of the petition were Negroes born free, twenty-seven of whom had served with Andrew Jackson in the War of 1812. They had already sent a petition to the military governor of the state, Brigadier General George F. Shepley, and to Major General N. P. Banks, commanding the Department of the Gulf, informing them that for forty-nine years colored New Orleanians had "never ceased to be peaceful citizens paying their taxes on assessments of more than nine million dollars." But the military had remained mum. Thereupon the colored men decided to send to the President and Congress their memorial for the ballot. The Negroes of New Orleans sent two of their number, Arnold Bertonneau and Jean Baptiste Roudanez, to Washington to present the petition in person.

The colored man's interest in securing the franchise was heightened with the approach of the Presidential election of 1864. The Negro wished to be numbered among those privileged to go to the polls and select a candidate for the nation's highest office. For the political pot had started simmering as early as February 22, 1864, when the Republicans announced that their national convention was to be held on June 7, at Baltimore.

A group of reformers who opposed Lincoln because they believed that he was slow and hesitant in his emancipation measures and lenient in his attitude toward the Rebels, called a mass meeting in Cleveland for May 31, hoping to forestall his nomination by the Republicans. At this third party convention, the four hundred Lincoln critics adopted a platform calling for the abolition of slavery by constitutional amendment, and nominated John C. Frémont as president and General John Cochrane as vice-president. It was expected that this ticket would appeal especially to Negroes, to whom Frémont's name was held to be "potent and talismanic," and who would think of Cochrane as the nephew of Gerrit Smith, their generous benefactor. But the

Negro leaders had been strangely absent from the Cleveland convention and their followers were similarly lukewarm.

Negro voters planned to support the candidate selected at the Union (or Republican) convention which met in Baltimore a week after the reformers had thrown Frémont's somewhat shopworn hat into the ring. The satisfaction of the great mass of colored people over Lincoln's nomination was more than a belief that "it is not best to swap horses while crossing the river." Their approval came as a consequence of his steady growth in matters pertaining to freedom and from his unfailingly courteous treatment of Negro individuals and groups.

Lincoln's expanding horizon on freedom was illustrated late in 1863 when at Gettysburg he uttered "a half dozen words of consecration." Asked to make a few remarks at the dedication of a battlefield as a cemetery for the Union soldiers who fell there, he delivered a short address which was destined to become a classic of the English language.

Slowly rising and drawing from his pocket a paper, the President began to read in a treble voice the opening words of that memorable American scripture: "Fourscore and seven years ago . . ." Lincoln's measured phrases rang out, the opening and closing lines making the Negro prick his ears. The opening sentence was a ringing affirmation of this country's origin as a land conceived in liberty, as a haven where all men were created equal. Great words to Negroes, but Lincoln had more. In the long cadences of his closing sentence, the President bespoke the country's dedication to the task still remaining – that of grafting "a new birth of freedom" onto the living tissue of American democracy.

By the time of the Gettysburg Address, Negroes had come to believe Lincoln had a personal interest in their condition. At a meeting of New Orleans Negroes in January 1864, a resolution was passed expressing "unbounded and heartfelt thanks" to the President for his "palpable interest in the so unrighteously

oppressed people of Africa's blood." There were many evidences
of Lincoln's concern. "Learn what you can as to the colored
people," ran a White House dispatch dated February 15, 1864,
to Major General Dan E. Sickles, who was being sent on a tour
from Cairo to New Orleans, returning by way of the gulf and
the ocean and touching such points as Memphis, Helena, Vicksburg, New Orleans, Pensacola, Key West and Charleston Harbor.
Lincoln asked his emissary to find out how the Negro was getting
along as a soldier, as a military laborer, as a hired hand on the
leased plantations: "Also learn what you can as to the colored
people within the rebel lines."

When the 1000 New Orleans Negroes sent their two-man delegation to Washington in January 1864, Lincoln responded by
assigning James A. McKaye, of the American Freedmen's Inquiry Commission, to pay them a visit. At a mass meeting in the
Crescent City, Commissioner McKaye learned the desires of the
Negroes: to have public schools, to be recognized as men, and
to have the black codes abolished. They also made clear their
opinion of Lincoln; they offered a resolution petitioning the
"Great Being" to vouchsafe "the longer continuance of His
servant, Abraham Lincoln, in his present high and responsible
position." Impressed by the behavior of the Louisiana Negroes,
the President sent a private letter, dated March 13, 1864, to newly
inaugurated Governor Michael Hahn, suggesting that the ballot
might be given to Negroes who were "very intelligent," and
those who had served in the armed forces. Added Lincoln, in
beautiful prose befitting so significant a Presidential declaration,
"They would probably help in some trying time in the future
to keep the jewel of Liberty in the family of freedom."

Negroes were satisfied with Lincoln as President because he
was "approachable." Such old friends as William de Fleurville,
"Billy the Barber," felt free to write to Lincoln expressing in a
single letter concern over his health, condolences on the death
of his son Willie, and news of a former pet dog of the Lincoln

boys. Well-to-do Billy, who contributed heavily to Catholic and Protestant charities in Springfield, Illinois, advised his friend to accept the Presidential renomination if it came his way, and then to carry "matters through to their termination." When that day came, wrote the Haitian-born barber and realtor, "The oppressed will shout the name of their deliverer, and generations to come will rise up and call you blessed (so mote it be)."

No Negro who ever went to Lincoln's White House came away without great gratification over his cordial reception. "Lincoln treated me as a man," said Frederick Douglass after his second visit to the executive mansion in August 1864. "Did you ever see such nonsense," wrote Negro army surgeon John H. Rapier, in mock horror to James P. Thomas, on August 19, 1864, "The president of the United States sending for a 'Nigger' to confer with him on the state of the country!"

Another colored caller was Sojourner Truth. She was at that time — six weeks before election — busy, as she put it, "scouring copperheads," as once she had scoured brass doorknobs. At the White House, the gaunt, black-skinned woman unabashedly told Lincoln that he was the greatest President the country ever had. For a valid comparison she reached back into biblical times and bracketed him with Daniel. She then brought out a little autograph book which she carried around. On a blank page the obliging President penned his name:

> For Aunty Sojourner' Truth,
> October 29, 1864 *A. Lincoln*

As the ex-slave arose he took her hand and told her that she must come again.

War nurse Caroline Johnson, another woman who had fled from the house of bondage, presented Lincoln with a collection of wax fruits, together with an ornamented stem table. The President examined the gift, walking around and lightly touching the imitation products, and then thanked the artisan. "Mr.

President," said Mrs. Johnson, "I believe God has hewn you out of a rock, for this great purpose." Lincoln murmured a disclaimer: "the praise must not go to him — it belonged to God."

Lincoln's reply was the sort that appealed to Negroes, most of whom had a rustic and religious background. In Lincoln the colored people recognized a man who was at home in the Bible. He could refer to the Deity in forty-nine different ways; such a man knew of God at least by report. And of course in the presence of Negroes, the considerate Lincoln would not dream of illustrating a point by reciting from his collection of "darkey" stories.

Lincoln's treatment of colored people in groups was heartwarming. At the annual New Year's Day handshakings at the executive mansion during his incumbency, Negroes, for the first time, stood in line to be presented to the Chief Magistrate. When a delegation of Negro Baptist clergymen, disturbed over the thought that life in an army camp might be short on spiritual influences, sought an appointment with Lincoln, he had them shown in. He nodded his head up and down in assent to their request for permission to preach to the soldiers, and then wrote a blanket directive to military officials, asking that the clergymen be afforded facilities "which may not be inconsistent with or a hindrance to military operations."

On July 4, 1864, Lincoln gave permission to the colored schools of the District to hold a celebration on the White House grounds, the children of the Protestant schools gathering in one body on the grounds west of the Capitol, and those of the Catholic schools spending the day on that section of the grounds between the Executive Mansion and Seventeenth Street. "In our recollection," wrote the *National Intelligencer* for July 6, 1864, "that same space has never been used for such a purpose."

Exactly a month later the Negroes received Lincoln's special permission to assemble on the White House grounds in observance of the national day of solemn humiliation and prayer which he had proclaimed in accordance with the recommendation of Congress. The celebration was day-long, with preaching at eleven and three o'clock, and an address at four. Admission was twenty-five cents for adults and ten cents for children, the proceeds to go toward purchasing a "Banner of Freedom." The celebrators found it pleasant to listen while seated on roomy, sun-streaked benches, or in relaxed positions under the trees. If one wished temporary surcease from the speechmaking, he might stroll along the shaded, well-kept paths, or rock to and fro on the swings suspended from the tree-limbs. Just outside the grounds were lemonade stands. All in all, the colored keepers of the day of prayer contrived to enjoy some forms of amusement not inconsistent with the general religious nature of the program.

Some eight weeks later the White House grounds provided the scene for a little drama in which the Negroes were on the giving end. A gift was presented to Lincoln which gave him more genuine pleasure, according to Frank B. Carpenter, than any other public testimonial of regard that ever came his way. On August 26, 1864, James Tyson had written on behalf of the colored people of Baltimore, asking when it would be convenient for Lincoln to receive "a very elegantly bound edition of the Bible." At the hour designated for the presentation, a committee of five Negroes, three of them clergymen, met the President on the White House lawn. Their spokesman handed Lincoln the gift "as a token of respect for your active part in the cause of emancipation."

Lincoln lifted the Bible from its white-silk-lined walnut case, uttering "many expressions of admiration." Costing $580.75, it was indeed an impressive piece. A pulpit-sized volume, bound in violet-tinted velvet, its corners were of banded gold, with heavy gold clasps at top and bottom. On the front cover was a raised design representing Lincoln in a cornfield striking the shackles from the wrists of a slave, who held one hand aloft in a gesture as if to bestow a blessing upon his benefactor. Below the design was a scroll bearing the word, "Emancipation." The back cover bore a plate:

To
Abraham Lincoln
President of the United States
From
The Loyal Coloured People of Baltimore
as a token of respect and gratitude
Baltimore, 4th July 1864

Realizing that he was expected to express his feelings, Lincoln told the delegates that he could only say then as he had said several times before that it had "always been a sentiment with me that all mankind should be free." As for the Bible — it was "the best gift which God has ever given to man." After thanking the five representatives, Lincoln shook hands with each in parting.

Negro support for his re-election, already overwhelming, became practically 100 per cent when the Democrats named George B. McClellan as their standard-bearer. Faced by the alternative of a general who had returned fugitive slaves and who had taken a dim view of the Negro as a soldier, the colored voters rallied even more strongly to the banner of "the Great Emancipator." When John C. Frémont withdrew from the race late in September, the campaign as far as Negroes were concerned was reduced to its least common denominator. "We are all for old Abe. I hope he will be elected," wrote Sergeant James Ruffin from Folly Island on October 16, 1864, to his sister-in-law. "Let the colored men at home do their duty."

The Democrats reacted in time-honored political fashion. Writing off the Negro vote as lost, they attempted to "smear" Lincoln and the Republican party with the tar brush. One of their campaign pamphlets informed the electorate that the platform of the Republican party was:

Subjugation
Emancipation
Confiscation
Domination
Annihilation
Destruction, in order to produce
Miscegenation!

The enemies of Lincoln had coined a new word: miscegenation. They issued a pamphlet in explanation of it. On the cover of this little brochure titled, *What Is Miscegenation?* was a woodcut of a Negro man and a white woman in fond embrace. It was unnecessary, reported the pamphleteer, L. Seaman, to enter into a lengthy definition of the word inasmuch as the artist had portrayed "that which our pen fails to accomplish."

Our illustrator represents an "intelligent gentleman ob color" affectionately saluting a pretty white girl of sixteen with auburn hair and light complexion; the different shades of complexion of the two contrasting beautifully and lending enchantment to the scene. . . . The sweet, delicate little Roman nose of the one does not detract from the beauty of the broad, flat nose of the other — while the intellectual, bold and majestic forehead of the one forms an unique, though beautiful contrast to the round, flat head, resembling a huge gutter mop, of the other.

The pamphlet was not done with the colored brother. Pulling out all stops, the sheet asserted that public sentiment for the past few years had been setting in Pompey's favor to the extent that soon dark complexions would become fashionable. Women would apply charcoal, rather than powder, to their faces; already the ladies in Washington had commenced "to friz their hair *à la d'Afrique.*" Instead of "a small, delicate foot being the rage, big flat understandings, with projecting heels, will be all the go."

Fully aware that they had a potent weapon of psychological

warfare, the Democrats launched a full-scale attack along the mis-cegenation front. Party headquarters picked up and publicized such rumors as that of young white women parading the streets with banners inscribed, FATHERS, PROTECT US FROM NEGRO EQUALITY. Democratic newspapers gave wide cir-culation to the story that sixty-four white schoolteachers at Port Royal had given birth to mulatto babies. From a reading of the Democratic and Copperhead press, one gathered the im-pression that the main plank of the Republican party was com-pulsory intermarriage.

If this appeal to folklore was so effective in politics, reasoned Petroleum Vesuvius Nasby, "Pastor uv the Church uv the Noo Dispensashun," might it not have transfer value in the pulpit? He had a pointed bit of advice to a young Democratic student of the ministry, "a youth of much promise who voted twice for Bookannon." Counseled Nasby to the novitiate: "Allez preech agin the Nigger. Preech agin amalgamashun at least 4 Sundays per month. Lern to spell and pronownce 'Missenegenegenashun.' It's a good word."

Such tactics by the Democratic and Copperhead campaign strategists confirmed the Negro in his allegiance to the opposi-tion party. The election of 1864 marked the cementing of the staunch affiliation of the colored man with the Republican party, a political fellowship destined to last for three quarters of a century.

In the months immediately following Lincoln's nomination, his Negro supporters spent many anxious moments. A Republican victory seemed imperiled as a desponding gloom enveloped the North. Grant had not taken Richmond, Sherman was not en-camped in Atlanta, and Sheridan had not swept the Shenandoah. Peace-at-any-price sentiment was strong, and men high in the councils of the party did not conceal their despair of a victory at the polls. Such a doubt had seeped up to the White House it-self; in a memorandum to his cabinet on August 23, Lincoln

observed that it was "exceedingly probable that this Administration will not be elected."

Fearing that he might have to conclude the war by a negotiated
peace in the closing months of what might prove to be a one-
term Presidency, Lincoln pondered over the probable fate of
the slaves. What would become of them if the North found itself compelled to grant peace terms to the Confederacy? Lincoln decided to talk this question over with the most prominent Negro of the day.

To the White House came Frederick Douglass on August 10.
First Lincoln asked his opinion about drafting a public letter
stating that the President would not make the abolition of slavery
a prior condition to the re-establishment of the Union. Lincoln
raised this question, said he, because many advocates of peace had
been critical of a recent Presidential note to Horace Greeley,
stating that Lincoln would receive and consider "any proposi-
tion which embraces the restoration of peace, the integrity of
the whole Union, and the abandonment of slavery."

"Shall I send forth this letter?"

"Certainly not," replied Douglass. "It would be given a
broader meaning than you intend to convey; it would be taken
as a complete surrender of your antislavery policy, and do you
serious damage."

Lincoln then passed on to his major topic. He asked the Negro
leader his reaction to establishing an unofficial agency which
would urge slaves to escape prior to the completion of possible
peace negotiations. For this government-sponsored underground
railroad the President suggested the need of a general agent with
twenty-five assistants. These men would conduct squads of runaways into the Union lines.

Douglass was startled by the proposal. Even the thought that
he would likely be chosen by Lincoln for the job of general
agent did not awaken his enthusiasm. For by this proposal Lincoln revealed that in his thinking his proclamation of emancipa-

tion was valid only as long as war existed, and that if peace were arranged before the South was decisively whipped, only such slaves would be free as had managed to escape.

Perhaps as Lincoln was unfolding his plan Douglass's thoughts may have darted back to a faintly similar proposal made to him by John Brown at Chambersburg, Pennsylvania, one hot August day on the eve of Harpers Ferry. Douglass had not thought Brown's scheme sound, and he was likewise cool to this plan of Lincoln's. The President and his guest talked at length — "We were long together and there was much said," wrote Douglass — but there was apparently no meeting of minds. Douglass asked the President to give him time to think it over.

Nearly three weeks later Douglass wrote a lengthy letter informing the Chief Executive that since their discussion he had conversed freely with several trustworthy and patriotic colored men concerning the proposal of running fugitives into the Union lines. "All with whom I have thus far spoken on the subject, concur in the wisdom and benevolence of the Idea, and some of them think it practicable." In this rather lukewarm tone, Douglass proceeded to outline a series of seven "ways and means" whereby slaves might be wrested from the enemy and conducted to places of safety.

Douglass's proposals were stillborn. His letter reached the President's desk on the same day that General William Tecumseh Sherman wired a pregnant sentence: "Atlanta is ours, and fairly won." Later that day Washington received the additional glorious news that torpedo-damning Admiral Farragut had forced his way into Mobile Bay and won a notable naval victory. The success of Northern arms insured Lincoln's re-election, and wiped out all fears of a negotiated peace. By the Tuesday of ballot-casting, November 8, Lincoln was a shoo-in: election day, wrote Goldwin Smith, a visitor from the British Isles, "passed off like an English Sabbath."

The Republican-Union success at the polls swept into office a preponderant party majority in both houses. The one-sided victory left no doubt about one thing: if the existing Congress failed to pass the constitutional amendment abolishing slavery, the next Congress, the Thirty-ninth, would have the required two-thirds Republican majority for such action. And the President could call a special session of the new Congress long before its scheduled date of convening in December 1865. Unquestionably, then, the amendment abolishing slavery would soon pass Congress. And such a measure should not have too much trouble getting the necessary ratification by three quarters of the states. After all, the Lincoln-Johnson ticket had carried twenty-two of the twenty-five states which voted.

The Negroes and their supporters were ecstatic over the results of the balloting on that God-sent Tuesday. "Since the re-election of Mr. Lincoln, the Royal Blood of Africa – the *crème de la crème* of colored society – have been extremely jubilant," wrote Copperhead pamphleteer, L. Seaman. "*Soirées d'Afrique* are being held throughout the country." Seaman's scribblings were meant to be barbed, but unquestionably things were picking up along the color line as Congressional mail pouches bulged with petitions to abolish slavery. Lydia Maria Child, a long-time worker in the reform vineyard, took note of the changing order of things:

> New anti-slavery friends are becoming as plentiful as the roses in June. Sometimes, when they tell me they have always been anti-slavery, I smile inwardly, but I do not contradict the assertion; I merely marvel at their power of keeping it a secret so long.

❖

In the North as the colored people and the other friends of freedom girded themselves for the final struggle, their watchword, "Equality before the law," the Negroes in the South, Rebel-held and Union-controlled, were also adjusting their sights to new horizons. Note will next be taken of the Negro under the Stars and Bars in the last phases of the war, as the Confederacy lived its life of unquiet desperation.

I well recollects when my master went to war. He called us all in the kitchen and told us he had to go over there and whip those sons of bitches and would be back 'fore breakfast. He didn't return for two years. I says, "Master, we sure would have waited breakfast on you a long time." He said, "Yes; they's the hardest sons of bitches to whip I ever had dealings with."

JERRY BOYKINS, TROUPE COUNTY, GEORGIA
(*Lay My Burden Down*)

CHAPTER XII

Toll de Bell

As THE STAR of the Confederacy waned, the Negroes within its shrinking orbit continued to enact the roles in which they had cast themselves. Those who had an opportunity to break their bonds promptly did so; the others bided their time. Exhibiting shrewdness and prudence, those who had only a slim chance of reaching the Union lines did not involve themselves in untimely mass uprisings. For they could sense that the day of deliverance could not be delayed much longer. Many understood the nature of the revolution going on around them, and they were convinced that the fated hour of freedom was drawing nearer by the minute.

Those slaves who might be best fitted to lead an insurrection were the house servants, and they tended to sympathize with the plight of their stricken "white folks." Many of them took pride in the increased responsibilities that fell to them in the absence of the master of the household. House servants were closer in the confidence of their mistresses and hence were influenced by their notable efforts to win the good will of the bondsmen.

Until the war's last drum, the white women showed no letup in their efforts to relieve the war-created deprivations of food and clothing which the slave, and everyone else in the South, was forced to undergo. The mistresses continued to sow among the slaves the seeds of distrust concerning Northerners, describing them as devils incarnate. This propaganda was not very effective, although when the Federal troops landed in the Port Royal region, Sea Islander Sammy Roberts shook his head in puzzled bewilderment over the taillessness of the Yankees.

On the whole the field hands on the plantations in the interior behaved much the same as though the masters were not away. Most mistresses could relate stories about the loyalty and fidelity of some "Faithful Old Nancy," or some "Cheerful Aunt Carrie H.," or some "Good Old Uncle Bobby." Mrs. Mary Rhodes, whose Alabama plantation was more than four miles from the nearest post office, looked upon the blacks as "my protectors." One of her slaves "slept in the nearest outhouse and I could call him if I needed him. But during the four years I was never disturbed." Mrs. C. B. Howard, who was left alone with two hundred slaves on a plantation in middle Georgia, praised their behavior to the skies:

> Can history produce such a parallel. Women and children left alone on an isolated plantation for years with Negroes whose faithful services continued as unchanged as if the lurid cloud of war had not arisen above our once peaceful horizon. Such was my case, yet never a disrespectful word or look did I observe.

Among Negroes there was some continuing response to the home-front campaigns put on for Johnny Reb by the patriotic women's groups. Boxes for the soldiers often contained articles contributed by colored women and children. At a Charleston raffle which netted $200 for the benefit of the garrison at Fort Sumter, $8 came from the sale of toys donated by two Negro girls. Also on display at the raffle were the contents of several "substantial" boxes sent by the slaves in the village of St. Helena. At Charleston a group of "Colored Abandoned Women" procured $450 "in a short time." This sum their leader delivered to "the pious ladies who meet daily at the rooms of the Young Men's Christian Association."

Leading all other Negroes in fidelity were the body servants. They almost never deserted. If they vanished for several days they usually showed up laden with forage. Among the steadfast family servants was Ned Haines, who accompanied three Virginia Dooleys during the war. "Ned Haines is still with me, having remained faithful during the whole campaign, and there was nothing to prevent him from going over to the Yankees had he any such idea," wrote twenty-year-old John Dooley, who had left Georgetown College in his sophomore year to don the gray.

Another tried-and-true black, John Scott, spent three and a half years on the war front, the body servant of Charles Minor Blackford of the Second Virginia Cavalry. The battlefield was nothing new to free Negro Scott — he had been the servant of "Captain Gardener in the Mexican War." Although quiet, Scott was always in good humor. He never gave Blackford a moment's worry: "In camp, on the march, even under fire, he never forsook me when he thought he could be of any use."

Some of the body servants were "in the know" concerning impending military developments, but their knowledge was deductive. An example was the attendant of the celebrated and well-loved Thomas J. ("Stonewall") Jackson. The general was famous for being tight-lipped about his plans, rarely divulging them even to his immediate subordinates. His servant, however, appeared to be in the general's confidence, since he invariably seemed to know precisely when the army was to be ordered to march. Asked how he seemed to be so well informed, the Negro replied, "Massa says his prayers twice a day — morning and night, but if he gets out of bed two or three times in the night to pray,

I just commences packing my haversack, for I know there will be the devil to pay the next day."

Some personal servants assisted their masters in attempting to escape, most notably the retainers of President Davis and Secretary of War John C. Breckinridge. When Davis fled from Richmond on Sunday evening, April 2, 1865, he was accompanied by James A. Jones, his Negro-Indian valet and coachman. The escaping party went first to Danville in southwestern Virginia and from there through the Carolinas into Georgia. At Irwinsville, seventy-five miles southeast of Macon, the small mounted escort was captured by a detachment of Union cavalry in the dawn of the morning of May 10.

The capture of Davis was effected despite Jones's efforts. When the approaching Yankees came within earshot, the coachman had aroused the party and awakened his master from a troubled sleep. Davis's horse was saddled and ready, Jones having taken that precaution the night before. As the Federal troops rode up, the servant threw over Davis's shoulders "the famous raincoat which Mr. Stanton's imagination magnified into a female costume." Jones was forever indignant at the charge that his master was attired in a woman's dress while trying to escape; throughout the rest of his long life Jones lost no occasion to disprove the allegation. At the unveiling of the Jefferson Davis monument in Richmond in June 1907, the loyal Jones was an honored guest, being warmly greeted by public notables and former wearers of the gray.

More successful than Davis in making good his escape was Secretary of War Breckinridge, formerly vice-president of the United States. Breckinridge had separated from the Davis entourage in middle Georgia only a few days before its capture. Breckinridge's party of six included his twenty-year-old servant, "Faithful Tom" Ferguson. An old campaigner despite his tender years, Ferguson had "cooked everything from a stalled ox to a crow." Of erect carriage and "good person," Ferguson accompanied his master

and four other Confederates as they crossed through heavily popu-
lated northeastern Florida, and then sailed down the Indian River,
eluding the camps of the Union guards. When they reached the
southern tip of the river, they seized from its owners a sea craft
better than their own. With this piratically acquired sloop, about
the size of a lifeboat, they put out into the Atlantic. After six
highly adventurous days adrift in the storm-driven Gulf Stream,
the party sighted the northern coast of Cuba. Starved and exhausted, they landed at Cárdenas on a quiet Sunday morning,
creating a sensation among the town's 13,000 inhabitants. After
receiving a truly Latin welcome at Cárdenas, the party proceeded overland to Havana. From that city the New York
Herald's correspondent posted a dispatch, dated June 21, 1865,
stating that the escape of the Confederates "savored of the
romantic, and may yet form the groundwork of an exciting novel
or thrilling drama."

Doubtless some of the Negro body servants actually were
pressed into emergency military service in firing on the enemy.
Blacks made excellent sharpshooters, and some of them perhaps
took an occasional pot shot at a lurking enemy figure. Indeed
the widespread belief in the North that the Confederacy was
using Negro soldiers undoubtedly originated from the closeness
of the body servants to the firing line. At historic Yorktown the
last Rebel gun discharged from the town was fired by a Negro,
according to Yankee reporter George Alfred Townsend.

One of the greatest contributions by the Negro in camp was
the humor and jollity that he radiated. General John B. Gordon
related that Robert E. Lee often told with relish the story of his
chat with an aged Negro who called to see him at headquarters.
"General Lee," said the ancient one, pulling off his hat, "I been
wanting to see you a long time. I'm a soldier."

"Ah? To what army do you belong — to the Union army or to
the Southern army?"

"Oh, General, I belong to your army."

"Well, have you been shot?"

"No, sir; I ain't been shot yet."

"How is that? Nearly all of our men get shot."

"Why, General, I ain't been shot 'cause I stay back whar de generals stay."

Many of the Negro military servants met with the Confederates in their reunions, and one of them delighted in repeating from memory the roll call of the company to which his master belonged. White-thatched blacks garbed in Confederate gray were honored at these reunions. Mississippi granted them pensions. Their role in the Confederacy may be summed up in the terms which Major General John C. Breckinridge used in writing a recommendation for Tom Ferguson:

> In many occasions of peril and hardship he has proved himself courageous and faithful. I have found him at all times honest and devoted.

✤

The slaves and free Negroes on the home front revealed their innermost sympathies by the all-out manner in which they assisted Union soldiers who escaped from prison pens. In the vast autobiographical literature of escaped war prisoners there is almost no instance in which the blacks do not come in for fulsome praise. " 'God bless the Negroes;' say I, with earnest lips," wrote the New York *Tribune* special war correspondent, Junius Henri Browne, who had seen the inside of a succession of Rebel jails, including the well-known stronghold at Salisbury, North Carolina, and the notorious Richmond pens, Libby and Castle Thunder. "During our entire captivity," he continued, "and after our escape, they were our firm, brave, unflinching friends. We never made an appeal to them they did not answer."

Another of the assisted prisoners, Melvin Grigsby of the

Seventh Wisconsin Infantry, entitled his book, *The Smoked Yank*, after those who had given him aid and succor, and dedicated it to them:

To the Real Chivalry of the South,
the old "Aunties" and "Uncles" and Valorous Young Men
who so generously and bravely
at the risk of Cruel Punishment and sometimes of Life
Fed and Warmed and Aided and Guided
Escaped Union Prisoners
As a Token of Gratitude this Little Volume
is Tenderly Dedicated

Among the Northern soldiers there was a fixed belief that "the Negroes, and especially the field hands, are all Union darkeys." In prison the captured Yanks thought and talked of one thing — escape. "To them, freedom is everything; all else, nothing." Their burning desire to make the dash for freedom was heightened by the knowledge that once they got outside the prison yard they would find scores of allies on whom they could depend. They had no hesitancy in approaching Negro cabins. They felt as safe from betrayal as though they were knocking on the door of a trusted friend.

These Negroes were in a position to give marked assistance. A long familarity with the operations of the underground railroad had given them valuable experience in the techniques of flight and concealment. The slaves knew the bypaths and short cuts in the woods, where the patrol guard made its nightly beat, where the Confederate pickets were stationed, and whether the cavalry scouts were in the vicinity searching for escaped Yankees. The slaves could furnish information as to the whereabouts of whites who secretly sympathized with the Union cause, and in the mountainous areas of western North Carolina and eastern Tennessee where the black population was sparse, Negro guides knew just where to go in order to deliver the escaping soldiers into the safekeeping of the white Union outlaws who roamed in exile for the very purpose of assisting Federal soldiers and Confederate deserters.

When a Union soldier making his getaway reached a Negro cabin, he was famished as a rule. He needed to whet his whistle and "fill up the vacuum below the diaphragm." Invariably the cabin occupants showed an eagerness to share their last crumb of cornbread and their last strip of bacon. Word would soon spread via the grapevine of the new arrival, and before long the Negroes in the neighborhood would be stopping by the cabin leaving their donations of food and hurrying away. But for his Negro hosts, many an escaped Union soldier would have starved to death.

Andrew Benson related that it was at a slave cabin that he had such a banquet as he had never enjoyed before in his life. When he knocked at the door, there had been no response. Pushing in and seeing an old couple sitting on the bed, he told them he was hungry.

"We haven't got anything, Massa, we are very poor."

"Can't you give me a piece of pone or something? I don't care what it is."

"We haven't anything."

"Haven't you a piece of bread, or a piece of meat, or anything?"

"No, we can't give you anything, we haven't anything."

"Then perhaps I will ask you another favor — do you suppose you could keep a secret, if I told you something. I am a Union officer, escaped from prison at Columbia, South Carolina, and we are trying to work our way up into our lines at Knoxville."

The aged couple immediately got up — the woman went into a corner and from a little box took a wooden tray and some meal and seasoning. The old man raked open the coals upon the hearth and uncovered a turkey wing. In no time a pone had been "nicely moulded" and placed on the coals, Benson's mouth watering. He would never, he wrote, forget that meal.

Three escaped lieutenants had a similar experience whose memory lingered on. Eluding the guards at their Charleston prison in December 1863, officers W. H. Shelton, Edward E. Sill and A. T. Lawson reached Pickensville, where they found a host of "sable benefactors." Shelton described the feast in his *A Hard Road to Travel Out of Dixie:*

> The great barn doors were set open and the cloth was spread on the floor by the light of the moon. The central dish was a pork-pie, flanked by savory little patties of sausage. There were sweet potatoes, fleecy biscuits, a jug of sorghum, and a pitcher of sweet milk. Most delicious of all was a variety of corn-bread having tiny bits of fresh pork baked in it, like plums in a pudding. . . . We filled our haversacks with the fragments.

The slaves took pains for the safety of their guests. When night fell they spirited the soldiers off to an old still, a corn-fodder house or an abandoned barn where they could lie down without having to keep one eye open. "Negro families stood guard while we slept," wrote Lieutenant James M. Fales who, with two other officers, had broken out of a Charleston prison on the night of November 9, 1864.

Flight-bound soldiers invariably needed something to put on their backs, since their Confederate prisonkeepers had been unable to make issues of clothing. Torn by bushes and ruined by waters, the rags worn by many of the Yankees were soon ready to fall off in tatters. The slaves took their annual clothing allowance and shared it with their half-naked guests, gladly giving what they could. A common gift was socks, one old woman taking the stockings from her own feet for a barefooted officer. While the soldiers slept, their clothes were washed and sewed. Black cobblers mended shoes for the foot-traveling fugitives. Some Negroes furnished them with hunting knives, and one buxom female, anxious to do her bit, contributed a fine-tooth comb.

After holding a prayer meeting for their white guests, the slaves assisted them in reaching the next post. A Negro ferryman would put them across the Pedee or the Santee, navigating soundlessly (sweet stream, run softly) under a night-darkened sky. Once on the opposite bank, the escaped prisoners would be furnished with a dugout canoe, or turned over to a waiting guide.

These slave guides played an important role. In his diary for December 2, 1864, Lieutenant Hannibal A. Johnson, of the Third Maine Infantry, lists seven Negroes who during the course of a single evening acted as guide for his party of three:

> At dark we were taken to Widow Hardy's plantation. Here Jim took us eight miles and turned us into the care of Arthur, who, after going with us fifteen miles, gave us to Vance who hid us in the woods. At dark Vance brought us more chickens for our evening meal, then started on the road with us, going eight miles, then Charles took us, he going five miles; then David took us four miles, he giving us to Hanson, who took us a short distance and left us at Preston Brooks' plantation. . . . Here one of the Brooks' Negroes who goes by the name of Russell took us in charge.

At the latter plantation, the three soldiers were shown the famous cane which Congressman Brooks had used in belaboring Charles Sumner ten years previously. The Yankee soldiers were then given a good supper. "God bless the poor slaves," exclaimed Lieutenant Johnson, "if such kindness does not make one an abolitionist, then his heart must be made of stone."

In cases where the Negroes could accompany the escaped soldiers no further, they mapped out the bypaths in the woods and the location of the next "station." They furnished information as to the whereabouts of Confederate pickets. When in February 1864, 109 officers in Libby, conceiving the idea of effecting their own exchange, succeeded in breaking out, they were able to reach Union lines because they followed the advice of Negroes who gave them specific directions as to the spots where the Rebel pickets were posted.

Soldiers in Southern prisons were often the recipients of food packages from Negroes. Susie King Taylor relates that under cover of night the colored women of Savannah used to go to the stockade in the suburbs of the city and pass boxes of food through the fences into the outstretched hands of the ravenous prisoners.

On the long and weary marches through Dixie, many infantrymen would become exhausted and have to fall out. The Union army would have to leave them by the wayside — a forced march into and through enemy country is no time for dalliance. These abandoned soldiers dragged themselves to a cabin and peered through to see whether the faces inside were white or black. A Yankee scout cut off from the main body followed the same precautions — if he saw a black face he presumed he had found a friend.

The role of the Negro as expediter of Yankee prisoner escapes moved George Ward Nichols, whose *Story of the Great March* was read more widely than any other Civil War narrative, to observe that "the faith, earnestness, and heroism of the black man is one of the grandest developments of this war." Aide-de-camp to William Tecumseh Sherman, soldier-author Nichols continues his tribute, dated January 1, 1865, at Savannah:

> When I think of the universal testimony of our soldiers, who enter our lines every day, that in hundreds of miles which they traverse on their way, they never ask the poor slave in vain for help; that the poorest Negro hides and shelters them, and shares the last crumb with them — all this impresses me with a weight of obligation and a love for them that stir the very depths of my soul.

❖

If the slaves helped thousands of escaping Yankee soldiers to reach friendly soil, their services to the Confederacy were nonetheless of marked importance. "Much of our success," wrote Jefferson Davis, "was due to the much-abused institution of African servitude." White men were enabled to go into the army, explained Davis, by leaving to those "held to service or labor" the cultivation of the fields, the care of the flocks and the protection of the women and children. Ulysses S. Grant shared this opinion of the role of the Negro. He described the whole South as a military camp. Because slaves were required to work in the fields without regard to sex or age, "the 4,000,000 of colored noncombatants were equal to more than three times their number in the North, age for age and sex for sex."

The Negro's home-front contribution to the Southern cause was incalculable. The Negro was "the stomach of the Confederacy," producing its crops of potatoes, corn, peanuts, oats, barley and wheat. As the factories stepped up their output, a plea went out from the armories and munitions plants for skilled Negro laborers — an armory in Macon advertised for 100 at $25 a month and subsistence; a naval gun foundry at Selma sent out a call for 200, and the Tredegar Iron Works in Richmond wanted 1000. The demand was great for Negro blacksmiths, harness makers, shoemakers, carpenters, wheelwrights and miners.

So pressing was the need for Negro labor that the Confederate Congress was forced to expand its impressment legislation. With the failure of the system of voluntary contract, the central government felt that there was no alternative. On March 20, 1863, Congress had passed a law legalizing impressment by military authorities. Impressment was to be made in conformity to state law; in the absence of such law, the Secretary of War could prescribe regulations. Seven months later Secretary Seddon issued a general order implementing the act. Commanding officers were given permission to determine the need for impressment, but they were to take no slaves who were in domestic service; they were to take no slaves from plantations where there were fewer than four slaves of the age specified, and they were not to exceed a quota of 5 per cent of the slave population of any county at any one time.

The army's need for an additional supply of black laborers led

Davis, in his message of December 7, 1863, to request further legislation. Ten weeks later (February 17, 1864) Congress passed a
measure which provided for the hiring of as many as 20,000 Negroes between the ages of eighteen and fifty for service in war
factories and military hospitals and in erecting fortifications.
Slaves who were impressed would receive clothes and rations;
their owners would be paid $25 a month, and would be com-
pensated for slaves lost through death or flight. A master's only
slave could not be taken.

But this effort by the central government to impress black
labor brought forth only a token response. The opposition of the
masters became more marked, widening the growing breach between the Confederate and state authorities. It would have seemed
that the masters would have been willing to hire out their bondsmen since in many instances the problem of feeding and clothing
them had become acute. The stoppage of the cotton crop had left
on the hands of many planters an unprofitable supply of non-
producing consumers.

But the slave owners did not care to run the risk of turning their
black chattels over to army officers who might overwork them.
And even well-intentioned commanders were unable to guarantee
good care. Brigadier General Josiah Gorgas, Chief of the Ordnance Bureau, found Negro laborers indispensable and treated
them as well as conditions permitted. But as he found out, conditions were not highly permissive; if the Confederate Army could
not provide its soldiers with full rations, sufficient clothing and
adequate medical care, it certainly could not provide them for
impressed Negroes, and this the planters knew.

Additional reasons for their reluctance to forward their slaves
were stated by James H. Rives, private secretary to Mississippi
Governor John J. Pettis, in a letter dated March 31, 1863, to
Lieutenant General J. C. Pemberton. Impressed Negroes had
been kept waiting at railroad stations for several days, alleged
Rives, because "it is said that the State must send them to the point

of destination." Moreover, the payments to the masters had not been forthcoming. Furthermore, the overseers sent by the masters were ignored and the slaves were "placed under the control of strangers, and in many cases badly treated."

Secretary Rives did not mention the greatest fear held by the masters — that of the slave taking to his heels. "The impressment of Negroes has been practiced ever since the war commenced," wrote General Joseph E. Johnston on January 4, 1864, to Senator Louis T. Wigfall of Texas, "but we never have been able to keep the impressed Negroes with an army near the enemy. They desert." Following the Confederate Impressment Act of 1864, no fewer than 1200 sequestered Negroes at Mobile fled in a mass desertion.

To placate the planters, the Confederate Congress passed a bill in April 1864, upon the recommendation of Secretary of War Seddon, appropriating $3,108,000 to compensate owners whose impressed slaves had died or escaped. Seddon got this figure from Acting Chief of the Engineering Bureau, Alfred L. Rives who, on January 22, 1864, estimated that Virginia's approximately 2000 losses in impressed slaves might be calculated at the minimum sum of $708,000. "Reasoning by analogy," wrote Rives to Seddon, "and for want of absolute data, and extending the calculation to the other states of the Confederacy, in all of which heavy losses have been sustained among the Negroes impressed for labor on the defenses, the Bureau has arrived at the sum of $3,108,000 as the minimum probably required to meet this class of expenditures."

This measure, which priced a slave at the ridiculously low figure of $354 in inflated Confederate currency, did little to mollify the slaveowners. Impressment thus undermined the morale of the class from which the government drew its chief support — the planter aristocracy. Men of property looked upon impressment as another hateful manifestation of the usurpation of power by the Richmond cabal, and the storm of criticism over the sequestration of slaves was stilled only with the collapse of the South.

✣

It was another controversy over the use of the slave population that brought on the final shattering internal convulsion that racked the Confederacy. This was the bitter debates over the question of enlisting the slave as a soldier. The heated discussions of this issue in the halls of Congress were matched by an equally excited succession of discussions in town or country wherever two or three were gathered.

Proposals to arm the blacks had multiplied as the war dragged on, the loudest clamors coming from those areas threatened by Yankee invasion. By the autumn of 1863 newspapers in the lower South were editorially debating the question, and the Alabama legislature sent a petition to President Davis recommending that the experiment be tried.

The first definite proposal by a high army officer was made by Major General Patrick R. Cleburne, a divisional commander of the Army of Tennessee. Cleburne had given the matter careful thought and had written out a lengthy report recommending the enlisting of Negroes. On December 28, 1863, Cleburne had outlined his proposals at length to his close friend, Captain Thomas J. Key, half convincing him. Four days later Cleburne described his plan to the officers of the Army of Tennessee who had been summoned to General Joseph E. Johnston's headquarters at Dalton, Georgia.

To arm the slave, said the Irish general with great earnestness, would provide the Confederacy with material and moral support. The North would be stripped of its supply of black laborers and soldiers, and the nations abroad would make manifest to the Confederacy their sympathy and assistance. Such a measure would take the wind out of the sails of the abolitionist fanatics in the

North. Cleburne's cogent report was long but not repetitious. In answer to the question, "Will the slaves fight?" Cleburne had a little lesson in history to recite to General Johnston and the assembled regimental commanders and general officers of all grades:

> The helots of Sparta stood their masters in good stead in battle. In the great sea fight of Lepanto where the Christians checked forever the spread of Mohammedanism over Europe, the galley slaves of the fleet were promised freedom and called on to fight at a critical moment in the battle. They fought well and civilization owes much to those brave galley slaves. The Negro slaves of Santo Domingo, fighting for freedom, defeated their white masters and the French troops sent against them. The Negroes of Jamaica revolted, and under the name of Maroons, held the mountains for 150 years; and the experience of this war has been so far that half-trained Negroes have fought as bravely as many other half-trained Yankees.

A copy of Cleburne's paper was sent to Richmond. President Davis immediately sent word to General Johnston that the report should be kept private — he deemed it "injurious to the public service that such a subject be mooted." Johnston received a similar dispatch from Secretary of War Seddon ordering "suppression of the memorial and discussion concerning it." Johnston hastily passed the word down the line. Obeying orders, Cleburne henceforth held his peace, although he had already said enough to prevent his promotion to lieutenant general when such a vacancy occurred some months later.

Davis and Seddon were unrealistic in hoping to stifle discussion of the issue. The South needed soldiers. As 1864 wore on, the ranks grew thinner and thinner. Desertions were depleting the Confederate columns. The contest at arms had long since lost its glamour — "When This Cruel War Is Over" was one of the most popular songs in the South. A conscription officer was reluctant to show his face in the mountainous regions, being detested even more than a revenuer. Many of the plain people of the Confederacy were becoming disaffected. Themselves possessed of few slaves ("if they doubled the number of slaves they had and added one more, they would own one Negro"), they were becoming influenced by the charge that the war was being waged to protect the property of the planter aristocracy.

With the unveiling of this somber picture, the Confederate politicians and military officers began to chew the bitter cud of reflection. Again stocktaking, they went over the objections to a policy of arming the slaves — it would be a repudiation of the traditions of the South, it would give offense to the white soldiers, and it would mean the abolition of slavery, for if a Negro were fit to be a soldier, he should not be a slave. The hoe was the weapon for the black man, and it was in the condition of a slave that "he obtained his best development, his maximum of happiness and civilization." Moreover, the slave was no warrior. When a gun is fired, he trembles: remember the story of the officer who told his slave to look after his property, and when some shot fell nearby, the Negro fled, and when the master reprimanded him he said, "Massa, you told me to take good care of your property, and dis property (placing his hand on his breast), is worf $1,500."

The South, in truth, faced a cruel dilemma. As moral men of sensible feelings, white Southerners wished to maintain an acceptable degree of congruence between their consciences and their actions. But they were enslaved by a system of values which stamped the blacks as inferiors, and to make the Negro a soldier would be to call into question the very foundation of their mythology, or compel them to invent new myths.

But familiar arguments and folklorist consistency concerning the role of the slave paled before the hard fact of military necessity. Manpower in the army was badly needed, and there was no other source of supply. The state governors took the first big step. Meeting at Augusta in October 1864, the titular heads of North Carolina, South Carolina, Georgia, Alabama and Mississippi

passed a resolution recommending the use of bondsmen as
soldiers.

The Confederate Congress, however, was still tending to delay,
as the die-hards fired their final volleys against slave soldiers.
Congressman H. C. Chalmers of Mississippi declared that "all
nature cries out against it," and Senator Wigfall confessed that
he had no desire to live in a country "in which the man who
blacked his boots and curried his horse was his equal." But these
denunciations had lost much of their potency — the public mind
had become resigned to the necessity of the momentous step.

The tide turned in February 1865. Davis had come to see the
light, his conversion being hastened by Sherman's northward
thrust from Savannah. Moreover, approval came from an influential quarter — Robert E. Lee, the most highly respected
figure in the Confederacy. Early in January he informed Andrew
Hunter, a Virginia state senator, that in his opinion slaves could
make effective soldiers. The commander put his finger on the
heart of the matter: "I think, therefore, we must decide whether
slavery shall be extinguished by our enemies and the slaves used
against us, or use them ourselves at the risk of the effects which
may be produced on our social system." Five weeks later Lee
again went on record: "I think we could do as well with them as
the enemy, and he attaches great importance to their assistance.
Under good officers and good instructions I do not see why they
should not become good soldiers."

As anticipated by the proponents of arming the blacks, the
recommendations of the revered Lee broke the back of the opposition. On March 6 the Virginia legislature enacted a law for the
enlisting of the slaves in the Old Dominion. A week later Davis
signed the "Negro soldier law" passed by the Confederate Congress. This measure authorized the acceptance of slaves to perform
military service in any capacity the President might direct. Such
soldiers were to receive the same rations, clothing and pay as were
allowed others in the same branch of the service.

The results of the Negro soldier bill were nil. The Confederacy hoped that the measure would induce England to extend diplomatic recognition. In January 1865 Secretary of State Benjamin sent Duncan F. Kenner to England as a high commissioner empowered to make commercial treaties and to pledge the Confederacy to slave emancipation. The emissary may as well have remained in Richmond. He soon discovered that the work of the abolitionists had been so effective that it was impossible to dislodge from the British mind the identification of the South with slavery. Moreover, John Bull's fat war profits in surplus stored cotton, and the spurt in his other industries created by Northern wartime buying, had weakened any economic motive to intervene on behalf of the South. And with the Confederacy's fortunes at a low ebb the time had gone by when a policy of voluntary emancipation might have had any influence in the British Isles.

On the domestic front the Negro soldier bill had a trial of about three weeks. Hit-or-miss efforts were made to enlist the blacks. The superintendent of the Virginia Military Institute offered to the state legislature the services of the Institute's cadets as instructors for colored soldiers. War Clerk Jones, in a diary entry dated March 17, noted that "letters are pouring into the department from men of military skill and character, asking authority to raise companies, battalions, and regiments of Negro troops." One of those desiring a commission in black volunteers was Walter Clark, later chief justice of the North Carolina Supreme Court. Young Clark preferred being an officer in a Negro company rather than remaining a private, "tho I know on all occasions these colored Troops will be in the forefront of the battle."

Richmond was the only place at which any appreciable number was enlisted. Here two companies of mixed free Negroes and slaves were recruited. As a means of inducing other Negroes to sign up, these companies were put on exhibition in the city. Uniformed in Rebel gray, they held parades in Capitol Square before thousands of curious onlookers. White Richmonders were fascinated by the spectacle of blacks marching in perfect step and going through the manual of arms with clocklike precision. But within a week after the drillings and paradings had begun, Richmond was abandoned; it had become too late for soldiers of whatever hue or previous condition of servitude.

Would Negroes have fought for the Confederacy? Perhaps so, but without their hearts being in it. Most of them had come to look on the Union soldiers as their friends and deliverers. "What will you do when they get you into their army and put a musket in your hands, and tell you to shoot the Yankees?" asked George Ward Nichols of a contraband. "I nebber will shoot de Yankees," he replied, "de first chance I git I run away."

❖

As the Negroes in the Confederacy listened to the bell toll for a day that was fading and an institution that was dying, the Negroes in those parts of the South held by the Union forces were making the transition from slavery to freedom. They found the experience exhilarating. Making good in their new status was a source of pride, something to be pleased over, a medal to be worn. It may be next in order, therefore, to submit a progress report on the freedmen as they worked to improve their condition in field and cabin, in classroom and church, on the war front and in the battle line.

> "Well, George, how is you?"
> "All right now for de fust time in my life."
> The Whip, Hoe, and Sword

CHAPTER XIII

Badges of Freedom

LIFE WAS hardly a pink tea party at the contraband camp in Washington. The overcrowded wooden barracks were little more than lean-tos, leaving their tenants at the mercy of the capricious Washington weathercock. If she were to describe the conditions at the contraband hospital, wrote Cornelia Howard on November 15, 1863, to her sister, "it would not be believed." The "maternity ward" averaged a birth a day, and as there were no baby clothes, the newborn were wrapped up in an old piece of muslin, "that even being scarce."

Despite these hardships the camp's inhabitants displayed little of the downcast or hangdog air. On the contrary, "old women, with their wool white with age, bent over the wash tub, grinned and gossiped in the most cheerful manner," observed war nurse and spy, S. Emma E. Edmonds. Smiling mothers fondled their babies, and most everyone seemed to be singing, whether "of heaven, or of hoe-cakes."

To these Negroes, now free and self-supporting, song came more easily. The poor facilities of the camp did not make them despondent as long as they could be on their own. Anxious to make enough money to leave the camp and set up housekeeping for themselves, husbands and wives pooled their small incomes. The men left the camp in the mornings to go to their jobs in the city, mainly in the employ of the army, and many of the women came into town to do domestic work.

There seemed to be no desire on anyone's part to go back to old master: "I never found a single one that would exchange their present condition for their former one," wrote Superintendent D. B. Nichols, whose observation was similar to that of others who worked with contrabands throughout the South. One of the camp's tenants, a Point Lookout mulatto with "considerable pretensions to beauty," described the general attitude to an interested visitor, Mary A. Livermore, of the Sanitary Commission. "We'd rather be jes' as po' as we can be, if we's only free," said the contraband — placing a finger in the palm of her other hand for emphasis — "than to belong to anybody, an' hab all de money ole massa's got, or is eber gwine ter hab."

One of the many ways in which the contrabands showed their love of liberty was in their desire to own land. To the predominantly rural Southern Negro the ownership of real estate was the chief mark of a free man. If he could purchase land on the plantation of his birth and own the very land he had cultivated as a slave, so much the better. But wherever it might be located, he wanted a piece of mother earth. Nor did it matter too much whether the plot of ground was swampy, scrubby, sandy or wooded. First a house would go up, then a well would be sunk. Pigs and chickens would soon appear, followed later by a cornfield and a cotton patch flanking the rows of sweet potatoes.

The Negro question, wrote Chaplain Horace James, Superintendent of Negro Affairs in North Carolina, in his annual report for 1865, "need give political economists no more perplexity. Make them lords of the land, and everything else will naturally follow." At Roanoke Island in the first year of their freedom, the contrabands built 591 houses, multiplying the value of the land 37 times. In the Sea Islands late in 1864 when the abandoned lands were put up at auction by the United States Direct Tax Commissioner for nonpayment of taxes, Negro heads of families eagerly sought to purchase the twenty and forty acre lots. By June 1865 Negroes on St. Helena's had made 347 land purchases.

To permit Negroes to buy land, however, was not the common practice. Throughout the South the prevailing pattern was for the Federal government to take title to the land and in turn lease it to whites, either resident planters who took the oath of allegiance or Yankee lessees come South for gain. However, despite the opposition of the white planter-speculators, some Negroes in the Valley of the Mississippi were permitted to lease land on their own account. In July 1864 Negroes were operating plantations on which 4000 acres of cotton had been planted.

The efforts of these colored agriculturalists were notable in demonstrating the possibilities of Negro enterprise. "Of all the elements represented in the Valley," wrote General Superintendent of Contrabands John Eaton, "the independent Negro cultivator was without doubt the most successful." Some cultivators were especially prosperous; Chaplain Asa A. Fiske, Superintendent of Contrabands at Memphis, reported that Robert Minor cultivated eighty acres in cotton opposite Milliken's Bend in 1864, making forty bales, a half-bale to the acre. "He also made 40 acres of good corn." At Helena, Arkansas, the aggregate income of the colored lessees was $40,000 in 1864.

Negro cultivators invariably made enough to keep themselves in comfort during the winter. Some of them acquired sufficient funds to purchase teams and agricultural implements. They were more cautious than whites in leasing land subject to Rebel attack, and they seldom contracted for plots that were too extensive for their labor supply. Samuel Thomas, assistant general superintendent to John Eaton, gave additional reasons for their success: "Their wants are simple, and easily supplied; they do full work themselves, and being of the same race with those they hire, they succeed in getting good and steady work out of them."

In the fall of 1863 in one region in Mississippi, James E. Yeatman discovered fifteen freedmen lessees all of whom had made from four to fifteen bales of cotton. Yeatman supplied a description — the first four of his fifteen vignettes suggest the complete picture:

> Granville Green (colored) on the Beard place, works a number of hands, and is supplied by the Government with rations, to be paid for when the crop is sold. I was informed that he would make from ten to twelve bales of cotton.
>
> Tom Taylor (colored) was working with seven hands on the Savage place, the Government furnishing rations until the crop is sold.
>
> Luke Johnson (colored) on the Albert Richardson place, will make five bales of cotton, and corn sufficient for his family and stock, and has sold $300 worth of vegetables. He has paid all expenses without aid from the Government.
>
> Bill Gibson and Phil Ford (colored) commenced work last May, and will make nine bales of cotton. They occasionally hire a woman or two, and have paid their hands in full, and found their own provisions.

The best known of the plantations under Negro lessees was Davis Bend, a pear-shaped strip of land on the elbow of the river twenty-five miles below Vicksburg. Formerly the property of Jefferson Davis and his brother Joseph, the fertile stretch had caught the attention of Ulysses S. Grant as a site for a "Negro paradise." By the spring of 1864, seventy-five free Negro heads of families, representing a total population of some six hundred, had set themselves up as cultivators, working plots of from five to one hundred acres. Rations and teams were furnished by the government, to be paid for when the crop was marketed. The colored lessees proceeded to raise the crop, make the sales, pay their bills and pocket the profits, which in some cases amounted to $1000. Davis Bend was practically self-governing, the military officers in charge permitting the Negroes to handle court procedure and prescribe penalties for wrongdoing.

During the year 1865 Davis Bend had 180 Negro heads of family lessees who handled their own business affairs straight across the board. According to the report of Colonel Samuel

Thomas, these Davis Bend cultivators raised 12,000 bushels of corn worth $12,000, a quantity of vegetable and melon produce worth $38,500, and 1736 bales of cotton worth $347,200. Of the total amount brought in by this diversified crop ($397,700), the expenses amounted to $238,500, leaving a profit balance of $159,-200 for the black farmers. The unprecedented success of the Davis Bend Negroes stemmed in part from the good treatment they had received as slaves from the Davis brothers, Joseph and Jefferson, who had encouraged their bondsmen to be enterprising and self-respecting. After the war Davis Bend was destined to become the all-Negro town of Mound Bayou, founded by Benjamin Montgomery who had managed the plantation before the war as a slave of Jefferson Davis.

Many of the nonfarming contrabands did well in small businesses which, wrote Dr. Joseph Warren, General Superintendent of Refugees in the Valley, they conducted "successfully on principles of honor that would do credit to any men." At New Bern, North Carolina, "some are becoming rich," reported Superintendent James. Port Royal Negroes sold sweet potatoes, hogs, chickens, eggs and fish to the soldiers and the commissary, receiving as high as ten cents a quart for fine oysters. The greatest marketman at Hilton Head was Limus, a contraband who had "not the slightest drop of white blood." Besides owning a number of guns and dogs, boats and seines, Limus traded in horses with great profit and planted cotton on a large scale. At St. Helena's an equally enterprising ex-slave owned 315 acres, 58 of which produced sea-island cotton, and 52 of which produced corn. He hired 20 laborers, and owned 12 cows, a yoke of oxen, 4 horses and 20 swine.

In addition to their attempts to become proprietors of land and operators of small businesses, the contrabands desired to acquire the comforts and conveniences of household living. Now that they owned their cabins and were less crowded than in slavery, they initiated cleanup and paintup campaigns. Cabins were scrubbed and whitewashed and pictures from the illustrated newspapers were pasted on the walls. Windows with glass panes became more common.

Now that they themselves determined the hour for their uprising and downsitting, the whole family could assemble for a meal together, with the father presiding at the head of the table and pronouncing the grace. The fare was more abundant and varied than heretofore — the corn, potatoes and fish of slavery days were supplemented by pork, molasses, sugar and coffee.

In their new status as free men the former chattels showed an increased respect for the law. Good behavior was the rule among them — "the family instinct of the Negro proved a tremendous power in maintaining order and regularity in our camps," reported Superintendent Eaton. Even at the contraband depots, which were badly overcrowded as a rule, there was almost no violence. The common vices of stealing and lying took a change for the better when slaves became free, reported the American Freedmen's Inquiry Commission in its preliminary draft to the Secretary of War, dated June 30, 1863. Under slavery the Negro had "a tendency to ignore the distinctions of *meum* and *tuum*," but this habit was found not to be deeply rooted.

Another mark of the new status of the Negro was the use of a family name. Under slavery the Negroes had first names only; in antebellum South Carolina and Florida, slaves were flogged for assuming a family name. The wholesale system of surnames for ex-slaves was inaugurated as early as the spring of 1862 by Major General Ormsby M. Mitchel at the town named after him, Mitchelville, a few miles from Hilton Head. The Union commander told the heads of the seventy Negro families in the settlement that they were entitled to two names and advised them to take the names of their former masters. Hence on the plantations of the Sea Islands there soon sprang up a crop of black Peter Beauregards, James Trenholms, Julia Barnwells and Susan Rhetts. The original owners were not always happy at this borrowing. "I used to be proud of my name," wrote Carolina R. Ravenal, of the Seneca plantation in the Palmetto State, "but I have ceased to be so, as the two meanest Negroes on the place have appropriated it. The old coachman is now Nat. Ashby Ravenal, & another man is Sempie Bennett Ravenal."

Not all slaves cared to follow the example of the Ravenal retainers. When recruiting officer Henry Romeyn was signing up Negroes at Gallatin, Tennessee, he overheard the following exchange between an army officer and a Negro volunteer who had just passed his medical examination, and had given his full name as "Dick":

"But every soldier, black or white, has two names; what other one do you want?"

"Don't want none — one name is enough for me."

"You *must* have two. Some of these men take their mother's name, and some take their old master's. Do you want to be called by your old master's name?"

"No, suh, I don't. *I'se had nuff o' ole massa.*"

Often the former slaves would try a name for sound and then after a few days decide to change it. This free-wheeling substitution of names was confusing to teachers and others who dealt with the contrabands, but to the ex-slave it was another proof that he was now his own master.

The use of surnames for Negroes was accepted by whites, but there was little willingness to call a Negro by the titles of "mister," "mistress," or "miss." A Quaker nurse writing from City Point, Virginia, on December 15, 1864, felt obliged to advise her mother to prefix "Miss" to the letters she sent, or else missives bearing the untitled name, "Cornelia Hancock," would be delivered to the contraband camp at the Point.

Another mark of freedom and elevation assumed by the contrabands was that of legal marriage. Under slavery, parents were unable to discharge the full responsibilities of parenthood since slave marriages were not legal and slave families daily faced the threat of separation. Hence among many slaves the idea of chastity was undeveloped, and they had loose ideas on marriage. Some colored women considered it less disgraceful to be illegitimate than to be dark-skinned.

With the coming of freedom, marriage was regarded as a privilege betokening their new status, and the former slaves showed their readiness for this obligation. "Please send me a hundred engraved marriage certificates, such as are sold in Nassau street," wrote the Reverend L. C. Lockwood to the American Missionary Association on September 30, 1861, a few weeks after his arrival at Fortress Monroe. One of Thomas Wentworth Higginson's soldiers, getting ready to marry a girl in Beaufort, asked for a loan of $1.75 to buy a wedding outfit. Colonel Higginson cheerfully advanced the sum, feeling that "matrimony on such moderate terms ought to be encouraged, in these days." In a mass ceremony in the Memphis district, Chaplain Fiske married 119 couples in an hour. Many of these newlyweds had long lived together in slavery, and they were happy to legalize their previously formed unions. Elizabeth H. Botume, witnessing the legal marriage of Sea Island ex-slaves who had long lived as man and wife, found it "touching to see the eager, expectant look on the faces of old couples." Commonly husbands or wives who had been forcibly separated sought out their former mates, going from one plantation to another. At Vicksburg during an eight months' period in 1864, of the more than 3000 couples married, one sixth had been forcibly separated by the operations of slavery.

Under slavery some of the men had been bigamously "married" to more than one wife, having remarried every time they were sold to another plantation. When freedom came the question arose as to which of the women should the much-married husband legally wed. Logically it might seem that he should marry the first of his roster of plantation mates, but in the Sea Islands General Rufus Saxton advised that it might be wisest for the man to marry the "wife" who had borne the most children. The other wives would have to hunt up other husbands.

Typical of the attitude of the majority of ex-slaves toward legal marriage was the step taken by the congregation of the First African Baptist Church of New Orleans, a church with a crisis-laden history dating back to its founding in 1826. When, in September 1864, Louisiana ratified a constitution abolishing slavery, the congregation held a conference meeting late the next month and adopted a new rule "for the government of our church":

> Any persons wishing to become members of this church who may be living in a state of illegitimate marriage shall first procure a license and marry.

To the contrabands one of the chief badges of emancipation was book learning. They placed a high value on literacy — one who had learned to read and write felt that he was thereby guaranteeing his freedom. The former bondsmen remembered that under the slave codes a Negro caught with a pencil in his hand was subject to the lash.

The drawbacks and difficulties in going to school were many. Suitable buildings and equipment were lacking, "sometimes the mere shade of a tree was the only shelter afforded to a school." Books, charts, crayons and slates were inadequate in number and kind. In the absence of primers and spellers the students learned their alphabet from anything in printed form, frequently the Bible. At St. Helena's a sympathetic visitor found the children reading in the seventh chapter of John and stumbling a little on words like "unrighteousness," and "circumcision."

But the undiscouraged Negroes, young and old, flocked to the schoolhouses. They started from scratch: "Us ain't know nothing, and you is to larn we," said an expectant Port Royal beginner to Elizabeth H. Botume. At the Mills plantation another young Sea Islander, who proved not to know one letter from another, said to his teacher, "I larn a little in Secesh, but come away 'fore I finish my edecation."

Sometimes the students answered questions in unexpected ways. When Charlotte Forten asked her class what their ears were for one bright-eyed lass of blessed innocence answered, "to put rings on." Another South Carolina lowland pupil, in response to a question in geography, informed the class that the world was bounded on the north by Charleston, on the south by Savannah, on the west by Columbia and on the east by the sea. William Wells Brown told of an elderly woman at a Jackson, Mississippi, school who when asked who made her, replied, "I don't know, 'zacly, sir. I heard once who it was, but I done forgot de gent-mun's name."

As might be expected, sometimes the learners gave highly in-dividual twists to their lessons. An aged contraband to whom the instructor had presented an old spelling primer with alphabetical couplets, proceeded to compose twenty-six verses of his own. His B, G, K and Q are illustrative:

> *Buchanan* he
> Did climb a tree
> And dar he be.

> *God* fix all right
> Twix' black and white.

> *King* Cotton's ded
> And Sambo's fled.

> *Quashee* was sold
> When blind and old.

But despite the inadequacy of the school buildings and equip-ment, and the flavorful responses of the students, the schools for freedmen flourished to a truly remarkable degree. The former slaves were generally eager to learn and attentive. "None were dull, stupid or uninterested," reported a visitor to the school at

Lawrence, Kansas, composed of colored emigrants from Missouri and Arkansas. These students got their lessons because they were possessed by the crucial factor in the learning process: motivation. Four reasons for their eagerness were listed by J. W. Alvord, Inspector of Schools and Finances of the Freedmen's Bureau, who in the fall of 1865 traveled 4000 miles in eight Southern states. Reported Alvord to Commissioner O. O. Howard on January 1, 1866:

1. They have the natural thirst for knowledge common to all men.
2. They have seen power and influence among white people always coupled with *learning* — it is the sign of elevation to which they now aspire.
3. Its mysteries, hitherto hidden from them in written literature, excite them to the special study of books.
4. Their freedom has given wonderful stimulus to *all effort*, indicating a vitality which augurs well for their whole future condition and character.

Young and old alike responded to the lure of learning. "Children love the school as white children love a holiday," wrote a Port Royal schoolteacher. Negroes far advanced in years showed the same zeal for self-improvement. One of the beginners at Port Royal was a Negro 105 years old, who had been the personal servant of General Nathanael Greene of Revolutionary War fame, who died in 1786. At Oakland's on St. Helena island, Charlotte Forten's man-of-all-work, Cupid, "feared" he was almost too old to learn, but according to a letter from Miss Forten appearing in the *Liberator* for November 22, 1862, "Cupid is now working diligently at the alphabet." J. Miller McKim observed an old woman laboriously spelling out monosyllables from a primer: "Tamar," said I, "why, at your age, do you take so much trouble to learn to read?" "Because I want to read de Word of de Lord." Union officer George E. Sutherland witnessed a sight that was both comic and touching. By the light of a pine knot a former slave had bent his old gray head over a spelling book, and after "wrinkling his forehead, contorting his countenance, and twisting his whole frame as if he were solving the problem of the ages," at last exclaimed, "Which of you uns is A, anyhow?"

The colored people's desire for education led them to take action on their own initiative. "One of the first acts of the Negroes, when they found themselves free, was to establish schools at their own expense," reported the Freedmen's Inquiry Commission, headed by Robert Dale Owen. When James McKaye visited New Orleans in March 1864 to interview the Negro inhabitants, he was informed that one of their chief desires was that "their children shall be educated." Negro parents found no sacrifice too great to send their offspring to school. In 1864 the "Baltimore Association for the Moral and Educational Improvement of the Colored People" operated sixteen flourishing schools with 1957 students. Of the many other schools for Negroes in that city, two were supported by a legacy given ten years earlier by Nelson Willis, a colored man. In Washington the basement of every colored church became a free school.

Throughout the entire South, colored people made great efforts to finance their own education. J. W. Alvord reported that he often heard them say, "We want to show how much we can do ourselves, if you will only give us the chance." Within five weeks after General Sherman swept into Savannah there were five hundred Negro children in schools which were supported wholly by the Negroes themselves. In Tallahassee a visitor in 1865 found five schools "gathered and taught," by the preachers of the place. In Texas in 1865 there were ten day schools and six night schools for freedmen, with a total enrollment of 1091. "They are all self-sustaining," wrote Alvord. Negroes in Little Rock formed a Freedmen's School Society in March 1865 which provided free schools in Arkansas, the first of their kind, whether for blacks or whites.

The work of the Little Rock Negroes points up a noteworthy

fact: the pioneering efforts of the freedmen to establish schools helped to lay the basis for free public education in the South. The poor whites did not care to listen to the Negroes read while they remained unlettered. And the efforts of the freedmen made the ruling class in the South realize that when the schools would open after the war, provisions would have to be made for the rank and file. The American ideal of free public education was measurably furthered by the effort of the former slaves.

The South could not escape the beneficent impact of this mass educational enterprise. For by the end of 1865 there were 90,589 former slaves going to schools conducted under the auspices of the Freedmen's Bureau, with 1314 teachers and 740 buildings. In 1865 the daily attendance at the public schools in New York state averaged 43 per cent; in Alabama among the Negroes the average was 79 per cent in school, and in Virginia 82 per cent. And this did not include the thousands of uncounted black pupils who learned the alphabet by meeting with some literate young man or old preacher in a cellar or shed and passing a torn spelling book from one to the other. "Only an enthusiastic desire for improvement could lead any people to put forth the efforts which the freed people are making to procure instruction," reported Dr. Joseph Warren in 1865. Inspector Alvord, after his trip through eight Southern states observing the activities of the freedmen, summed up his findings: "What other people on earth have shown, while in their ignorance, such a passion for education?"

Thus the former slaves were far from merely wishing for an education — they sought to translate their aspirations into realities. Their efforts were aided immeasurably by the numerous benevolent societies, religious groups and freedmen's aid committees formed to relieve the pressing needs of the newly emancipated. The notable and generous labors of these organizations were superseded by the Bureau of Refugees, Freedmen and Abandoned Lands, popularly known as the Freedmen's Bureau, established in March 1865 by act of Congress. Under the able leadership of

Commissioner O. O. Howard, the Bureau was destined in its seven years of existence to accomplish great good in helping many of the ex-slaves make the transition to freedom. But the Freedmen's Bureau, and its forerunners, was needed "not because these people are Negroes," as Robert Dale Owen's committee phrased it, "but because they are men who have been for generations despoiled of their rights."

This does not mean that the more than a thousand white teachers who came to the South prior to the establishing of the national Bureau did not deserve the deepest gratitude of the contrabands. Taking a personal interest in the welfare of the ex-slaves, these dedicated men and women contributed greatly to the Negro's desire to go to school and to improve his lot. Inspired by the Christian imperative in human relations, these whites went uncomplainingly about their varied duties — instructing in the alphabet, teaching Sunday school, visiting cabins to inform mothers of the simple rules of health and cleanliness, and writing letters for the wives of soldiers.

These teachers had their problems. Salaries were small, barely covering expenses. Sneers came their way from Southern whites who objected to book learning for blacks. "Nigger teachers" faced social ostracism. When Henry Martin Tupper, founder of Shaw University, came to Raleigh, North Carolina, in 1865 to take up missionary work among the freedmen, a locally prominent Baptist clergyman advised him like a brother to catch the first Seaboard Air Line train going back North. Turning to Tupper's young bride, he said, "I hope, young woman, you have brought a generous supply of handkerchiefs with you, for you will certainly need them."

Nothing daunted, these teachers brought to their labors courage and endurance. One of them, Elizabeth James, sent out by the American Missionary Association to Roanoke Island in October 1863, worked for three months alone and unattended. In planting New England schoolhouses among the unlettered sons and daughters of the South, Elizabeth James and others like her took heart because the former slaves so obviously appreciated their sacrifices. Teachers' tables were loaded, morning and noon, with oranges, apples, figs and candies. "It is a great happiness to teach them," said Charlotte Forten, whose affection for her pupils was reciprocated in full measure. Laura M. Towne, who for nearly four decades lived among the freedmen and their offspring, knew every day of her life that she was loved. On a plot of ground in the center of windswept St. Helena's stands a single stone with a few brief words:

In Memory of
LAURA M. TOWNE
1825–1901
She devoted thirty-eight years of her life to
the colored people of St. Helena Island and
employed her means in their education and care.

Miss Towne would not have minded this restrained statement. She had received roses while she was living.

✤

Another badge of freedom proudly displayed by the ex-slave was military service. The Negro took stock in the adage that they who would be free must themselves strike the blow. By bearing arms on the field of battle the freedman could demonstrate his devotion to the cause of liberty. In the closing year of the war black soldiers gave many such demonstrations.

The Virginia theater, more than any other, witnessed the actions in which many Negro troops participated during the war's last twelve months. Ulysses S. Grant, commissioned lieutenant general on March 9, 1864, and appointed general in chief of the military forces, transferred nearly 20,000 Negroes from other fronts to the armies of the James and the Potomac. In addition to these blacks from the southern and western armies, there were in Virginia a host of recently recruited colored troops ready to assist in the final thrusts designed to knock out Lee's veteran army and capture Richmond. These colored volunteers included the nine regiments which comprised the fourth division of Ambrose Burnside's Ninth Army Corps, the eight regiments constituting the third division of the Tenth Corps, and the thirteen regiments, one of them cavalry, making up the third division of the Eighteenth Corps, the two last corps comprising the Army of the James.

Burnside's colored division had trained at Camp Stanton in Annapolis. Breaking camp early in April 1864, the Negro regiments joined the rest of the corps for a parade through Washington en route to Alexandria. On the cool and clear spring morning of April 25 the blue-clad soldiers, white and black, moved through the densely crowded streets of the capital, bands playing and drums beating. From a balcony above the entrance to Willard's Hotel, President Lincoln and a party of Congressmen viewed the columns of troops, which returned a marching salute as they filed past the Presidential box. This was Lincoln's first review of blacks in uniform, and he seemed pleased as he watched regiment after regiment of ex-slaves march in perfect step, their platoons stretching from curbstone to curbstone. Perhaps this impressive spectacle would come into his mind's eye a few weeks later when he received reports of the steadiness shown by the raw Negro recruits while under severe fire during the bitter Wilderness campaign and at Cold Harbor.

During May and June while Burnside's blacks were fighting north of Richmond, the Negroes in the Army of the Potomac, commanded by General Benjamin Butler, saw action below the besieged capital. On May 5 they seized Wilson's Landing, on the north side of the James, which they held despite a bitterly waged counterattack by Major General Fitzhugh Lee and his famous cavalry force, the eyewitness New York *Times* correspondent reporting that "the chivalry of Fitzhugh Lee and his cavalry division was badly worsted in the contest last Tuesday with Negro troops composing the garrison at Wilson's Landing." Four days after the fall of Wilson's Landing, General Butler sent a dispatch to Washington describing another operation involving Negroes: "With one thousand seven hundred cavalry we have advanced up the Peninsula, and forced the Chickahominy. . . . These were *colored cavalry*, and are now holding our advanced pickets toward Richmond."

In mid-June Grant decided to make a surprise attack on Petersburg, a vitally important railroad center, twenty-two miles below Richmond. The Eighteenth Corps, under General W. F. Smith, was ordered to do the job. One of "Baldy" Smith's three divisions was General E. W. Hinks's Negro brigade, consisting of four regiments of infantry, two regiments of cavalry and two batteries.

Shortly after daybreak on June 15 as the Union columns approached the City Point and Petersburg turnpike, at a place known as Baylor's farm, a Rebel battery opened fire behind a line of heavy thickets. The black troops struggled forward through the swampy woods, the Rebels shelling them without stint every step of the way. Then the colored soldiers charged up the slope through the murderous fire. A hundred men went down, but the slope was taken, the Rebels fleeing in confusion. The fifth and twenty-second colored regiments had carried the enemy's outpost and cleared the road for the entire corps.

Confident now in their ability, the 3000 colored volunteers steeled themselves for the attack on the main line of the Confederate works. To reach their assigned position 800 yards away, the Negro soldiers, so runs a contemporary account, "were obliged to advance across an open field, exposed the whole distance to a deadly fire, completely enfilading their two lines of battle, to a fire from two batteries directly in front, and to a cross-fire from an intermediate battery." At 1:30 P.M. their ordeal ended as they gained their position, having advanced a few nerve-racking rods at a time. Then for five hours they lay in the shadow of the

enemy guns, while General Smith made a reconnaissance preparatory to launching the general assault.

Finally at 6:30 the charge was ordered. Following an exchange
of heavy cannonading, and the sending out of a detail of colored
skirmishers, the Union troops made a dash toward the formidable
Rebel works. The advancing line was greeted by a torrent of
bullets, but the Negro soldiers kept coming on the run, their
bayonets glistening obliquely in the fading sunlight. Despite a
devastating fire, they pressed forward until they had gotten so
far under the enemy's long-range guns as to be sheltered. The
Rebels then took to their rifle pits. To no avail. Led by a color
sergeant who waved them on, the black troops scaled the breastworks and made a dash for the Confederate infantrymen. The
latter fought till the last moment and then, shortly after nine
o'clock, swiftly withdrew. However, the fleeing Rebels had taken
a sizable toll. The Fourth U. S. Colored Troops alone lost "about
250 out of less than 600 men," wrote Christian A. Fleetwood, a
company sergeant.

The black soldiers were elated at having proved their mettle. Of
the 15 pieces of artillery captured, they took 9; of the 300 prisoners taken, they accounted for 200. Their gallantry had amazed
their white fellow soldiers, who were loud in their expressions of
admiration. "No nobler effort has been put forth today, and no
greater success achieved than that of the colored troops," said the
usually uncommunicative "Baldy" Smith to a reporter. His order
of the day bore additional testimony:

> To the colored troops comprising the division of General
> Hinks, the General commanding would call the attention of
> his command. With the veterans of the Eighteenth Corps,
> they have stormed the works of the enemy and carried them,
> taking guns and prisoners, and in the whole affair, they have
> displayed all the qualities of good soldiers.

An hour after the Rebels had withdrawn, Smith appeared before
the colored volunteers and told them that he was proud of their

courage and dash. They had no superiors as soldiers, added he. The general spread the news. "Smith told us that the Negro troops fought magnificently, the hardest fighting being done by them," wrote Assistant Secretary of War Charles A. Dana, who was escorted to the Petersburg front by General Grant on the morning after the action.

When Lincoln visited Grant's camp six days later to review the Virginia commands, the general suggested that they "ride on and see the colored troops, who behaved so handsomely in Smith's attack on the works in front of Petersburg last week." "Oh yes," replied Lincoln, as related by Horace Porter, Grant's personal aide, "I want to take a look at those boys. I read with the greatest delight the account given in Mr. Dana's dispatch to the Secretary of War how gallantly they behaved."

Despite the bravery of the blacks on June 15, however, Petersburg was not taken. General Smith did not follow up the success of the day's fighting; instead he bivouacked for the night, despite a clear sky and a nearly full moon. Thus given an unexpected breathing spell, the defenders of the hard-pressed city mounted twenty guns. At dawn they were further re-enforced by the arrival of Lee's iron-sided veterans. The Union Army had lost a golden opportunity.

Smith's tardiness in following up his thrust necessitated a siege. Among the troops brought up and stationed in front of the city were the eight black regiments comprising the fourth division of the Ninth Army Corps. Commanded by Brigadier General Edward Ferrero, this division was destined to sustain more losses than any other in the Battle of the Crater, one of the most spectacular as well as one of the most bloody and brutal actions of the war.

Encamped 150 yards from the enemy, the Union forces were confronted by a fort projecting beyond the Rebels' main line. If this outlying bastion could be reduced, a successful general assault on Petersburg might be quickly effected. To achieve this end, the Union high command decided to run a mine under the fort and blow it up. Under Colonel Henry Pleasants, an experienced mining engineer, the Forty-eighth Pennsylvania, composed largely of men from the anthracite coal regions of the Schuylkill Valley, began tunneling on June 25. Screened from the enemy's observation, the regiment worked steadily for five weeks, scooping out the earth under the unsuspecting Confederates and charging the mine with 8000 pounds of gunpowder in 320 kegs. The mine completed and the two galleries charged, operation "springing" was set for the morning of July 30 at the pitch-black hour of three-thirty.

Then came an even more crucial question: which of the four divisions of the Ninth Corps should lead the attack? For this action, Burnside had selected the black phalanx, and for some days had been drilling them in preparation for the initial dash into the chasm to be opened by the explosion. "We had expected we were to lead the assault, and had been for several weeks drilling our men with this idea in view, particular attention being paid to charging," wrote the captain of the Nineteenth U. S. Colored Troops. "Only the day before, our regiment was drilled by Major Richwood in forming double columns and charging. There was not an officer but would have staked everything that we would break through their lines and go on to Cemetery Hill, as proposed."

But Burnside's decision was questioned by George G. Meade, who felt that the Negro troops were not sufficiently seasoned to lead the assault, and that if the venture proved a failure, "it would be then said, and very properly, that we were shoving those people ahead to get them killed because we did not care anything about them." Burnside appealed this decision. Ulysses S. Grant, following military propriety, upheld Commander Meade, although later, in his testimony before the Committee on the Conduct of the War, he confessed that he believed that had Burnside's recommendation been followed, the assault "would have been a success." Just a few hours before the assault was to be made, the fourth division was told of the decision. Burnside ordered the three white divisions to draw lots for the lead position.

Then came the moment for the explosion. The fuses were lighted and every eye was turned to the Rebel fort three hundred feet distant. The Confederates were sleeping, the sentinels pacing their rounds. The Union troops watched in silence, scarcely a murmur rising from the massed divisions, the first division in the center, the second and third divisions on the right and left sides, and the black contingent in the rear, assigned to follow over the center route taken by the first division. Back of the lines stood General Grant, flanked by his officers, peering toward the mine.

Some minutes passed, and Grant looked at his watch. It was past the time — ten minutes, then half an hour, then an hour, and no explosion. Dawn was breaking and the enemy camp was showing signs of bestirring itself. Grant waited impatiently for his officer-messengers to return and explain the cause of the delay. They brought back word that the match had been applied, but that the fuses had failed, and that two brave volunteers of the Forty-eighth Pennsylvania had entered the mine to resplice the fuses. A few minutes after this report was made a second match was struck, and at 4:50, over an hour behind schedule, the mine exploded.

No one present ever forgot the spectacle. The shock was like that of an earthquake, accompanied by a dull, muffled roar. Then came the incredible sight of men, guns, and caissons being vomited two hundred feet in air. The spot where these objects had stood but a moment before was now an inverted cone with forked tongues of flame. The first thunderous report had not yet died down when a loud clap was heard as great blocks of clay, rock, sand and timber, all interspersed with mutilated human bodies, descended around the periphery of the exploded area. Four Rebel companies were shattered by the eruption and partly buried in the debris. "The first I knew of the crater, be-

HARPER'S WEEKLY.

A JOURNAL OF CIVILIZATION.

VOL. V.—No. 260.]   NEW YORK, SATURDAY, DECEMBER 21, 1861.   [SINGLE COPIES SIX CENTS.

BUILDING ROADS

GOVRNT. BLACKSMITHS' SHOP

ON PICKET

COOKING IN CAMP

UNLOADING GOVT. STORES

IN THE TRENCHES

SCOUTS

TEAMSTER OF THE ARMY

DRIVING GOVT. CATTLE

WASHING IN CAMP

THE WAR IN VIRGINIA—THE EIGHTEENTH ARMY CORPS STORMING A FORT ON THE RIGHT OF THE CONFEDERATE LINE
BEFORE PETERSBURG, JUNE 15th, 1864.

THE WAR IN VIRGINIA.—THE TWENTY-SECOND COLORED REGIMENT, DUNCAN'S BRIGADE, CARRYING THE FIRST LINE OF
CONFEDERATE WORKS BEFORE PETERSBURG.—FROM A SKETCH BY OUR SPECIAL ARTIST, EDWIN FORBES.

yond the tremendous report of the explosion," wrote Confederate General William Mahone — an able commander, but one not given to unnecessary self-exposure — "came from a soldier, who, from thereabouts, hatless and shoeless, passed me, still going, and only time to say, 'Hell has busted.' " Pieces of Confederate artillery were tossed fifty feet away. The clearing of the dust and smoke revealed a yawning crater, 30 feet deep, 60 feet wide and 170 feet long. Simultaneously the Union guns, 110 cannon and 50 mortars, opened up all along the line, and the first division was ordered to charge.

As soon as the blue-clad soldiers rushed toward the crater, some fatal errors became apparent. The ground obstructions placed by the enemy had not been removed, thus causing the loss of twenty precious minutes in clearing a path. When the Yankees reached the side of the crater they found that the sides were so steep that, once in, it would be almost impossible to get out. The element of surprise had been diminished by the delay, and the Rebels recovered their wits much more quickly than anticipated.

When the men of the first division attempted to rush up the side of the crater, the Rebels opened a deadly fire. As the Union soldiers fell back, the enemy sharpshooters picked them off, and soon the Rebel artillery had the range. But worse was to come for the milling men in the pit. The third division, failing in its assignment to move to the left, fell back into the crater. The second division, assigned to the right, was caught in a withering fire from enemy guns planted on each side of the crater, and they too sought refuge with their already crowded predecessors.

But military ineptitude had one final crowning touch. The supporting reserve column of Negro troops, which had been standing for over an hour crowded in the covered ways leading to the breastworks, was ordered to charge. Faced by musketry fire in front and a cross fire of shell and grape from the flanks, the Negro troops moved forward rapidly, some of them going into the pit, as originally planned, and others skirting around it. The Forty-third Colored Troops moved over the lip of the crater and engaged the enemy in close combat, taking two stands of colors and 200 prisoners, for the only Union success of the day.

The hand-to-hand fighting continued without quarter. The Negro troops were meeting a keyed-up enemy. Moreover, his murderous fire, from front and flank, could not be long withstood. From their untenable position, the stricken blacks soon fell back in disorder, some into the crater, already choked with dead, and some all the way back to the Union lines.

The failure of the black brigade ended any hope of success. In the early afternoon Burnside gave the order to retreat. But this proved difficult: the crater had become a hell. Thirsty and sun-baked, the blue-clad boys tried to break out of the deathtrap and make a dash for the Union lines. The Confederates, fresh and victory-flushed, decided to ring down the curtain. Advancing into the slaughterhouse, they killed or captured those who had been unable to scale the sides.

The Negro brigade's casualty list of 1327 was greater than that of any other division, the first division aggregating 654, the second 832, and the third 659. Rolled in blankets, the dead were laid in long, deep trenches, several bodies deep. The wounded blacks were rushed to City Point, where noble-spirited nurse Helen Gilson, in her somber, gray-flannel gown, had established an efficiently run Colored Hospital Service. Thus ended the most costly military experiment in the four years of battle: "It was the saddest effort I have ever witnessed in the war," reported Grant.

The crater experience by no means demoralized the Negro soldiers in the Virginia theater. At Deep Bottom two weeks later, four black regiments incorporated into the Tenth Corps distinguished themselves in an action designed, as Grant put it, "to call troops from Early and from the defenses of Petersburg." The Negro volunteers bore the enemy assault gallantly. "The Colored Troops behaved handsomely, and are in fine spirits," reported corps commander, Major General D. B. Birney, on August 19, 1864. General Butler added a like comment:

> The loss in the four colored regiments is about three hundred. The Seventh U. S. C. T. on the first day, carried with fixed bayonets, a line of rifle-pits, and carried it without a shot, but with a loss of 35. It was one of the most stirring and gallant affairs I have ever known.

Six weeks later at New Market Heights, the key to the Rebel flank on the north side of the James, the black soldiers under Birney added to their laurels. Ordered to take Fort Harrison, the Negroes reduced that stronghold and secured the New Market Road. They had advanced at dawn and pressed up the slope, the axemen hacking the lines of abatis. When the last line was reached, the Rebels fled without waiting for the bayonet charge. The Negro column swept over the parapet and took possession. Their losses had been severe. General Butler, riding along the line of charge, counted 543 dead bodies in a space 300 yards long and "not wider than the clerk's desk."

Black soldiers saw their share of action in nearly all the military engagements around Richmond and Petersburg in the closing year of the war. On Virginia battlefields "the Negro stood in the full glare of the greatest search-light, part and parcel of the grandest armies ever mustered upon this continent," wrote Christian Abraham Fleetwood, "competing side by side with the bravest and best of Lee's army, and losing nothing by comparison." Congressional medal winner Fleetwood could speak from first-hand knowledge: his own regiment, the Fourth United States Colored Infantry, had an impressive record, seeing action at Yorktown, Petersburg, New Market Heights and Fort Fisher.

❖

Matched by the role of the Negro in the Virginia campaign was the work of his black brother in the battle of Nashville —

the military engagement that put an end to effective Confederate resistance in the West. When this two-day encounter ended, one of the South's two armies was completely broken, its regiments in flight as a disorganized rabble.

In early December 1864 this deservedly proud Army of Tennessee, consisting of about 44,000 men of all arms and commanded by John B. Hood, had encamped in position on the outskirts of Nashville. Its earthworks were constructed and its siege guns were mounted in preparation for the attack on the Union forces which William T. Sherman had left behind when he started his march to the seaboard. The object of the proposed assault against Nashville, as stated by General P. G. T. Beauregard, was "to deal rapid and vigorous blows — to strike the enemy while dispersed, and by that distract Sherman's advance into Georgia."

The Army of the Cumberland was quite ready for the wager of battle with the Confederates. Commanding officer George H. Thomas had been ordered to take the initiative from the Rebels. Battlewise Thomas, "the Rock of Chickamauga," had decided on a ruse: to make a strong demonstration against the enemy's right wing so as to withdraw his attention from the flanking main assault against his left. "Old Pap" Thomas, as he was affectionately known among the colored soldiery, had come around to the belief that Negroes would fight; hence the brigade selected for this opening feint attack was formed almost entirely by blacks — five regiments of them, recruited mainly from Tennessee, with a few dozen volunteers from Missouri. To assist in this attack designed to mislead the enemy, three additional Negro regiments — the second brigade, commanded by Colonel Charles R. Thompson — were given the assignment to carry the line of Rebel fortifications on the Nolensville turnpike, which cut across the railroad running from Nashville to Murfreesboro.

On the night of December 14, Colonel Thomas J. Morgan, commander of the first brigade of five black regiments, was summoned to the headquarters of General James B. Steedman, com-

mander of the Provisional Detachment which included the two
colored brigades, and informed that he was assigned to open up
the hostilities in the battle by making a vigorous assault on the
Rebel right flank, intended to betray Hood into the belief that it
was the main attack. On his way back to camp, Morgan thought
through a plan of action, then gave orders for the brigade to have
an early breakfast and be ready for combat immediately thereafter.

On the following morning at eight, when the dense fog that
curtained the landscape had lifted, the Union battery opened up
on the enemy, and then "the Negroes came out with a rush,"
wrote a Confederate officer, "first sending out a cloud of skirmishers to draw our fire." The oncoming blacks drove the pickets
to cover and then passed over the crest of the rising ground and
onto the slope reaching down to the Nashville and Chattanooga
railroad. So vigorous was the attack that the black soldiers carried a portion of the works, the impetuosity of their thrust
turning the action into more than a mere feint.

Once on the enemy's works, however, the Negro troops were
exposed to severe fire from close-range artillery and from the
shells of a battery placed in position on a hill. "When a colored
brigade, led by white officers, was within 200 yards of our line,
our batteries opened upon them," wrote Confederate Captain
Thomas J. Key, in his diary for December 15, 1864, "leaving
quite a number of the fuliginous skins lifeless and vimless on the
cold ground." What the assaulting troops were up against, in the
words of another Confederate officer, was "the hottest fire men
ever faced, white or black." Thereupon General Steedman sent
word to order the black detail back behind the crest.

The colored brigade was immediately re-formed for an attack
on a Rebel detachment occupying an earthwork east of a habita-
tion known as the "Raine's house." At 11 o'clock, the Negro
troops, raising a yell, carried the works at the point of the
bayonet. They took the house and the adjacent brick buildings,

perforated them with openings for guns, and camped there until next morning, their assignment executed smoothly.

While Morgan's troops were engaged, Colonel Thompson's second brigade was not idle. As soon as the first guns were heard, they waded across Brown's Creek, swept past the Lebanon Pike, and advanced to the ground between the Nolensville and Murfreesboro turnpikes. Here they carried the left of the Rebel front line of fortifications, resting on the Nolensville Pike. Their orders successfully executed, they waited at the pike, making slight shifts now and then in order to protect themselves from the enemy fire.

By their soldiership these eight Negro regiments enabled General Thomas to execute the grand strategy of the battle. The vigor of their attack convinced the Confederates, as Thomas had hoped, that the main thrust was to be made at their right wing. Hood thereupon had weakened his left to meet what he believed was an attack in force, rather than a diversionary tactic. Thomas seized the coveted opportunity, assailing the weakened Rebel left flank, doubling it up, and taking 1200 prisoners. It was a memorable day for the Union forces. Lying on their arms, the boys in blue bivouacked with complete confidence of finishing the job the next day.

On the following morning at six o'clock Steedman's brigades moved toward the enemy works, only to discover that Hood had drawn back his right line during the night. The Confederate commander had taken up a new line above a crest of hills and had spent the night in fortifying his position. Soon after breakfast the black brigade moved toward the enemy stronghold, pushing out on the Nolensville Pike.

At one o'clock Steedman's command joined that of General T. J. Wood for an attack on strongly fortified Overton Hill. Thompson's black regiments were assigned to attack the extreme right of the Rebel line. The assaulting troops were instructed to move steadily across the field of corn stubble until they were near to the entrenchments, 600 yards away, and then to dash up the ascent and leap over the obstructions and over the parapets.

As the Union columns moved up the slope of the hill, the Thirteenth U. S. Colored Infantry led the line. Greeted by a tremendous fire of canister and musketry which tore wide gaps in their ranks, they continued to thread their way upward, slowed down by the abatis — a tangled intricacy of sharpened branches and palisades which tore their flesh into ribbons. Stumbling, tripping and falling, regaining their feet to fall again, many of them got through.

When the front line neared the crest, the Rebel reserves rose and poured into the thinning line a devastating fire. The assaulting column was fearfully cut up, "its right wing melting away like snow falling into a stream." In the space of thirty minutes the black regiment lost 25 per cent of its enrollment. The official report of Confederate General James T. Holtzclaw indicated something of the high death toll among the Negroes:

> At 12 m. the enemy made a most determined charge to my right. Placing a Negro brigade in front they gallantly dashed up the abatis, forty feet in front, and were killed by the hundreds. I have seen most of the battlefields of the West, but never saw dead men thicker than in front of my two regiments.

Facing such a volley as the most battle-hardened veteran would dread, many of the Negro troops pressed on, and actually succeeded in mounting the parapets. Confederate General Henry D. Clay reported that "five Union color bearers were shot down within a few steps of our works, one of which, having inscribed on its folds, 'Eighteenth Regiment U. S. Colored Infantry: presented by the colored ladies of Murphreesboro.'" These color bearers and others who reached the parapet were soon forced back, having no support. The retreat of one of them was described by an eyewitness:

I saw the color corporal of the 12th, the only man left on his feet, and [while] loading and firing, a glancing shot struck the side of his head, and pulling up the flag, he drew from beneath the dead sergeant the stars and stripes. With both under one arm and his musket in the other, with blood streaming down his face, he strode back to the supporting line.

General Steedman immediately re-formed the troops for a second try. But it was unnecessary. At about three o'clock, as the brigade readied itself for the command to charge, the Rebels suddenly abandoned the works all along the defending line. What had happened soon became evident. The Confederates had thrown a disproportionate share of their strength into repelling the assault on Overton Hill, with the result that they had so weakened their left wing that the pressing Union forces on that front had achieved a complete breakthrough which soon spread all along the line. The Army of Tennessee took to headlong flight in what soon became a rout of major proportions. "I beheld for the first and only time a Confederate army abandon the field in confusion," said the sorrowing Hood. Routed from the field and ingloriously pursued for ten days was an army that had acquitted itself with distinction at such historic Southern shrines as Donelson, Shiloh, Chickamauga, Lookout Mountain, Missionary Ridge and Reseca.

To the headquarters of General George H. Thomas came telegrams of congratulations from President Lincoln and Secretary of War Stanton. A message from Lieutenant General Grant sped its way: "The armies operating against Richmond have fired two hundred guns in honor of your great victory. . . ." A salvo of one hundred guns had been the salute discharged in honor of other victories.

On the night of December 16, as his troops pursued the fleeing enemy, modest General Thomas had good reason to be proud. In this great battle which clearly marked the doom of the South, his own generalship had been in the tradition of the masters of military strategy and execution. Moreover, his entire army had displayed the highest military virtues, living up to his complete confidence. He had never doubted any of his regiments. As he rode over the littered battlefield in the gathering dusk and saw the strewn bodies of black soldiers up with the foremost, the Virginia-born general turned to his staff and said, as if in confirmation of something that he had known all along, "Gentlemen, Negroes will fight."

In the final four months of the war, as Sherman moved upward from Georgia and Grant hammered harder at Richmond, the nation got ready to write "finis" to a stirring chapter in its history, a chapter to which Americans of color were contributory.

WILLIAM TECUMSEH SHERMAN: *"Well, now, old man, what do you think about the war?"*

UNCLE STEPHEN: *"Well, Sir, what I think about it, is this — it's mighty distressin', this war, but it 'pears to me like the right thing couldn't be done without it."*

CHAPTER XIV

Jubilee – Jubilanus – Jubilatum!

LATE IN 1864 when Admiral David D. Porter visited a plantation twenty miles above Vicksburg, he found only one Negro out of a former population of nearly four hundred. "Uncle Moses," with whom he had conversed on a previous visit many months before, informed him that all the young "bucks" had gone on the warpath, having joined the army or enlisted on board "Mr. Linkum's gunboats." The ancient retainer asked the admiral what a contraband was. Porter told him. Delighted with the explanation, the old ex-slave said that henceforth he would insist that the younger generation address him as "Mister Contraban' Moses." Admiral Porter remembered his farewell words, "Good-by, Massa Cap'n, I's mos' sorry de war so nigh ober, cos I's 'fraid de niggers won't be no more consekence."

That the Negro was *persona grata* in the closing months of the war could hardly be disputed. He was the subject of laws passed by state legislatures and Congress, he contributed to the success of General W. T. Sherman's armies as they swept into Savannah, and then northward, he was with the vanguard of triumphant troops that marched into Charleston and Richmond, and he took part in the victory celebration held at historic Fort Sumter four years from the day on which Major Robert J. Anderson had run up the white flag. These roles may be considered in turn.

Toward the close of the war, a number of states acted on be-half of the Negro. Early in January 1865 the Missouri legislature declared free "all persons held to service or labor" in the com-monwealth. At the same time Tennessee also joined the ranks of the free states and the governor of Delaware, William Cannon, urged his legislature to go and do likewise. During the same month Illinois repealed her notorious laws discriminating against the colored population.

The national government also took action concerning the Negro. By the end of January 1865 both houses had passed the amendment abolishing slavery and the measure had gone to the states for ratification. Early in March the President had signed a bill freeing the wives and children of colored soldiers and later in the same month the Freedmen's Bureau was established. And on February 1, 1865, an hour before noon, Charles Sumner stood before the highest tribunal in the land and said in tones strangely muted: "May it please the Court, I move that John S. Rock, a member of the Supreme Court of the State of Massachusetts, be admitted to practice as a member of this Court." The massive head of Chief Justice Chase moved with an assenting nod, and the reluctant clerk of the court swore in a man "with hair of an aggravating kink, and with no palliation of complexion, no let down in lip, no compromise in nose," from the pure Negroid.

In the South the Negro was of consequence during the war's terminal stages, his role being that of an actor rather than some-thing acted upon. One of the curtain-lowering scenes in which he appeared was Sherman's march to the sea, perhaps the most celebrated campaign in the whole war. The Negro did not shoulder a gun in this great movement — Sherman never changed his opinion about the Negro as a soldier. But in this memorable seaward thrust, Sherman's army was noted far less for any fight-ing it did than for its long marches in Rebel territory, cutting through the land like a giant scythe. The fame of Sherman's troops rested primarily on their resourcefulness in living off the enemy country, and in their ability to lay bridges and build or tear up roads and railways with speed and efficiency. In doing these things they were measurably assisted by Negroes.

Atlanta had fallen to Sherman early in September 1864, and six weeks later he was ready to move on, destination Savannah. His thoroughly sifted troops — 60,000 infantry and 5500 cavalry — had received their instructions. Supplies and ammunition had been accumulated. On November 15, after setting off a tremendous bonfire, the Union troops rode out of the stricken city, their bands playing "John Brown's Body."

Before Sherman was one day out he was faced with a problem that with all his meticulous planning he had not foreseen and that his armies were to encounter during the entire four weeks' journey — the coming of a dark human cloud. Every day as the troops covered the miles they could see hundreds of Negroes, in all shades and sizes, threading along through the roads and cutting across the fields. At every encampment flocks of blacks appeared, as if drawn like a plague of moths by the huge campfires. From one plantation near Covington — that of the Lunts — every slave had left except one whose wife was in service on a nearby estate. So great were their numbers that Sherman's officers were certain that the knowledge of the coming of the Federals had been carried by swift black runners traveling during the night from plantation to plantation.

These Negroes greeted the Yankees effusively. Some danced a jig, some gave fervent and embarrassing hugs to the nearest soldiers, and some stood by the roadway, politely and gravely saluting everything that came along. Walt Whitman ("as under doughty Sherman I marched toward the sea") described one of them in "Ethiopia Salutes the Colors":

Who are you, dusky woman, so ancient hardly human,
With your woolly-white and turban'd head, and bare bony
feet?
Why rising by the roadside here, do you the colors greet?

One of the ex-slaves, waiting in awe for the long line of marching soldiers to come to an end, exclaimed, "Dar's millions of 'em,
millions." Then he asked, "Is dare anybody lef' up Norf?" After
paying their respects, the Negroes waited till the column passed
and then fell in at the rear, ready to follow the bluecoats wherever
they went.

These uninvited blacks brought with them all their earthly
goods, and some goods which were not theirs. Many carried
bundles packed with clothes and a small stock of groceries. Livestock, carts and old family carriages all took their places in the
refugee train. One cart drawn by a pair of lean, broken-down
oxen, "contained no less than nineteen pickaninnies, the oldest of
them not over three years," their anxious mothers walking in
procession on each side.

Mules and horses were laden with hampers and bags, stuffed
with children and wearables, balanced on each side. Sometimes
on one side of the mule, a dark head would be peeping out, its
weight counterpoised by a sack of hams and turkeys on the
other. Major General Henry W. Slocum, commanding the Fourteenth and Twentieth Corps, related that one day a large family
came through the fields to join the left wing. The head of the
family was mounted on a mule, the latter covered by a blanket
to which pockets had been attached. Stowed away in these pockets were two little Negroes, one on each side. This gave rise,
wrote Slocum, "to a most important invention, i.e., 'the best way
of transporting pickaninnies' ":

On the next day a mule appeared in column, covered by
a blanket with two pockets on each side, each containing
a little Negro. Very soon old tent flies or strong canvas was
used instead of the blanket, and often ten or fifteen pockets
were attached to each side, so that nothing of the mule
was visible except the head, tail, and feet, all else being
covered by the black woolly heads and bright shining eyes
of the little darkies.

General Sherman was not happy as he looked toward the rear. Feeling that these trailing swarms of Negroes would slow down his line of march, he pondered on how he might arrest the tide. He decided on the personal approach — talking directly to the refugees.

At a plantation just outside of Covington, near the Ulcofauhachee River, the commander noticed among the swarm that came to greet him "an old, gray-haired man, of as fine a head as I ever saw." Addressing his remarks to this spokesman, Sherman asked him if he understood "about the war and its progress." "Yes, suh!" said the old man, adding that he had been looking forward to the day of deliverance since he was knee-high. Did the Negroes understand, continued Sherman, that slavery was the cause of the war and that Union triumph on the battlefield would be their freedom? Yes, they knew this, answered he of the impressive head. These things cleared, Sherman then explained that he wanted the Negroes to stay put and not to load the armies "with useless mouths." The strong and unmarried he could employ as laborers, but if the others tagged along it would cripple him in the task of winning freedom for all.

Sherman believed that the old man spread this message, which was then carried by grapevine, thus saving the army from the danger of "swelling our numbers so that famine would have attended our progress."

With this incident on the Ulcofauhachee, Sherman set the pattern for his dealings with Negroes — sitting down and presenting the issues in plain terms and asking their co-operation. "Along the whole line of our march," wrote George Ward Nichols, "General Sherman has never lost an opportunity of talking with and advising the Negroes who came to our camp, and his great heart has overflowed in kindly counsel to these poor people."

Like Sherman's soldiers, the Negroes idolized the general. "They gather round me in crowds," wrote Sherman to H. W.

Halleck, "and I can't find out whether I am Moses or Aaron, or which of the prophets; but sure I am rated as one of the congregation." This commander of a great army found time to talk to former slaves, frankly and pleasantly. He put them at their ease by his informal, off-hand manner. Yet he did not talk down to them; he had that rare knack of being friendly without being familiar.

In Negro circles his fame was great. A Union soldier pointed him out to a contraband woman who "was smart as a steel-trap," having fed and hidden three escaped prisoners: "Dar's de man dat rules de world," she shouted. Another Negro approached the general, peered at him closely, and went away muttering repeatedly like a defective phonograph record, "He has the Linkum head, he has the Linkum head, he has the Linkum head." At the Howell Cobb plantation as Sherman was relaxing after supper, an old Negro with a tallow candle in his hand came up and scanned his face. Sherman asked what he wanted. "Dey say you is Massa Sherman." The general answered that such was the case and again inquired what he wanted. According to Sherman, the old Negro replied that "he only wanted to look at me, and kept muttering, 'Dis nigger can't sleep dis night.'" Just as the Sea Island Negroes reckoned time from the day "when the guns fired at Bay Point," the colored population at Savannah for half a century hence would date events by "the time when Tecumpsey was here."

Despite their genuflection at the mention of Sherman's name, some 35,000 Negroes ignored his advice about remaining where they were. Why wait until the end of the war for freedom, ran their reasoning, when they could have it right away by simply attaching themselves to the army? So on they came, across the bayous and lagoons of Georgia, by day trudging in the rear, and at night fringing the bivouacs with a hundred gypsy camps. Despite Sherman's orders, it was hard to turn them off and order them back. Here a woman begged that she might go to Savannah to see her husband and children from whom she had been sold many years previously. Another related that she had heard that her boy was in Macon, the son for whom she had been "done gone with grief goin' on four years." George Ward Nichols told of a woman who was threading her way among the teams, a child in her arms, when an officer called to her: "Where are you going, aunty?" The ancestral contraband looked into his face and replied, with a hopeful, beseeching look, "I'se gwine whar you'se gwine, massa."

But the role of the Negro was not confined to the receiving end. From the very beginning, blacks furnished valuable information to the onmarching Yankees. On his second day out, Sherman dispatched Major James C. McCoy to find a Negro resident in order to question him about roads and bridges. "Don't want [a] white man," said the general. McCoy brought back a "very intelligent fellow," who had a long talk with Sherman, both sitting before the campfire. "Grinning Negroes piloted the army, and appeared to be in their element," reported Sherman's aide-de-camp, David P. Conynham. The blacks helped the invader flush up hidden valuables, and they could be relied on to tell whether a newly made grave enshrouded a corpse or concealed a cache less other-worldly.

The assistance given by Negroes to the foragers was incalculable. One of the notable features of the march was the skill and success of the "bummers" in rounding up mules, horses, cattle, hams, bacon, poultry, bags of corn meal and flour, sacks of potatoes and other provisions. Indeed Sherman's success in feeding 65,000 men while on the march in enemy country was one of the most remarkable commissariat feats in history. Negroes helped locate these supplies, exhuming them from pits and cellars. Nothing escaped them, whether in barn, granary, smokehouse or kitchen garden.

Once the supplies were found, the former slaves were used in transporting them. Foraging on foot was impractical, but in cases where it became necessary, black backs carried the loads. On expeditions with animal transport, the drivers were usually Negroes. These colored teamsters, often riding with a rope for rein and a square of carpet for saddle, shared the dangerous and exciting life of path-breaking into the enemy country, serving as a screen of scouts. If attacked by Rebel infantry, the laden foragers would temporarily abandon their loot, snatch up their Springfield rifles and cluster behind trees. The Negroes with these expeditions quickly became skilled in shooting and cover, and if the party were pressed, at falling back and reassembling.

Sherman generally astounded his foes by his ability to move 65,000 troops, loaded army wagons and heavy artillery at a pace averaging ten miles a day in spite of rain-sogged roads, flooded lowlands, dense swamps, swollen streams and intersecting rivers. In this accomplishment of defying Generals Winter and Mud and making the most spectacular march in modern history, the Negroes accompanying the armies rated an assist. In his general order issued one week before leaving Atlanta, Sherman advised his commanders to "take along" able-bodied blacks:

> The organization, at once, of a good pioneer battalion for each army corps, composed if possible of Negroes, should be attended to. This battalion should follow the advance-guard, repair roads and double them if possible, so that columns will not be delayed after reaching bad places.

These Negro laborers were among the troops that lifted the bulky army wagons and cannons from the mudholes; physically fit to outlabor Hercules, they helped to construct the bridges and put the roads in repair. At untraveled places they improvised pathways, making corduroy roads by uprooting rail ties or felling young trees and depositing them across the way to be traversed. They helped in rebuilding the railroads, a work which the Federal troops did with such rapidity that many Rebels were wont to exclaim, "No use tearing up the roads, for old man

Sherman will come along and run trains before we are through twisting the rails."

Negroes were employed in tearing down as well as building up. Sherman's aim was to "make George howl." A believer in total war, he made it a point to destroy anything of possible value to the enemy. His plan called for the breaking up of all railway communication between Richmond and the Gulf States, and he went about this work with customary thoroughness. The Negro pioneers quickly learned the technique. They gathered at one side of the track and at the word of command, lifted together until the line of rail and ties was as high as their shoulders. At another command they would let everything drop, stepping aside as it fell. Many of the spikes would be loosed by the heavy fall and the men would pry off the rest, using the loosened rails as levers. The cross ties would be piled high and then set on fire. Into the fire would go the iron rails. When a rail was red-hot in the middle it was not difficult to seize it by the ends and twist it around a tree, or interlace it into great iron knots. The Union soldiers and their colored allies reduced this technique to an art, uprooting 300 miles of track and thereby breaking up the railway system of the South.

Under Sherman, everything else of military value was demolished — depots, mills, factories, machine shops, and stores of every kind. "Dem Yanks," said an old Negro, "is de most destructionist people I ever see."

Sherman was not unaware of the role of the black auxiliaries that accompanied his armies. "We employed a large number of them as servants, teamsters and pioneers," wrote he in his *Memoirs*, and they "rendered admirable service."

The entertainment value of the Negro while the great march was in progress was appreciated by the rank and file, if ignored in the official reports from headquarters. At night mirth and festivity reigned in the camps, the contrabands making "minstrelsy such as never heard in the North." Soldiers brought out

their violins and to the strains of the strings and the clapping of
hands, the Negroes "went tearing away like mad in the plantation jig and walk around." At one of the plantation dances staged
for the amusement of the Yankees, Major James A. Connolly
laughed "until my head and sides are aching." These particular
dancers required neither fiddle nor banjo, "but kick, and caper
and shuffle in the most complicated and grotesque manner their
respective fancies can invent, while all who are not actually engaged as dancers stand in a ring . . . clapping their hands, stamp-
ing their feet, swinging their bodies, and singing as loud and as
fast as they can." Their performance was as mirth-provoking as
"Christy's Minstrels."

Another service of a social character was that contributed by
the bevy of good-looking colored girls who traveled with the
troops, willing to take love where they found it. These daughters
of dalliance were the happy recipients of such tokens of esteem
as jewelry, plate, quilts and Madeira wine, generously given to
them by soldiers who, in ransacking the mansions of the planters,
had broadly construed Sherman's order to "forage liberally on
the country." Some of the enlisted men had in their entourage
such a large number of "dark houris," wrote Major Connolly, as
would have brought envy to the Grand Turk or Brigham Young.
In the higher echelons the story was the same. "I have seen officers themselves very attentive to the wants of pretty octoroon
girls," reported the major, "and provide them with horses to
ride." One touch of nature made the whole army kin!

The Confederates decided to evacuate Savannah, and on the
morning of December 21, Sherman's troops marched into the city,
accompanied by their corps of black laborers and followed by a
long train of more than 10,000 straggling contrabands. Cheering and happy, and bowing to everyone, these Negroes shared
fully the elation of the Union forces over this crowning triumph.

Sherman took up his residence in the two-story mansion of
Charles Green, a wealthy British banker. "The greatest in-door

feature of our residence in Savannah has been the General's new-found colored friends who have come by the hundreds . . . to see 'Mr. Sherman,'" wrote Hitchcock. As soon as word got around that the commander would see them "there was a constant stream of them, old and young, men, women and children, black, yellow, and cream-colored, uncouth and well-bred, bashful and talkative — but always respectful and behaved — all day long."

That Savannah Negroes regarded Sherman highly was demonstrated at a memorable meeting at which Secretary of War Stanton put a series of questions to twenty of their leaders. It was the first time in which a high government official had summoned a Negro group and asked, "What do you want for your people?" Needing rest and relaxation, and anxious to check on the disposal of the more than 30,000 bales of captured cotton, Stanton had made the trip to Georgia. Perhaps seeking to curry favor with the Congressional Radicals, staunch advocates of the suffrage for the colored man, Stanton asked Sherman to arrange a meeting with a group of Negroes. On the night of January 12, twenty colored men, predominantly of the clergy, assembled in Sherman's upstairs room to be questioned by Stanton.

In this singular interrogation, Stanton sat at a table making a note of the replies, and Sherman stood near the fireplace, occasionally pacing to and fro. Watching with curious gaze were Adjutant General E. D. Townsend, and Sherman's aide-de-camp, George Ward Nichols. In a meeting which lasted until "the small hours of the morning," Stanton posed twelve questions, to which Garrison Frazier, the spokesman for the Negroes, gave responses. Like fifteen of his colleagues, Frazier had been born in slavery, having purchased his freedom and that of his wife for $1000 in 1859. Frazier's words were written down and read to the other Negroes to be sure that there was common agreement.

Eleven of the questions were general. "State what you understand by slavery," ran one of the questions read by Stanton, "and the freedom that was to be given by the President's proclamation." The answer was quickly forthcoming:

> Slavery is receiving by irresistible power the work of another man, and not by his consent. The freedom, as I understand it, promised by the proclamation, is taking us from under the yoke of bondage, and placing us where we can see the fruit of our own labor, and take care of ourselves and assist the government in maintaining our freedom.

At such answers Stanton would put down his pen and finger his glasses in a surprised way, "as if he could not comprehend how these men came to possess such a clear consciousness of the merits of the questions involved in the war." To Stanton their replies seemed so phrased as to show that "they understood and could state the principles" of his questions "as well as any member of the Cabinet."

The final question directed to the twenty Negroes grouped around the room concerned Sherman. Before putting it, Stanton looked meaningfully at the general, obviously inviting him to leave the room. His heart seething, the surprised officer made for the door. It was a humiliation he would never forget — the idea, as he wrote in his *Memoirs*, that Secretary Stanton "should have catechized Negroes concerning the character of a general who had commanded a hundred thousand men in battle, had captured cities, conducted sixty-five thousand men successfully across four hundred miles of hostile territory, and had just brought tens of thousands of freedmen to a place of security."

When the huffed Sherman had left the room, Stanton asked a single question: What was the feeling of the colored people toward the general? The Negro delegation gravely formulated a reply:

> We looked upon General Sherman, prior to his arrival, as a man, in the providence of God, specially set aside to accomplish this work, and we unanimously felt inexpressible gratitude to him, looking upon him as a man who should

be honored for the faithful performance of his duty. Some of us called upon him immediately upon his arrival, and it is probable that he did not meet the secretary with more courtesy than he did us. His conduct and deportment toward us characterized him as a friend and gentleman.

With this answer, Stanton thanked the black conferees and sent them home "with words of kindness and counsel."

Although the Negro clergymen had complete confidence in Sherman, the suspicious Secretary of War was less sure. For three days he discussed the Negro question with Sherman, finally requesting him to draft an order to meet the situation. On January 16 Sherman issued a mutually agreed upon field order (Special Order No. 15) which was designed to encourage the freedmen to become soldiers and assist them to become farmers. For the benefit of the latter, agricultural settlements were to be established on the abandoned lands from Charleston south and "along the rivers from thirty miles back from the sea," in addition to the "country bordering the St. John's River, Florida." Under this plan of homesteading, Negro heads of families could reserve plots not exceeding forty acres nor "more than eight hundred feet water-front." To supervise this system of land distribution an "inspector of Settlements and Plantations" was to be appointed, an office which soon fell to Rufus Saxton, a man beloved by Sea Island Negroes.

Under Saxton's direction the thousands of Negroes who had followed Sherman's marching columns were settled on the abandoned lands. To assist these penniless camp followers in getting started, Inspector Saxton sent an urgent appeal to the North. The response was gratifying. Just as the citizens of Philadelphia, New York and Boston had sent two ships laden with food for the Savannah whites, so the charitable people in the North sent shoes and stockings, hats, underclothes, suspenders, utensils, medicines and money for the colored refugees.

After remaining in Savannah for some six weeks, resting and

refitting his army, Sherman moved northward, thrusting through the heart of South Carolina. He had decided on bypassing Charleston; this city would be forced to capitulate when the arteries that gave it life were cut. "If I am able to reach certain vital points," said Sherman, "Charleston will fall of itself." Powerless to halt this veteran Union Army, the Confederates could only put up minor delaying actions. On February 18, 1865, Sherman's troops captured a strategic center, proud Columbia, capital of the Palmetto State.

As Sherman entered the city the Negroes gave him a welcome that was "singular and touching," greeting his arrival, wrote George Ward Nichols, "with exclamations of unbounded joy." One Negro woman, fat and old, took possession of the general's hand and made a little speech. While proceeding down the main street Sherman was also greeted by a number of Union prisoners who had escaped months earlier, and "had been secreted in the town by the Negroes."

With Columbia fallen, Charleston and its harbor fortifications could no longer be defended. Sherman had conquered Charleston "by turning his back on it." Finding himself flanked, General J. W. Hardee, commanding the Confederate forces in South Carolina and Georgia, ordered the city evacuated. Resolving to leave as little as possible to the enemy, Hardee also ordered that the torch be put to buildings, warehouses and sheds that stored cotton, and that all torpedo boats, blockade-runners and vessels in shipyards be burned or scuttled. So thoroughly were his orders carried out by the detachment of cavalry assigned to set the fires that the breaking day revealed the ghastly spectacle of a scarred city, blackened by charred scaffoldings.

While the proud metropolis — the Confederate Holy of Holies — still smoldered, the Union forces took possession of the harbor defenses — Forts Sumter, Ripley, and Moultrie, and Castle Pinckney — which had so valiantly withstood all previous efforts. A few hours later, at ten in the morning, Lieutenant Colonel A. G.

Bennett, of the Twenty-first U. S. Colored Troops, reached the city by rowboat from Morris Island and demanded that the mayor formally surrender. The latter quickly sent word of his acquiescence. Bennett acknowledged the reply and added: "My command will render every possible assistance to your well-disposed citizens in extinguishing the flames."

Then into the stricken city marched the Union soldiers, the Twenty-first U. S. Colored Troops, followed by a detachment of two companies of the Fifty-fourth Massachusetts. The Bay State Negroes had distinguished themselves at Battery Wagner, where they had led the charge, and at Olustee, where they had held back the victorious enemy until a new battle line could be formed. And then for more than a year they had been lying in sight of Charleston. The other Negro soldiers who marched into the city were members of the old Third and Fourth South Carolina regiments, many of whom had been numbered in 1860 among Charleston's nearly 18,000 slaves. Now theirs was the high privilege of being the first Federal troops to enter the proud capital city of South Carolina, their own birthplace.

A reporter for the Boston *Journal* was moved by the drama of it all. The Negro soldiers had already proved their courage and heroism on the field of battle, observed Charles Coffin, "and on this ever memorable day they made manifest to the world their superiority in honor and humanity." Here were ex-slaves "with the old flag above them, keeping step to freedom's drum beat, up the grass-grown streets, past the slave shambles, laying aside their arms, working the fire-engines to extinguish the flames, and, in the spirit of the Redeemer of men, saving that which was lost."

As the black soldiers took their posts at the fire-pumps, some of them found themselves in the shadow of the auction block of J. B. Baker, on which they had once stood as chattels. From this vantage point they could see the familiar nearby buildings which still bore the lettered signs, "Theological Library," and "Sunday School Depository." Some of these Negro fire-fighters who viewed St. Michael's with its roofs now gaping, its pillars demolished, its pews filled with rubble, had once spent the night in the adjacent guardhouse for having disobeyed the law in ignoring the bell of the venerable church, which at curfew time had been wont to thunder out of its cavernous mouth to the slave: "Get you home! Get you home!" Perhaps these black troops took note that a shell had broken through the wall of St. Michael's pulpit, obliterating seven of the commandments, but leaving still untouched in their stone engraving those awe-inspiring words: "Thou shalt not steal," "Thou shalt not kill," "Thou shalt not commit adultery."

Three days after the arrival of the first Negro soldiers, the Massachusetts Fifty-fifth, the second colored regiment recruited under Governor John A. Andrew's auspices, entered the city. As they marched to their assigned quarters, singing the John Brown song, Lieutenant George Thompson Garrison, son of the noted reformer, halted his company in the street in order to greet James Redpath, confidant and biographer of the abolitionist whose name was now pouring from the throats of the Negro volunteers.

The arrival of the Union troops brought the customary response from the Negro populace — shouts, prayers and blessings resounded wherever blacks were congregated. There were some touching incidents. A soldier riding on a mule down Meeting Street at the head of an advancing column and bearing aloft a banner with the word "Liberty" inscribed, was nearly unseated when a Negro woman rushed up with outstretched arms, and unable to reach him in the saddle, hugged the mule, shouting, "Thank God."

Two newspaper reporters were accosted by a sixty-nine-year-older, wearing a brown dress and a roundabout, who seized their hands and danced for joy. Then she made a deep curtsy, and broke into a simple, unrhymed chant:

Ye's long been a-comin,
Ye's long been a-comin,
Ye's long been a-comin,
For to take de land.

"You are glad the Yankees are come, then?" asked one of the reporters.

"O chile," she said, "I can't bress de Lord enough. But I doesn't call you 'Yankees.' I call you Jesus' aids, and I call your head man de Messiah."

Two weeks after the beginning of the occupation, the colored women of Charleston presented the Negro regiments with three flags. The troops were drawn up in parade formation in front of the military academy, the Citadel, with the Stars and Stripes flying on high. The women presented a bouquet of flowers to the officers, and gave them a white swan fan to send to Lincoln. After the presentations the regiments staged an exhibition drill.

The next day, March 4, marked the opening of the first free public school in the city. It was located in a large building on Morris Street. With Superintendent James Redpath presiding, the opening exercises included a Scripture reading, a repeating of the Lord's Prayer, and a special prayer for President Lincoln. Then the children went to their rooms, the colored children going to the first and third floors, and the whites to the second floor. The Negro youngsters, "all lately slaves," numbered nearly one thousand; the whites, some two hundred. There was a common playground where at recess time all the boys joined together in games.

Charleston Negroes had scarcely gotten over the excitement of the coming of the Union troops when a black major arrived. This was Martin R. Delany, editor, medical practitioner, colonizationist and African explorer. Delany had been commissioned late in February, the first Negro field officer, and had been assigned to duty at Charleston to assist in recruiting and organizing colored troops. Delany's quarters were besieged by a constant stream of colored visitors, anxious to see a black man to whom advance rumor had given the rank of major general. A few days after his arrival he was officially greeted at an immense gathering of Negroes at Zion church, largest in the city.

To white citizens the presence of Delany and the colored troops was sorrow's crown of sorrow. "Can you conceive a bitterer drop that God's chemistry could mix for a son of the Palmetto State," asked Wendell Phillips, "than that a Massachusetts flag and a colored regiment should take possession of Charleston?"

For whites it was a novel experience not to have Negroes give them "the inside of the walk," and for a black man to address them without first removing his hat. It was particularly galling to see Negro sentinels stationed at the public buildings, examining the passes of all who would enter. Negro soldiers made up the provost guards, charged with maintaining law and order. The guard had its headquarters at the Citadel, and "whoever desired protection papers or passes, whoever had business with the marshal or the general commanding the city, rich or poor, highborn or low-born, white or black, man or woman," wrote Charles Coffin, "must first meet a colored sentinel face to face, and obtain from the colored sergeant permission to enter the gate."

One of the white South Carolinians, Mrs. Frances J. Porcher, in a wry letter to a friend, described the new dispensation:

> Nat Fuller, a Negro caterer, provided munificently for a miscegenat dinner, at which blacks & whites sat on an equality, & gave toasts and sang songs for Lincoln & freedom. Miss Middleln and Miss Alston, *young ladies of colour*, presented a coloured regiment with a flag on the Citadel green, and nicely dressed black sentinels turn back white citizens, reprimanding them for their passes not being correct.

But with rare exceptions did Negroes wittingly seek to humiliate whites; there were few instances in which former slaves showed any rudeness to their former masters. Indeed, in several instances, writes Harriette K. Leidling, a contemporary authority on Charleston, "Negro families moved in and occupied the homes of their white friends and thus preserved these places from being pillaged and destroyed. Later these homes were returned to their rightful owners after they had complied with the military requirements and taken the oath of allegiance."

❧

The whites and blacks in Savannah, Columbia and Charleston who were adjusting themselves to the changed order of things soon had illustrious company — no less than the inhabitants of the capital of the Confederacy. Like its sister cities, Richmond was evacuated, although more abruptly. It happened on a beautiful spring morning, the church bells pealing "unassailed by one single noise of battle." A little piece of paper conveying momentous news was passed to a man seated in a church pew halfway up the middle aisle, listening to a rector's sermon. "On Sunday, April 2, while I was in St. Paul's Church," wrote Jefferson Davis, "General Lee's telegram, announcing his speedy withdrawal from Petersburg, and the consequent necessity of evacuating Richmond, was handed me." As the Confederate President made his way to the rear, the St. Paul's congregation was too well bred to make a scene, but the incredulous news was quickly passed by word of mouth and soon became public property.

Signs of evacuation became only too apparent by afternoon, with trunk-laden wagons hurrying toward the railroad station, and Negroes carrying luggage as vehicles skyrocketed to a value of $100 in gold, with the banks open, and with the streets filled as if by magic. One slave broker had marched his fifty chattels to the depot, chained two by two, but there was no room on the overcrowded train, soldiers with fixed bayonets turning them back. Cursing his hard luck, the slave dealer was forced to unlock the handcuffs and witness $50,000 worth of property amble away, the last slave coffle in the United States.

By midnight the government officials were en route to Danville, and a few hours later the city was in flames, the fires lighted by order of Confederate General Richard S. Ewell, and gleefully spread by hoodlums. Wrote heavy-hearted Constance Cary, later the wife of Burton Harrison, private secretary to President Davis, "Hardly anybody went to bed. We walked through the streets like lost spirits till nearly daybreak."

But morning brought only the Yankees. About an hour after the last contingent of Rebel soldiers pushed through the smoke and burned the Fourteenth Street bridge behind them, Union officer Godfrey Weitzel's troops entered the burning city, marching with even, steady step by the direct route straight up Main Street, with colors waving and drums beating. The Fifth Massachusetts Cavalry, a colored regiment under command of Colonel Charles Francis Adams, grandson of President John Quincy Adams, shared with two white regiments the honor of being the first Union soldiers to enter the city. They were soon followed by companies C and G of the Twenty-ninth Connecticut Colored Volunteers, and the Ninth U. S. Colored Troops.

Richmond Negroes were beside themselves with joy. Here on horseback and afoot were men of color, in neat blue uniforms, their shoulders erect, their heads high, their eyes confident. The black admirers ran along the sidewalks to keep up with the moving column, not wishing to let this incredible spectacle move out of sight. In acknowledgment of their reception, the Negro cavalrymen rose high in their stirrups and waved their swords. The cheers were deafening.

Weitzel's troops soon reached the Capitol, and racing up the stone steps, they hauled down the red Stars and Bars and ran up the Stars and Stripes. Richmond, a city that had withstood one of the most unremitting sieges in the military history of the Western world, was in Union hands.

But the Federal soldiers had work to do before they could celebrate. They had to get the flames under control and protect property from looters. Stacking their guns and laying aside their knapsacks, they first went to work on the fires, springing to the engines, mounting the roofs, pouring buckets of water, tearing down some buildings and blowing up others. By afternoon the terrible roar of the conflagration had subsided and the dense pall of smoke had lifted — the fires were out, or under control. A few hours later the one-day carnival of lawlessness had been brought to an end, and the stricken city took on a quiet mien. Their share of the work done, the colored soldiers returned to Capitol Square and divided their rations with the half-starved Richmonders, who rolled their tongues over the long-lost taste of hot coffee sweetened with sugar.

While the white citizens and officials praised highly the spirit in which the Union forces restored order, they were, in the words of War Clerk Jones, "annoyed that the city should be held mostly by Negro troops." Here were soldiers the color of their former slaves guarding the crossings and walking up and down the pavements, their muskets bayoneted. Some of the whites raised a displeased eyebrow at the sight of the muscular, black-skinned newspaper reporter, J. Morris Chester, sitting in the hall of the Confederate Congress at the Speaker's desk, writing his dispatches to the Philadelphia *Press*. Clearly the world was out of joint! But as in Charleston, the Negro soldiers and civilians showed no tendency to try to lord it over anyone.

The fall of Richmond evoked rejoicing in the North beyond that of any other victory — Gettysburg, Vicksburg, Nashville, Atlanta, Savannah, Columbia or Charleston. For the surrender of the Rebel capital clearly marked the deathblow to the Confederacy. Hence all previous celebrations paled before the demonstrations that followed the message which the telegraph at the War Office clicked off on Monday, April 3: WE TOOK RICHMOND AT 8:15 THIS MORNING. At Washington the Secretary of War ordered an eight hundred-gun salute. As the distinguished-looking Mrs. Elizabeth Keckley made her way through the Washington streets, she noticed that the government clerks were enjoying the day "by getting gloriously fuddled," and toward evening she saw many "usually clear-headed men, in the street, in a confused, uncertain state of mind." Similar expressions of joyous high spirits took place throughout the North, with bells pealing from every church and schoolhouse, cannon roaring from every village green and city park, and men, women and children gathering in spontaneous celebrations — singing, cheering, praying and orating.

Negroes gloried in the news, finding intense satisfaction that colored troops were among the first to enter the city. "In West Broadway the American citizens of African descent turned out in great force," reported the New York *Herald* on April 4, "and indulged in the most demonstrative style of jubilee." Mrs. Keckley's work-girls reminded her that she had promised them a holiday when Richmond fell.

Not unmoved by the spirit of celebration and thanksgiving, President Lincoln decided to visit the captured city. On April 4, the day after the Federal occupation, the Presidential party, including young Tad Lincoln, started up the James River, but obstructions placed in the stream by the Rebels made it necessary for the *River Queen* to anchor. Lincoln then proceeded to the city by a twelve-oared barge provided by Admiral Porter.

There was neither escort nor guard for the Presidential party when it made its unexpected landing at the foot of the city, at a place called Rockett's. When Lincoln stepped ashore holding his son by the hand, the only persons around were a group of forty Negro laborers securing floating lumber. One of them instantly recognized the man in the tall black hat. Dropping his hook, the sixty-year-old Negro sprang forward, exclaiming, "Bress de Lord, dere is de great Messiah! I knowed him as soon as I seed him. He's ben in my heart fo' long yeahs an' he's cum at las' to free his chillun from deir bondage! Glory, hallelujah!" He fell on his knees before Lincoln, and others followed his example. In a few minutes Lincoln was surrounded, black people springing from corners that had seemed deserted. The streets "seemed to be suddenly alive with the colored race."

Porter requested the foremost Negro to fall back. "Yes, massa," said the old man, "but after bein' so many years in the desert widout water, it's mighty pleasant to be lookin' at las' on our spring of life." Unaware that they were detaining the President, the Negroes joined hands in a circle and sang a hymn:

> Oh, all ye people clap your hands,
> And with triumphant voices sing;
> No force the mighty power withstands
> Of God, the universal King.

Lincoln and his party listened respectfully, the crowd still swelling. The boat's crew was alerted to fix bayonets lest the throng crush the President to death. Lincoln thought it best to say a few words, otherwise he could not have budged. He urged the former slaves to live up to the laws, obey the Commandments, and prove themselves worthy of the boon of liberty. Thereupon his Negro audience shouted and cheered in approval.

Finally a path was cleared and the party got started toward General Weitzel's headquarters at the White House of the Confederacy. With a colored man as guide and with six sailors in front and six in the rear, with their round blue hats, short jackets and baggy pants, and each armed with a carbine, Lincoln and his party slowly moved forward. Surrounding them was a surging mass of men, women and children, running, shouting, dancing and swinging caps.

As the party walked along, the tall gaunt form of the President looming conspicuously, the crowds kept growing, newcomers pouring from every bystreet. "Wherever it was possible for a human being to find a foothold," wrote Colonel William H. Crook, "there was some man or woman or boy straining his eyes after the President."

Many of the spectators behaved as though at a religious revival. From a woman standing in a doorway came a vehement outcry, "Thank you, dear Jesus, for this! Thank you, Jesus!" Another colored glorifier was no less ecstatic, "I know I am free," shouted she, "for I have seen Father Abraham and felt him." Still another spirit-possessed sister snatched her bonnet, whirled it in the air, and screamed, "God bless you, Massa Linkum."

The walk was long, a mile and a half, and the Chief Magistrate paused a minute for rest. "May de good Lord bless you, President Linkum," said an aged Negro, doffing his hat and bending his head. Innately courteous, Lincoln removed his own hat and bowed in turn. Then he resumed his trudge through the dusty streets, the man of the people among the people, inclining his head in acknowledgment of the cheers and on one occasion putting his hand lightly on the head of a baby thrust in front of him for the distinguished touch.

At length the party reached General Weitzel's headquarters. After a rest, refreshments and an informal reception of Union officers, Lincoln went on a sight-seeing drive. He visited the Capitol building, the prison pens, Libby and Castle Thunder, and saw many of the nearly nine hundred charred buildings. In the evening an officer's ambulance rode him to the wharf, where a rowboat was waiting to transport him to the quiet of the flagship *Malvern*. Just as the small craft pushed off amid the cheering of the crowd, an old colored woman cried out, "Don't drown, Massa Abe, for God's sake."

❧

It was a bit more than a week later and the day was Good Friday, historically a day of mourning. But on this particular anniversary of the crucifixion of Christ there was a feeling of thanksgiving in the North. Five days earlier, on April 9, the two leading generals of the rival armies had met at a meagerly furnished parlor in a modest dwelling at the edge of Appomattox village, and there had negotiated the surrender terms of the Confederate Army of Northern Virginia. Peace had come; the Union was to be restored and swords could now be beaten into plowshares.

The North's thanksgiving found its chief expression in a ceremony at Fort Sumter in the Charleston harbor. Three weeks earlier Secretary Stanton, upon Lincoln's request, had ordered Robert J. Anderson, now a retired general, to raise over the battlements of Fort Sumter the identical flag which he had been forced to lower four years previously to the day.

Among the notables asked to attend the flag-raising ceremony was William Lloyd Garrison. Stanton's telegram of invitation was put into Garrison's hand on April 4, at a reformist gathering held in Chelsea, Massachusetts, just as the great abolitionist was mounting the steps of the auction block brought from the Charleston slave mart, and covered with a Confederate flag captured by his son's Negro regiment.

After a pleasant boat trip on the paddle-wheel transport, *Arago,* the distinguished party, including Judge Advocate General Joseph Holt, Supreme Court Justice N. H. Swayne, Senator Henry Wilson and Clergyman Henry Ward Beecher, arrived at Hilton Head on April 12. On the next evening the abolitionists making the journey, Garrison, Editor Theodore Tilton, Judge William D. Kelley, and the long-time English reformer, George Thompson, took a trip to the self-governing Negro settlement of Michelville, a mile and a half away. In the densely packed church, the floodgates of feeling opened wide: "from the most hysterical contraband to the dispassionate judge there was no reserve or restraint in the general flow of tears." Garrison was "rapturously welcomed," and began his address by reading Moses' triumphant song in Exodus. He was followed by the other guests, the audience singing songs fervently between speakers.

The next day, the fourth anniversary of the surrender of Sumter, the formal ceremonies took place. At eight in the morning the Charleston streets were thronged and the crowd got an *apéritif* as the harbor guns fired a salvo in celebration of the news of Lee's capitulation. Three hours later a host of boats, ships and steamers had gathered around the battered fort. Every vessel in the harbor was dressed in full color: "The whole bay seemed covered with the vast flotilla, planted with a forest of masts, whose foliage was the triumphant banners of the nation." Among the spectators massed at the fort were hundreds of Negroes, transported across the waters in the *Planter*. Captain Robert Smalls's passenger list included Major Delany and his son, Toussaint L'Ouverture Delany of the Massachusetts Fifty-fourth.

The hundreds of Negro onlookers witnessed a memorable scene. First came an invocation, delivered by the Reverend Matthias Harris, the same chaplain who had officiated at the raising of the flag over Sumter on December 27, 1860. Then Dr. Richard S. Storrs and the audience read antiphonally several verses from the Psalms, reading in unison the closing lines:

> Some trust in chariots, and some in horses: but we will remember the name of the Lord our God.
> We will rejoice in thy salvation, and in the name of our God we will set up our banners.

General E. D. Townsend, officially in charge of the proceedings, read Major Anderson's original dispatch to Secretary of War Simon Cameron, announcing the fall of the fort.

Then came the high moment. Just after the ships' bells had struck the hour of noon, the shot-pierced United States flag was taken out of its mail bag and handed to Anderson. The general let out its folds to the breeze, and adjusting the halyards, sent the flag up. As the banner reached its apex, the acclamation became ear-splitting. The bay thundered with the roar of cannon from ship and shore, every band burst into full-throated sound, every drum came alive, and the thousands of keyed-up celebrators shouted and screamed for joy. After several minutes of demonstration, the crowd quieted while Anderson said a few touching words. Then came the singing of "O say, can you see, . . ." It was now time for Henry Ward Beecher, orator of the day. Beecher's address had been carefully prepared and his congregation from Brooklyn was present, having chartered a steamer to come and hear their eloquent pastor. But the speech was a letdown after the flag-raising — even fiery Beecher was no match for the hundred-gun salute from Sumter and a national salute from every ship and fort in the harbor.

The next morning at ten o'clock more than 3000 Negroes assembled at a meeting in Zion church, with Rufus Saxton presiding. The gathering had been scheduled for Citadel Square, but had been moved indoors because Henry Wilson's voice did not permit an open-air address. Zion church was a logical substitute for the square. An immense structure costing $25,000, it was the most spacious religious edifice in Charleston, and the only Negro Presbyterian church building in the South.

When Garrison entered the building he was hoisted aloft and carried to the rostrum. "My reception," wrote he, "was beyond all description enthusiastic, and my feelings were unutterable." As he ascended the pulpit steps to speak, two little colored girls came forward with bouquets in their arms. Their father, Samuel Dickerson, accompanied them. A former slave, Dickerson had once had his daughters separated from him. He addressed the editor of the *Liberator* in moving terms, "I tell you it is not this heart alone, but there are mothers, there are fathers, there are sisters, and there are brothers, the pulsations of whose hearts are unimaginable. Thank you for what you have done." Deeply affected, Garrison accepted the flowers. He never doubted, said he, "that I had the gratitude and affection of the entire colored population of the United States." When the audience sang, "Roll, Jordan, Roll," the enthusiasm was intense. The mood of elation continued through the addresses of Henry Wilson and George Thompson, subsiding only when the crowd went out into the streets.

When the abolitionists boarded ship to sail from Charleston, the "wharf was all black." A *bon voyage* meeting was held at the waterfront, with James Redpath presiding. Samuel Dickerson said farewell for the group, and Major Delany spoke. Garrison, Thompson and Tilton responded. Then hundreds of children, dismissed from school by Superintendent Redpath for the occasion, sang a group of patriotic airs. The last notes had hardly died down when a number of women rushed forward, showering the reformers with bunches of roses, jasmines and honeysuckles. One woman presented them with a straw basket full of ground nuts; another came forward with some homemade cakes.

As the steamer eased out into the harbor, the departing abolitionists saw Dickerson kneeling at one end of the wharf, his left arm around his little daughters and the other arm waving the American flag. The sight moved the Reverend Henry Ward Beecher to a reflection in language theological:

> And when the boat moved off, I felt that it were better for a man that a millstone were hanged around his neck, and that he were drowned in the depth of the sea, than that he should lay one finger of harm on these little ones of Christ.

✤

"May I send an invitation to good Abraham Lincoln to come and visit you?" asked one of the *Arago* abolitionists to a group of 1000 Negro children assembled in the lower room of Zion church on the morning of the celebration honoring Garrison. A thousand little dark hands went up.

But the message never reached the President. For on the morning of April 15 when the Negro children held up their hands, the earthly pilgrimage of Abraham Lincoln had come to an end. . . .

Thus now, as always, the evils which men fear they shall be called upon to encounter as a result of doing what is just and humane, are discovered, when they are really encountered, not to be evils at all, but blessings pure and simple.

REPORT OF THE COMMITTEE FOR SECURING COLORED PEOPLE IN PHILADELPHIA THE RIGHT TO STREET-CARS (1866)

CHAPTER XV

Where Sleep Our Kindred Dead

OLD "SIS" THOMAS, who lived with her daughter and son not far from Ford's Theatre in Washington, was not afraid of the ghosts who were always dropping in for a visit, for she "knew how to talk to them." But when the dogs kept howling for several days, and the roosters kept crowing, she became uneasy. And finally "when a large picture of Lincoln fell off the wall and a bird flew into the room, she just knew someone was going to die in the neighborhood."

The awe-inspiring event came to pass on the morning of Saturday, April 15, at 7:30 in the morning. On the preceding night shortly after ten o'clock, "the sad, mad, bad John Wilkes Booth" had fired one lead ball from his eight-ounce derringer, and nine hours later President Lincoln had died.

The news transfixed Negroes with sorrow. As Secretary Welles, after a night of vigil at the deathbed, walked along the avenue in front of the White House, he observed "several hundred colored people, mostly women and children, weeping and wailing their loss." Throughout the day, the crowd of blacks hovered along the walk, unmindful of the cold, drizzling rain, some of them quietly sobbing, others paralyzed with grief. Their tear-stained faces affected Welles more than anything else in the whole calamitous business. The bells had started to toll, and by noon the town was shrouded in black drapes and decorations. "It was the gloomiest day I ever saw," wrote John H. Napier, the Negro soldier-surgeon.

Hastening to the White House that bleak morning was Elizabeth Keckley. "Is there no one, Mrs. Lincoln, that you would desire to have with you in this terrible affliction?" a cabinet member's wife had asked. "Yes," replied the anguished widow, "send for Elizabeth Keckley. I want her just as soon as she can be brought here."

Elizabeth Keckley found Mrs. Lincoln distraught and inconsolable, with Robert bending over her and Tad crouching at the foot of the bed, "a world of agony in his young face." Mrs. Keckley, who was to be Mrs. Lincoln's only companion while her husband's body was being borne 1700 miles in solemn state to its final resting place at Springfield, Illinois, bathed her patron's head with cold water.

When Mrs. Lincoln's sobs became less violent, her colored attendant stole away for a few minutes and sought the room where the martyred President's body lay in the majesty of death. As the tall, distinguished-looking mulatto entered, the members of the cabinet and the high army officials made an opening for her. She glided toward the body "and lifted the white cloth from the white face of the man that I had worshipped as an idol." Tears flooded her beautiful eyes, for to her "no common mortal had died":

> The Moses of my people had fallen in the hour of his triumph. Fame had woven her choicest chaplet for his brow. Though the brow was cold and pale in death, the chaplet would not fade, for God had studded it with the glory of the eternal stars.

A choking sensation in her throat, she turned away and walked back to Mrs. Lincoln's side, slowly, so as to regain her composure.

Later that day, the fateful April 15, the Baltimore Annual Conference of the African Methodist Episcopal Church, happening to be in annual session, drew up a series of resolutions expressive of the sentiment of the Conference concerning the dread event. This was one of the first, if not the first, such set of resolutions formulated by a religious group. With Bishop Daniel A. Payne in the chair, the Conference expressed its profound regret, "not unmingled with indignation," over "the cowardly assassination on the 14th day of April, in the City of Washington, of the Chief Magistrate of the Republic, the great and good Abraham Lincoln." Resolutions were passed extending to President Andrew Johnson "our hand and hearts," tendering to "the estimable Lady of the White House our profoundest condolence," and conveying "our sympathies to the Hon. W. H. Seward, Secretary of State, who has been inhumanly assaulted."

On the evening before the funeral ceremonies at Washington, D. C., the Negroes of Sacramento, California, held a great public meeting in commemoration of the President's passing. One of the speakers, the colored versifier, J. Madison Bell, captured something of the mournful spirit that pervaded the entire country:

> Wherefore half-mast and waving sadly
> And seeming ill-disposed to move,
> Are those bright emblems which so gladly
> Were wont to wave our homes above?

In Washington that same evening 25,000 people, many of them Negroes, filed through the East Room for a solemn look at the mortal remains of a beloved friend.

On the next day, after the impressive services at the White House, the coffin was carried to a funeral car and the vast procession moved to the Capitol — the black hearse followed by regimental bands, cavalry, artillery, naval and marine detachments, marching to the sound of muffled drums and dirge-tolling bells. Pacing at the head of the column was a regiment of black troops with arms reversed. In the civic procession that followed behind were thousands of Negroes, among them the entire membership of the Baltimore Conference of the A.M.E. Church. "Wearing a dejected aspect and many of them in tears," wrote *Harper's Weekly*, these colored marchers bore a banner inscribed, "We mourn our loss."

Negroes were prominent among the 60,000 spectators that lined the sidewalks and filled every roof and window along the mile of march. Their grief was apparent. "There were no truer mourners, when all were sad," wrote Welles in his diary, "than the poor colored people who crowded the streets, joined the procession, and exhibited their woe, bewailing the loss of him whom they regarded as a benefactor and father."

As the body rested for a day under the soaring dome of the Capitol rotunda, thousands of black men, women and children passed for a final gaze on the features of one whom they had come to regard with reverence. Perhaps their grief was lessened by the expression Lincoln wore — an expression, wrote his secretaries, "of profound happiness and repose, like that so often seen on the features of soldiers shot dead in battle."

At eight o'clock on the morning of Friday, April 21, the funeral cortege left Washington on its long journey to the prairies of Illinois, following much the same route over which President-elect Lincoln had traveled in the winter of 1861 to his inauguration. At every stopping place the sorrowful pageant was met by multitudes. At Philadelphia, where a third of a million people filed past the mahogany coffin, an ancient Negro woman laid a wreath thereon, crying, "Oh, Abraham Lincoln, are you dead? Are you dead?" At New York no less than 2000 Negroes, many of them in army blue, were numbered among those who marched in the procession from City Hall to the Hudson River Railroad Station.

On the third of May — twelve days after the journey began — the procession reached Springfield. For twenty-four hours the body lay in state at the Capitol, viewed by 75,000. On the fourth

of May as the hearse moved from the Capitol to Oak Ridge Cemetery, every colored person in the city stood in line to see the
procession pass by, practically every one of them wearing a flower
in remembrance. Hundreds of Lincoln's Negro fellow townsmen
followed the coffin to the cemetery. There they stood on the
green banks, and listened in subdued silence to the prayers and
hymns. Then came words which were more meaningful to Negroes than to anyone else — the incantatory phrases of the immortal Second Inaugural Address, read aloud before the open
grave:

> On the occasion corresponding to this four years ago,
> all thoughts were anxiously directed to an impending civil
> war. . . . And the war came.
> One eighth of the whole population were colored slaves,
> not distributed generally over the Union, but localized in
> the Southern part of it. These slaves constituted a peculiar
> and powerful interest. All knew that this interest was,
> somehow, the cause of the war. . . .
> Fondly do we hope — fervently do we pray — that this
> mighty scourge of war may speedily pass away. Yet, if God
> wills that it continue until all the wealth piled by the bond
> man's two-hundred and fifty years of unrequited toil shall
> be sunk, and until every drop of blood drawn with the lash
> shall be paid by another drawn with the sword, as was
> said three thousand years ago, so still it must be said, "The
> judgments of the Lord are true and righteous altogether."
> With malice toward none; with charity for all; with
> firmness in the right, as God gives us to see the right, let
> us strive on to finish the work we are in; to bind up the
> nation's wounds; to care for him who shall have borne the
> battle and for his widow, and his orphan — to do all which
> may achieve and cherish a just and a lasting peace among
> ourselves and with all nations.

Negroes in the South joined in the grief. At Beaufort the funeral
exercises were held in the schoolhouse, everyone wearing a
swatch of black as a mourning badge. One man who could find no

black cloth wore his coat inside out because it had a "mourning lining." Every one of Michelville's 3000 Negroes wore crepe on the left arm until the end of the month, April 30. The black drapes with which Zion church in Charleston had festooned its walls and pulpit were left hanging for an entire year.

The deep, nation-wide grief of the Negroes was an outward sign that their generation would hold the name of the martyred President in everlasting remembrance. The colored people beheld in Lincoln a father image; he was "the chieftest of ten thousand, and altogether lovely." His death burdened every black with a personal sense of loss: "in his perfect benignity and just purpose," wrote *Harper's Weekly*, "inflexible as the laws of seedtime and harvest, they trusted with all their souls, whoever doubted."

The colored people lost a friend and the nation lost a leader, but the legacy of the Civil War still abided. For the war, with all its bloodshed and sorrow, was an emancipating and uplifting national experience. Its most striking achievement was not its battle conquests on sea and land, but in the momentum it gave to the ideals of the freedom and the dignity of man. It made easier every subsequent battle for human rights. A proving ground, the war furnished illustration that free institutions had the energizing power to pose an adequate response to the greatest challenge of their day. America demonstrated the purpose and the strength to refashion the fabric of its democracy, broadening its weave.

The war left some unfinished business, as was to be expected. "Liberty is a slow fruit," said the all-knowing Ralph Waldo Emerson.

The Negroes of the Civil War knew only too well the validity of the philosopher's aphorism. But their faith in America never flickered out. "No people grow so rapidly in the right direction as Americans," wrote the Negro infantryman, George Washington Williams. "What a wonderful revolution!" exclaimed Civil War

nurse Susie King Taylor. "In 1860 the Southern newspapers were
full of advertisements for slaves, but now, despite all hindrances,
my people are striving to attain the full standard of all other races
born free in the sight of God." Nurse Taylor furnished an answer
to the question, What do the Negroes want? "Justice, we ask —
to be citizens of these United States, where so many of our people
have shed their blood with their white comrades, that the stars
and stripes should never be polluted."

Like soldier Williams and nurse Taylor, abolitionist lecturer
Frances Ellen Watkins Harper loved the land of her birth. A poet
of minor gifts, she could not rise to the vein of epic poetry com-
mensurate with one of her country's heroic ages. But although
her lay was simple, it voiced the song in her soul, and in the souls
of other black folks:

> God bless our native land,
>   Land of the newly free,
> Oh may she ever stand
>   For truth and liberty.
>
> God bless our native land,
>   Where sleep our kindred dead,
> Let peace at thy command
>   Above their graves be shed.
>
> God bless our native land,
>   Bring surcease to her strife,
> And shower from thy hand
>   A more abundant life.
>
> God bless our native land,
>   Her homes and children bless,
> Oh may she ever stand
>   For truth and righteousness.

❖

Everything flows; no man has ever crossed the same river twice,
said a young student in ancient Greece. No, not even once, re-

joined his old teacher gently, for by the time he has crossed it, it has already become a different river. "Each age is a dream that is dying, or one that is coming to birth," intoned a modern poet.

From this endless pattern of becoming and ceasing to be, is there any mark that is left indelibly, any deposit that is not washed away? That there was, nineteenth-century Americans were certain. Few of them would have disagreed with their greatest historian:

> On the banks of the stream of time, not a monument that has been raised to a hero or nation, but tells a tale, and renews the hope of improvement.

Bibliography

The best general history of the American Negro is John Hope Franklin's deservedly popular *From Slavery to Freedom* (New York, 1947), a well-written survey embodying the fruits of the most recent scholarship. Another very useful standard work is Carter G. Woodson's *The Negro in Our History* (Washington, 1945), which reflects the broad learning and the militant spirit of this great pioneer in revitalizing the study of the Negro past. A third title which also serves as a textbook is Merl R. Eppse's *The Negro, Too, in American History* (Chicago, 1943). Benjamin Brawley's *Short History of the American Negro* (New York, 1939) is a readily grasped introductory statement. Two nineteenth-century accounts which proved of some service in their time were George Washington Williams's panoramic and pathbreaking *History of the Negro Race in America from 1619 to 1860* (2 vols., New York, 1882), and Edward Johnson's simply told *A School History of the Negro Race in America* (Raleigh, 1891). Martin R. Delany's *The Condition, Elevation, Emigration, and Destiny of the Colored People of the United States* (Philadelphia, 1852) is typical of the antebellum general accounts in its episodic quality and its inclusion of thumbnail sketches of Negroes who stood out from the crowd.

Of the black man's participation in the Civil War there are three accounts by contemporary Negroes, two of whom bore arms in the conflict. Joseph T. Wilson's *The Black Phalanx* (Hartford, 1882) is a well-planned, but not always well-integrated study of the Negro on the battle front. Covering not so much ground is

George Washington Williams's *History of the Negro Troops in the War of the Rebellion, 1861–1865* (New York, 1888); however, its generally fast pace and vivid descriptions are sometimes interrupted by moralizing digressions. *The Negro in the American Rebellion* (Boston, 1867), by the abolitionist lecturer William Wells Brown, is a series of anecdotes and stories, not all of them verifiable, since Brown was more interested in the human-interest angle than anything else. His book, like the books of Wilson and Williams, is padded with lengthy quotations from unacknowledged sources. Another nineteenth-century writing with a pro-Negro point of view is James M. Guthrie's *Camp-Fires of the Afro-American* (Phila., 1889), a work of minor merit.

Contemporary scholars have been filling the picture in. Herbert Aptheker has brought four of his thought-provoking essays together under the title, *The Negro in the Civil War* (New York, 1938). Bell Wiley's *Southern Negroes, 1861–1865* (New Haven, 1938), is a revealing study, methodically planned and heavily documented. The opening chapters of W. E. B. Du Bois's *Black Reconstruction* (New York, 1935) describe the role of the Negro in the war with all of the author's moving literary power. The nearly forty volumes of *The Journal of Negro History* (Washington, 1916–   ), the great treasure house of scholarship on the black man, are indispensable for the Civil War period. The volumes of the well-edited *Journal of Negro Education* (Washington, 1932–   ) embrace articles on the Negro's role in the war.

Among the standard general works Edward Channing's *The War for Southern Independence* (New York, 1925; vol. 6 of his *A History of the United States*) reveals a most perceptive understanding of the role of the Negro. With characteristic objectivity, John B. McMaster includes the Negro in the panoramic, *A History of the People of the United States During Lincoln's Administration* (New York, 1927). Much earlier titles with pertinent data include Horace Greeley's *The American Conflict* (2 vols., Chicago, 1864–1866), Edward McPherson's *The Political History of the*

United States of America during the Great Rebellion (Washington, 1882), and Henry Wilson's works: *History of Anti-Slavery Measures of the Thirty-Seventh and Thirty-Eighth United States Congress, 1861–1864* (Boston, 1864), and *The History of the Rise and Fall of the Slave Power in America* (3 vols., Boston, 1872–1877).

Contemporary volumes with descriptive materials include: E. Merton Coulter's *Confederate States of America* (Baton Rouge, 1950); Robert S. Henry's readable *Story of the Confederacy* (Indianapolis, 1936); Margaret Leech's brilliant *Reveille in Washington, 1861–1865* (New York, 1941); J. G. Randall's standard work, *Civil War and Reconstruction* (Boston, 1937); Carl Sandburg's justly celebrated *Abraham Lincoln: The War Years* (4 vols., New York, 1939); and Charles H. Wesley's *Collapse of the Confederacy* (Washington, 1937).

Foremost of the printed documentary sources furnishing data for this study were the voluminous depositories, *The War of the Rebellion: A Compilation of the Union and Confederate Armies* (128 vols., Washington, 1880–1901), and the *Official Records of the Union and Confederate Navies in the War of the Rebellion* (26 vols., Washington, 1894–1922, and index, 1927). Also used extensively was *The Rebellion Record*, Frank Moore, ed. (12 vols., New York, 1861–1868), a miscellany including official reports, newspaper clippings, humorous stories and poetry. The pages of the *Congressional Globe* abound with speeches on the pros and cons of every significant question relating to the Negro.

In the choice of periodicals, the aim has been one of breadth. Three publications edited by Negroes were used: *The Anglo-African* (New York, 1859), *Douglass' Monthly* (Rochester, 1859–1863), and *L'Union* (New Orleans, 1862–1864), a French-English weekly. (Dates within the parentheses indicate period for which publication was used.) Also strongly pro-Negro was the *Pine and Palm* (Boston, 1861–1862), a vehicle subsidized by the Haitian government, and the old-line abolitionist sheets, *The Anti-*

Slavery Standard (New York, 1861–1864), organ of the American Anti-Slavery Society, and *The Liberator* (Boston, 1861–1863), the personal weekly of William Lloyd Garrison. Newspapers used which were not so extreme but which favored the cause of the Negro generally were: the Cincinnati *Gazette* (1862–1863), the *Independent* (New York, 1861–1862), the Philadelphia *Inquirer* (1862), the *National Intelligencer* (Washington, 1864), the Boston *Post* (1862), the Chicago *Tribune* (1861), the New York *Tribune* (1861–1863), the New York *Times* (1861–1863), and the two pictorials, *Frank Leslie's Illustrated Weekly* (New York, 1861–1864), and *Harper's Weekly* (New York, 1861–1865). Newspapers used which reflected a Southern point of view were: the Richmond *Examiner* (1863), the Charleston *Mercury* (1861), and three from New Orleans: the *Bee* (1860), the *Daily True Delta* (1862–1863), and the *Daily Picayune* (1861–1862).

Some dozen manuscript sources were consulted. The collections of antislavery letters written to William Lloyd Garrison and others (Boston Public Library), and the Garrison MSS. (BPL) are indispensable for the wartime activities of the reformers. The Felix Brannigan MSS. (Library of Congress) reveal the attitude of a typical white soldier in the ranks. The Christian A. Fleetwood MSS. (LC) have a few suggestive items concerning this Negro recipient of a Congressional Medal of Honor. Charlotte Forten's Diary (Moorland Foundation, Howard University Library) is the outpouring of a noble-spirited young colored woman who worked for the cause of the enslaved. The Lincoln MSS. (LC) were used which covered the closing three months of 1861 and the closing two months of 1862. At the National Archives, War Department, I thumbed through the collection of Confederate Records, and used portions of the Lorenzo Thomas Letterbooks and the records of the Adjutant General's Office, Colored Troops Division. Three collections of Negro papers at the Moorland Foundation proved of service: the John and James T. Rapier MSS., the George L. Ruffin MSS., and the Jacob C. White MSS.

Scattered items of information were gleaned from the Carter G. Woodson MSS. (LC). The wartime conduct of a Southern Negro church is reflected in the Minutes of the First African Baptist Church of New Orleans and its board of officers, January 11, 1857 to February 21, 1869 (used through the courtesy of Dr. R. W. Coleman, New Orleans, Louisiana).

In addition to the general works listed above, a few selected titles follow which are especially pertinent to the chapter named.

CHAPTER I

Specialized accounts of Battery Wagner include: Frank R. Butts, *A Cruise Along the Blockade* (Providence, 1881); Luis F. Emilio, *The Assault on Fort Wagner* (Boston, 1887); Robert C. Gilchrist, *The Confederate Defence of Morris Island* (Charleston, 1884); Horatio B. Hackett, *Christian Memorials of the War* (Boston, 1864); Garth W. James, *The Assault on Fort Wagner* (Milwaukee, 1891); H. D. D. Twiggs, *Defence of Battery Wagner, July 18, 1863* (Augusta, 1892).

CHAPTER II

For four accounts of the Tillman episode, plus illustrative engravings, see *Harper's Weekly*, Aug. 3, 1861; for the Garrick episode see *The Jeff Davis Piracy Cases: Trial of William Smith for Piracy* (Phila., 1861). The response of New Orleans Negroes to the war is shown in James Parton's *General Butler in New Orleans* (New York, 1864).

CHAPTER III

The treatment accorded to the free Negro in the Confederacy is indicated in two articles by Bernard H. Nelson, "Legislative Control of the Southern Free Negro, 1861–1865," *Catholic His-*

torical Review, XXXII (April 1946), and "Some Aspects of Negro Life in North Carolina During the Civil War," *North Carolina Historical Review*, XXV (April 1948). The role of Southern women is described by Francis B. Simkins and James W. Patton, *The Women of the Confederacy* (Richmond, 1936). A suggestive article on slave morale is G. P. Whittington's "Concerning the Loyalty of Slaves in Northern Louisiana in 1863," *Louisiana Historical Quarterly*, XIV (Oct. 1931). The attitude of former slaves, as they reported it to Union soldiers, is revealed in Charles C. Coffin, *The Boys of '61* (Boston, 1901).

CHAPTER IV

General Butler describes his first contacts with contrabands in his autobiographical *Butler's Book* (Boston, 1892). For the "Captain Hill" episode see J. W. Bissell, "The Western Organization of Colored People for Furnishing Information to United States Troops," in *Glimpses of the Nation's Struggle*, Second Series (St. Paul, 1890), p. 318. Smalls's exploit is imaginatively described in James M. Rosbow's "The 'Abduction' of the Planter," *The Crisis*, New York, April 1949; see also Samuel F. Du Pont's *Official Dispatches and Letters* (Wilmington, 1883), p. 168. Congress and the President took action to reward the Smalls's crew, *Globe*, 37th Congress, second sess., pp. 2186, 2187, 2364, 2440.

CHAPTER V

Allan Pinkerton in his *Spy in the Rebellion* (New York, 1883) describes Scobell's work. The "Brutus" story is related by David L. Porter, *Incidents and Anecdotes of the Civil War* (New York, 1885), pp. 98–103. The contributions of Brutus of the Quincy A. Gillmore dispatch are noted in R. M. Thompson and R. Wainwright, eds., *The Confidential Correspondence of Gustavus Vasa Fox, 1861–1865* (New York, 1918), p. 92. Vincent Colyer's estimate of the role of the Tarheel blacks is outlined in his pamphlet, *Report of the Services Rendered by the Freed People to the United States Army, in North Carolina, in the Spring of 1862 after the Battle of Newbern* (New York, 1864).

CHAPTER VI

For the entire Hunter-Stanton-Wickliffe episode see Charles G. Halpine, *Baked Meats, By Private Miles O'Reilly* (New York, 1866), pp. 171–189. The Trowbridge episode is treated in Thomas W. Higginson, *Army Life in a Black Regiment* (Boston, 1870). Butler's conversation with the New Orleans Negroes is reported in the *Private and Official Correspondence of Benjamin F. Butler* (Norwood, Mass., 1917). A sketch of Mrs. Peake is furnished by Lewis C. Lockwood, *Mary S. Peake, the Colored Teacher at Fortress Monroe* (Boston, 1862?). Yeatman's journey is described in his *Report on the Condition of the Freedmen in Mississippi* (St. Louis, 1864). Mrs. Keckley's activities are related in *Behind the Scenes* (New York, 1868), the authorship of which the title page ascribes to her. An account of the services of the National Freedmen's Relief Association of the District of Columbia may be found in its *First Annual Report* (Washington, 1863).

CHAPTER VII

Lincoln's Negro acquaintances in Springfield are presented by John E. Washington, *They Knew Lincoln* (New York, 1942). Bishop Payne tells of his White House visit in *Recollections of Seventy Years* (Nashville, 1888). The findings of the House committee to inquire into gradual emancipation were published in pamphlet form as the *Report of the Select Committee on Emancipation and Colonization* (Washington, 1862). James Mitchell gave an account of Lincoln's interview with the Negro group of five in his *Report on Colonization and Emigration Made to the Sec-*

retary of the Interior by the Agent of Emigration (Washington, 1862). For Lincoln's colonization schemes see Warren A. Beck, "Lincoln and Negro Colonization in Central America," *Abraham Lincoln Quarterly*, VI (Sept. 1950). Pro-emigration points of view by Negroes include: Alexander Crummell, *The Relations and Duties of Free Colored Men in America to Africa* (Hartford, 1861), and Edward W. Blyden, *Liberia's Offering* (New York, 1862).

CHAPTER VIII

Bates's decision was printed as a pamphlet, *Opinion of Attorney General Bates on Citizenship* (Washington, 1863). The emancipation day celebrations of the Boston Negroes were recorded in the Boston *Transcript*, Jan. 2, 1863. See also Frederick Douglass's, *Life and Times* (Hartford, 1884). Whittier's letter to Charlotte Forten appears in Samuel T. Pickard, ed., *Life and Letters of John Greenleaf Whittier* (2 vols., Boston, 1895), II, 473.

CHAPTER IX

Negro efforts to spur the enlistment of fellow blacks are described in *Record of the Action of the Convention Held at Poughkeepsie, N. Y., July 15th and 16th, 1863, for the Purpose of Facilitating the Introduction of Colored Troops into the Service of the United States* (New York, 1863), and John Mercer Langston, *From the Virginia Plantation to the National Capital* (Hartford, 1894). Many of the whites who officered Negro troops left accounts of recruitment techniques: see J. M. Addeman, *Reminiscences of Two Years with the Colored Troops* (Providence, 1880); Frederick W. Browne, *My Service in the United States Colored Cavalry* (Cincinnati, 1908); Joseph M. Califf, *Record of Services of Seventh Regiment, United States Colored Troops* (Providence, 1878); Augustus L. Chetlain, *Recollections of Seventy Years*

(Galena, 1899); Robert Cowden, *Brief Sketch of the Fifty-Ninth Regiment of the United States Colored Infantry* (Dayton, 1883); George M. Dennett, *History of the Ninth United States Colored Troops* (Phila., 1866); N. P. Hallowell, *Record of the Fifty-Fifth Regiment of the Massachusetts Volunteer Infantry* (Boston, 1868); George H. Hepworth, *The Whip, Hoe, and Sword* (Boston, 1864); Henry O'Reilly, *First Organization of Colored Troops in New York to Aid in Suppressing the Slaveholders' Rebellion* (New York, 1864); James H. Richard, *Services with Colored Troops in Burnsides' Corps* (Providence, 1885); James Shaw, *Our Last Campaign and Subsequent Service in Texas* (Providence, 1905). Fred A. Shannon's *The Organization and Administration of the Union Army, 1861–1865* (2 vols., Cleveland, 1928) includes a chapter on the recruiting and the treatment of the black volunteer. The War Department prepared, and Lincoln approved, a manual, *United States Infantry Tactics for the Use of Colored Troops* (New York, 1863). For additional notes on Negro recruiting, see Robert D. Reid, "The Negro in Alabama During the Civil War," *Journal of Negro History*, XXXV (July 1950), and Roland C. McConnell, "Concerning the Procurement of Negro Troops in the South During the Civil War," *ibid*. Brainerd Dyer discusses "The Treatment of Colored Union Troops by the Confederates, 1861–1865," in *ibid*., vol. XX (July 1935).

CHAPTER X

A sidelight on the Port Hudson encounter is found in J. S. Bangs, *The Ullman Brigade* (Portland, 1902). A particularly revealing description of the action at Milliken's Bend is found in Cyrus Sears, *The Battle of Milliken's Bend* (Columbus, Ohio, 1919). Charles Dana's comments on Milliken's Bend are recorded in his *Recollections of the Civil War* (New York, 1898). Susie King Taylor has left an account of her experiences, *Reminiscences of My Life in Camp* (Boston, 1902). For the Negro tar, see

Herbert Aptheker's signal article, "The Negro in the Union Navy," *Journal of Negro History*, vol. XXXII (April 1947).

CHAPTER XI

A most recent account of the white laborer's attitude toward the Negro is Albon P. Man's "Labor Competition and the New York Draft Riots of 1863," *JNH*, vol. XXXVI (Oct. 1951). A graphic sketch of the colored orphan asylum is presented by Helen Havener, "Passing the Hundredth Milestone," *Opportunity* (New York, Nov. 1936). There is a published account of the efforts to assist the victims of the draft riots: *Report of the Committee of Merchants for the Relief of the Colored People Suffering from the Late Riots* (New York, 1863). The work of ladies' aid societies is touched upon in George Washington Williams's *History of the Twelfth Baptist Church* (Boston, 1874), and the *Autobiography of James L. Smith* (Norwich, 1881). The George L. Ruffin MSS. have a penciled account, in Ruffin's handwriting, of the 1864 colored convention. L. Seamon's race baitings were issued in pamphlet form: *What Miscegenation Is* (New York, 1864). For the coining of the word, see Sidney Kaplan, "Miscegenation Issue in the Election of 1864," *JNH*, XXXIV (July 1949).

CHAPTER XII

Slave assistance to escaped Union soldiers can be abundantly documented; the following sources have been used in this volume: Andrew M. Benson, *My Capture, Prison Life and Escape* (Boston, 1900); Linus P. Brockett, *The Camp, the Battle Field and the Hospital* (Phila., 1866); Junius Henri Browne, *Four Years in Secessia* (Hartford, 1865); Melvin Grigsby, *The Smoked Yank* (Sioux Falls, S. D., 1911); Hannibal A. Johnson, *The Sword of Honor* (Providence, 1930); Albert D. Richardson, *The Secret Service, the Field, the Dungeon and the Escape* (Phila., 1865);

W. H. Shelton, "A Hard Road to Travel Out of Dixie," *Famous Adventures and Prison Escapes of the Civil War* (New York, 1893); George E. Sutherland, "The Negro in the Late War," *War Papers of the Commandery of Wisconsin* (Milwaukee, 1891). See also William B. Hesseltine, "The Underground Railroad from Confederate to East Tennessee," *East Tennessee Historical Society's Publication*, II (1930). There are two widely quoted articles on the controversy over using Negro soldiers: Thomas R. Hay, "The Question of Arming the Slaves," *Mississippi Valley Historical Review*, VI (June 1919), and N. W. Stephenson, "The Question of Arming the Slaves," *American Historical Review*, XVIII (Jan. 1913). See also Albert B. Moore, *Conscription and Conflict in the Confederacy* (New York, 1924).

CHAPTER XIII

In the form of the annual reports of freedmen's aid societies, there is a voluminous literature on the wartime activities of the emancipated Negroes. More readily available accounts include: Elizabeth H. Botume, *First Days Among the Contrabands* (Boston, 1893); John Eaton, *Grant, Lincoln and the Freedmen* (New York, 1907); S. Emma E. Edmonds, *Nurse and Spy in the Union Army* (Hartford, 1865); Mrs. A. M. French, *Slavery in South Carolina and Ex-Slaves* (New York, 1862); Charles Nordhoff, *The Freedmen of South Carolina* (New York, 1863); and *Preliminary Report Touching the Condition and Management of Emancipated Refugees, Made by American Freedmen's Inquiry Commission, June 30, 1863* (New York, 1863). The crater fiasco is vividly described in Alfred P. James, "The Battle of the Crater," *The Journal of the American Military History Foundation*, II (Spring, 1938). The role of the Negro volunteer in the Tennessee theater is recounted in Henry Romeyn, *With Colored Troops in the Army of the Cumberland* (Washington, 1904).

CHAPTER XIV

For Sherman's marches, see Henry Hitchcock, *Marching with Sherman* (New Haven, 1927); Dolly Summer Lunt, *A Woman's Wartime Journal* (New York, 1918); George W. Nichols, *The Story of the Great March* (New York, 1865), and the *Memoirs of General William T. Sherman*, II (New York, 1889). For the Massachusetts Fifty-fifth in Charleston, see *Record of the Fifty-fifth Regiment of Massachusetts Volunteer Infantry* (Cambridge, 1868); for Negro troops in Richmond, see George M. Dennett, *History of the Ninth United States Colored Troops* (Phila., 1866).

Index

Index

Other DA CAPO titles of interest

BLACK ABOLITIONISTS
Benjamin Quarles
310 pp.
80425-5 $13.95

THE CIVIL WAR DAY BY DAY
An Almanac 1861-1865
E. B. Long with Barbara Long
1,135 pp., 8 pages of maps
80255-4 $19.95

ENCYCLOPEDIA OF
BLACK AMERICA
Edited by W. Augustus Low
and Virgil A. Clift
941 pp., 400 illus.
80221-X $35.00

LINCOLN AND THE NEGRO
Benjamin Quarles
275 pp., 8 illus.
80447-6 $13.95

THOMAS MORRIS CHESTER,
BLACK CIVIL WAR
CORRESPONDENT
His Dispatches from the
Virginia Front
Edited, with a biographical essay
and notes, by R.J.M. Blackett
375 pp., 3 photos, 1 map
80453-0 $13.95

TRAGIC YEARS 1860-1865
A Documentary History of the
American Civil War
Paul M. Angle and
Earl Schenck Miers
1108 pp.
80462-X $23.95

Available at your bookstore

OR ORDER DIRECTLY FROM

DA CAPO PRESS, INC.

1-800-321-0050